ANDREW DEMPSTER has walked ar[...]
Highlands and Islands for over twer[...]
Munros in 1988 and has since then[...]
such as Corbetts and Grahams, and longer walks taking up to a
month to complete, one of which is the subject of this book. In
1989 he walked from the Mull of Kintyre in south-west Scotland
to the north-western tip at Cape Wrath through some of
Scotland's wildest, remotest terrain, a journey of some 350 miles.
This walk laid the foundation for his Skye coastal walk.

Andrew's life-long love of Skye and in particular of the Cuillin,
a scrambler's paradise, sowed the seed for his first book, *Classic
Mountain Scrambles in Scotland*, published by Mainstream in
1992. His second book, *The Munro Phenomenon*, examined the
peculiarities and personalities of the Munro-bagging cult and was
published in 1995, also by Mainstream. On completion of the
Grahams (Scottish peaks between 2,000 and 2,500 ft), Andrew
produced *The Grahams – a Guide to Scotland's 2,000 foot Peaks*,
the first ever guide to these hills (Mainstream, 1997).

Andrew taught mathematics at the Fort Augustus Abbey
School, now sadly closed, before taking up his present position as
Head of Mathematics at Kilgraston School, Bridge of Earn, fifteen
years ago. His wife, Heather, also teaches at Kilgraston and he has
a stepdaughter, Laura, and son, Ruaraidh.

Skye 360
Walking the coastline of Skye

ANDREW DEMPSTER

Luath Press Limited

EDINBURGH

www.luath.co.uk

First Published 2003

The paper used in this book is recyclable. It is made from low-chlorine
pulps produced in a low-energy, low-emission manner
from renewable forests.

Printed and bound by
Creative Print and Design, Ebbw vale

Typeset in 10.5 point Sabon by
S. Fairgrieve, Edinburgh

To Ruaraidh and Laura

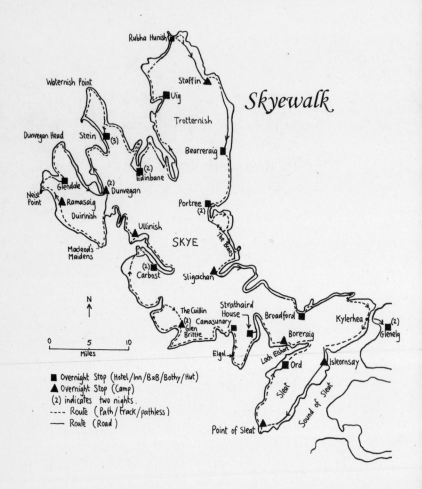

Skyewalk

- Rubha Hunish
- Staffin
- Uig
- Trotternish
- Waternish Point
- Dunvegan Head
- Stein (3)
- Bearreraig
- Edinbane (2)
- Glendale
- Dunvegan (2)
- Neist Point
- Ramasaig
- Duirinish
- Portree (2)
- Ullinish
- SKYE
- The Braes
- Macleod's Maidens
- Carbost (2)
- Sligachan
- The Cuillin
- Strathaird House
- Broadford
- Kylerhea
- Camasunary (2)
- Glen Brittle
- Boreraig
- Glenelg (2)
- Elgol
- Loch Eishort
- Isleornsay
- Ord
- Sleat
- Sound of Sleat
- Point of Sleat

N

0   5   10
Miles

■ Overnight Stop (Hotel/Inn/B&B/Bothy/Hut)
▲ Overnight Stop (Camp)
(2) indicates two nights.
---- Route (Path/Track/pathless)
—— Route (Road)

Contents

An t-Eilean Sgitheanach (The Winged Isle)

An t-Eilean Sgitheanach
Many-winged bird
Of the restless sea
An t-Eilean Sgitheanach
Your spirit resides in me.

Frozen phoenix of the waves
Rising from the ashes
Of a troubled past
I pass your blackhouse graves
Where no memories will last.

Skye, from whence you came
Escaping landward clutches
Of purest flight to stay
No concrete span can tame
This wondrous bird of prey.

Acknowledgements

I WOULD LIKE TO THANK all the people who helped, in any way, to make the Skye coastal walk and this book a reality. Firstly, my wife, Heather, who supported me wholeheartedly during her pregnancy while I swanned off for a month. I hope Heather and Ruaraidh will forgive me for my neglect during the long hours writing this book.

Thank you to Tony and Bridget La Trobe at Fiordhem and Christine and Roddy MacKinnon at Bearreraig for a wonderful Skye welcome. Also to the Chisholms at Glenelg for a hearty Highland welcome and for kindly providing me with a home for my car for four weeks.

Much gratitude is due to the hosts of various inns and guesthouses who allowed me to leave donation bottles to collect money for Save the Children Fund.

Thanks also to the trusted companions who joined me on Skye either to walk or wine and dine or both; in particular, Ken Black, Mike Wilson, George, and Jim and Lucy Scanlan. Finally, thanks to Joan Blue for her fast and efficient typing of the manuscript.

Note for potential Skyewalkers

ALTHOUGH THIS BOOK IS in essence a personal account of my own four-week trek around Skye's coastline, it should also be useful to those who, for various reasons, might wish to tackle only parts of the walk, or all of the walk on a piecemeal basis. To this end, each chapter finishes with a brief summary of the route covered in that chapter, together with additional information on accommodation, shops, etc.

Walking part of a coastline is not generally conducive to returning easily to the point of departure, and judicial use of one or two cars will be required in many cases. Public transport on Skye is scanty to say the least and usually restricted to the main roads only. Post-buses and hitch-hiking are possibilities but cannot be relied on. What can be relied on in Skye is the good nature of the local people, and I say this through many years of personal experience.

Introduction

SOME LIKEN SKYE TO a great bird, some to a fragile butterfly breaking away from the confines of mainland Scotland. In fact, for almost two thousand years Skye has been known in the Gaelic as An t-Eilean Sgitheanach or the Winged Isle. The far more recent label of Eilean a' Cheo (Isle of Mist) is a throwback to Victorian times when mist-shrouded moors and mountains were regarded as mysterious and romantic. This notion, like the mist, still lingers in the hearts of many, and Skye has been stuck with this fanciful half-truth.

To the privileged few who are lucky enough to know the island intimately, it is simply An t-Eilean, The Island. True intimacy cannot develop through fleeting visits but requires more prolonged encounters to sample its many and varied moods. Over the last twenty five years I have visited the island many times and have slowly but surely surrendered to its subtle spell. The great bird holds me powerless but placid in its talons. From this captivation by and addiction to one of the most remarkable islands in the world grew the idea to walk the coastline – an idea which was to become an irresistible obsession.

Skye is an island of superlatives. With an astounding variety of landscapes, it is unquestionably the most scenic of all the Scottish islands. It contains the finest and most demanding range of mountains in Britain: the rough crystalline gabbro of the Cuillin is renowned the world over. The northern 'wing' of Trotternish, with its tottering rock spires of the Quirang and the Storr, is geologically unique and one of the most extraordinary landscapes in Britain. Skye probably has more myths associated with its turbulent past than any other part of Scotland. Its history is romantic and poignant. Its weather can range from cloudless blue sky to driving squalls within the space of a few minutes. The quality of light in these conditions can be breathtaking, and it is little wonder that Skye is one of the most photographed islands in the world. It is also the most written about, but this book is one with a difference.

'Skye has little body and more arms than the Goddess Kali' wrote distinguished Scottish mountaineer Bill Murray. The Winged Isle is indeed an appropriate term for an island whose coastline is so indented that it is out of all proportion to its land area of 670 square miles. Skye has been described as a collection of peninsulas. So just how long is the coastline? This question is not nearly as easy to answer as it would initially appear, and indeed was the very stumbling block which delayed my first attempt to walk it. Incredibly, published figures for the total length vary between 300 and 1,000 miles. Now, as all good chaos theory mathematicians know, from a fractal geometrical perspective all coastlines are of infinite length, so I would require an infinite amount of time to complete the walk – somewhat longer than a school summer holiday during which it would have to be undertaken. The 'real' upper limit of 1,000 miles is obtained by extremely accurate measurement on exceedingly large scale maps and almost literally takes in every twist and turn and localised contortions, probably also with the tide out! Certainly not compatible with the holiday – even for a teacher!

So the idea of a pedestrian circumnavigation of the Winged Isle was shifted on to the back-burner to await a more suitable time in my life: perhaps retirement, or (perish the thought) perhaps never. Then one dark February evening I was leafing through a copy of the *Scots Magazine* when I came across an article by renowned outdoor enthusiast Hamish Brown entitled 'The Lost World of Rubha Hunish' about the northern tip of Skye. In it he declared that 'years ago I thought a walk round the coast of Skye might be a good ploy'. More to the point, he made the bold assertion that its coastline was around 400 miles in length. Two minutes later I had fished out os Landranger maps 31, 32 and 33 and began a systematic measurement of the length of Skye's coast with a pair of dividers and a dram. Half an hour later I confidently came up with a figure of 366 miles – and promptly refilled my glass wishing it was Talisker rather than Bowmore. In an instant the idea had moved off the back-burner to become a foaming froth at the front – I knew what I had to do that summer: Skyewalk was born. There is a wonderfully euphoric flush of excitement in realising that a distant dream has been delivered into the realms of reality. I felt exorcised and purified as in my mind's eye I could see the challenge crystallising into a consummate whole. The contorted coastline on the map ceased to be an inanimate wavy line and instead became a writhing snake-like thoroughfare – the embryonic stage where my dream would be acted out. I began to look at the coastline through the eyes of a traveller, scheming and planning as to possible nightly stops, daily mileages and potential hazards.

I had already undertaken the planning of a long-distance walking route for that same summer holiday, only this one was for to an east to west crossing of Scotland finishing at Neist Point on Skye. Had I not read Hamish Brown's article, I would almost certainly have completed that route rather than the Skye coastal walk.

Two major differences are immediately apparent between a linear backpacking route and a circular coastal walk. Firstly, on a long-distance linear route (like the Pennine way or a trans-Scotland route) beginning at the beginning and ending at the end is common sense – most official long-distance routes are usually walked in one direction. On a circular coastal walk there is a multitude of possible starting points and finishing points. Secondly, there is the question of direction – clockwise or anti-clockwise? Having done some coastal walking on Skye previously, almost totally with the sea on the left, I had already made the unconscious decision that I would make a clockwise circuit. This decision required some soul searching however.

On a purely logistical basis the start/finish would almost certainly have to be either a main ferry point or a centre of population such as Kyleakin, Kylerhea, Armadale, Portree or Broadford. On the other hand, my sentimental and romantic urges demanded a more remote and wild spot, preferably one with which I was well acquainted. There is one particular place on Skye to which I have made several pilgrimages over the years. It is where time seems to stand still, and all notions of the real world dissolve spontaneously to be swept away on an off-shore breeze. It is where I have always experienced inner peace and calm, contentment deriving from its spectacular coastal position and the company of like-minded souls. It is where the idea of walking the Winged Isle originated. It is called Camasunary, or more correctly, Camas Fhionnairigh, the Bay of the White Sheiling.

The bay in fact contains two white sheilings, one a fine bothy and the other a private lodge, and both have been the scene of many happy carefree days smitten by and steeped in the magic of Skye. However, after much deliberation I decided not to begin at Camasunary. The main reasons for this decision were that it was not a natural starting point from a geographical viewpoint; and, I felt that starting and ending there really demanded a homecrowd of gangrels for a send-off and a welcome back and this was not easily forthcoming.

So where on the coast was there a place that satisfied the logistical requirements and was geographically significant but also retained an element of simple romanticism? The answer had to be Kylerhea, the tiny ferry terminal situated at the heel of the Winged Isle, the closest point to the mainland and the oldest ferry crossing to the island. Some readers may wonder why Kyleakin, a dozen miles round the coast from Kylerhea and endpoint of the ill-disposed Skye bridge, was not a contender. It is certainly sound from a logistical angle and a geographical one – but romantic? No. Besides, being something of an anti-toll person I invariably avoid the bridge and use the Kylerhea ferry. Indeed, even before the advent of the bridge, I always preferred turning left at Shiel Bridge to drive over the spectacular Mam Ratagan Pass with its hairpin bends, single track road and glorious views of Glen Shiel and Loch Duich. The descent to Glenelg and Klyerhea is equally fine and is to my mind the only way to arrive on the island. Skye is worth more than daylight robbery at a toll booth and a concrete connection. The ferry may only be a few pence cheaper than the bridge but I have no hesitation in saluting Roddy Macleod who has successfully given a two finger salute to the Skye Bridge Company with his efficient running of the only 'Skye Connection' worth considering.

With the start and end point selected I was now in a position to plan the walk in detail. The route was obvious – follow the coastline – so the planning revolved around factors such as daily mileage, nightly accommodation, booking hotels or guest houses, depositing caches, arranging meetings with friends and family, and countless other details. I was not a newcomer to long-distance walking and had already completed several backpacking expeditions lasting up to four weeks. One of these, dubbed Scotwalk '89, had entailed walking from the Mull of Kintyre to Cape Wrath, a distance of about 350 miles through some of Scotland's wildest terrain. I had purposely chosen the route to pass through the very best of West Highland scenery such as Glen Etive, Glencoe, Ardgour, Knoydart, the Fisherfield Forest and Coigach. Such was my love of Skye that I had seriously considered a diversion to include it, but due to several factors decided not to. The walk lasted four weeks and was probably the most enjoyable and satisfying experience of my life up to that point. The self-reliance, independence and delicious freedom which resulted from simply putting one foot in front of the other for a month was a feeling which grew into a passion, which took root within me to blossom into future ventures, one of which was Skyewalk.

Skyewalk would only be marginally longer that Scotwalk '89 both in distance and time but the similarities ended there. Apart from the linear nature of the one walk and circular nature of the other, there was the fact that Skyewalk essentially followed a rigid route – the coastline – and the inflexibility of this, though simplifying some aspects of the planning, made other aspects complex. Scotwalk '89 consisted mostly of excellent hill-tracks, paths and roads with only very minor sections of totally trackless terrain. By its very nature Skyewalk had to contain many trackless sections which would prove far more difficult to negotiate than following a path. Obviously this would considerably affect the daily mileage which on the 1989 walk had averaged about 14 miles per day. I did not take this fully into account during the planning stages, with the result that there were some profound logistical changes during the course of the walk.

Walking a coastline is not as simple as it sounds. For instance, sticking religiously to the coast (i.e. walking and stumbling on sand, seaweed and rocks for four weeks) is impossible – not only that, but the actual mileage would then be of the order of the 1,000 miles mentioned previously. After pondering on various self-invented rules such as never straying more than half a mile from the sea at any time, or being able to see the sea at all times, I finally decided to adopt no rules, though I knew this could be dangerous. A long coastal walk teases with temptations in a way that a linear A to B walk does not – cut across a peninsula here, take a shortcut there. In short it demands much more mental and physical discipline. Eventually a happy medium is found, somewhere between blatant disregard of any rules and a strict adherence to every twist and turn of the coastline. Where this medium actually lies depends on a multitude of factors such as individual mood, weather, load carried, time, etc. When the contorted nature of the coastline, with at least seventeen sea lochs and six major peninsulas together with dozens of smaller ones, is taken into account, the true enormity and challenge of the venture begins to sink in. It was precisely this challenge which made the proposition of a coastal walk so enticing. No other Scottish island has such a long coastline in relation to its area and no other Scottish island has such a diverse and numerous collection of coastal attractions.

A rough analysis from map combing had shown that approximately half the intended route could be accomplished on marked paths/tracks or roads with the rest being wild trackless terrain. The word 'wild' is to some degree a misnomer. In no sense could a walk around the coastline of Skye could be regarded as a 'wilderness walk'. Skye, like the rest of the West Highlands, is not a true wilderness in the vein of northern Canada or the Arctic tundra, but a man-made wilderness where human greed, malice and downright mismanagement have exerted a heavy toll over the last few hundred years. The clearance of native woodland is mismanagement on one scale; the clearance of native people is an offence so immoral that it goes off any scale of injustice. It was only in the aftermath of the walk that the sheer scale of denudation reflected in the empty shells of stone dwellings all along the coast really began to sink in. Canadian novelist, Hugh MacLennan, descendant of a West Highland emigrant, embraced the notion perfectly on returning to the place from which his ancestors had been evicted: 'But this highland emptiness only a few hundred miles above the massed population of England, is a far different thing from the emptiness of our own North-West Territories. Above the 60th parallel in Canada you feel that nobody but God had ever been there before you. But in a deserted Highland glen you feel that everyone who ever mattered is dead and gone.'

This recurring theme of walking through long since deserted settlements and their abiding and haunting reminder of past atrocities, which even to myself who tends to appreciate the more natural features of a landscape, became an hallmark of the whole experience. It would of course be wrong to conclude from this discourse that Skye has little wild country. A vast proportion of Skye is spectacularly wild and lonely, but this wildness and loneliness is very much a result of a wilful and methodical man-made process. It would be fair to say that with the exception of the Cuillin Ridge and some of the more remote parts of the coastal cliff areas, no region of Skye is in its original natural condition.

In my view, the abiding beauty of Skye resides within its very form and structure and the interrelation of its parts. The physical geography and geology of the Winged Isle which are reflected in such stark and grand features of the Cuillin, the Durinish cliffs and sea-stacks, the Trotternish ridge and countless other natural wonders is, from a human perspective, eternal. As Derek Cooper succinctly puts it:

'But Skye is no longer the place it was ten years ago and ten years from now it will no longer be the place it is today. This need not give rise to either regret or alarm or even misplaced tears of nostalgia. The beauty will be there long after we are gone and long after we are gone the magic will remain.'

This is an important and far-sighted observation. To many people, the beauty of Skye is transient and ephemeral and too fragile to weather the vagaries of its turbulent past. Yet through the clearance of the trees, the clearance of its very lifeblood, the arrival of sheep, the steady increase of tourism and the recent bridge construction, the Winged Isle has graciously acknowledged these graceless times. Its feathers may be ruffled but the great bird of prey still has that piercing gleam in its eye, an eye trained unwaveringly to the future and belief in itself. Skye is going places – and so was I.

CHAPTER I

The Heart is Highland

(Monday 6 July)

To Glenelg

'From the lone shieling of the misty island
Mountains divide us, and the waste of seas,
But yet the blood is strong,
The heart is highland,
And we in dreams behold the Hebrides.'

A STRANGE BITTER-SWEETNESS possessed me as I sped up the A9 on a soft July afternoon. Thoughts recoiled in my head like a pinball in a games machine and there seemed to be no coherence in my mind's musings. Every train of thought which gained momentum was immediately derailed, to be replaced by another equally as fleeting and lacking in substance.

Less than an hour before I had said goodbye to my wife Heather and stepdaughter Laura at our cottage nestling cosily in the Perthshire countryside. Heather and I had celebrated our first wedding anniversary only the day before and here I was en route to Skye to begin a four-week trek round the coastline – it would be the longest period we had been apart since our wedding day; and to top it all she was already six months pregnant! There had been the odd direct and indirect comments from people expressing their incredulity at me leaving my wife in her swollen state. 'Heather will be joining you, won't she?' one would say. 'Yes, probably for a day or two,' I would reply, which was in fact true although she declined to indulge in any actual walking.

Right from the start of our relationship Heather had understood and accepted my need to escape to the hills on occasions and she realised the spiritual nourishment thus provided was essential to my well-being and to our marriage. She has often made the comment that I would not be the same person if I didn't go off hillwalking on a regular basis and that she always wanted me to be the person she first remembered. I was extremely grateful to Heather for this unselfish and liberal outlook without which I would probably not have been speeding toward Skye on that July afternoon.

Despite this, it would have to be a fairly uncaring, selfish individual who did not experience some glimmer of conscience and guilt at shirking his domestic responsibilities for four weeks to wallow in a self-indulgent dream. Yes, I did feel a shade guilty, but there was also the stark reality of leaving my loved one for several weeks, and the knowledge that she would be missing me dreadfully. At least I hoped so!

In those last few tender moments we had spent together, tears had continually welled up in her eyes, and I felt a profound sense of togetherness tinged with sadness and shame – shame that I was choosing to leave the most wonderful woman in my life for a month of backpacking round a tortuous piece of coastline. Such is the absurdity of man's petty visions – or as Heather was fond of saying: 'Boys and their toys!'

The actual moment of departure had been paradoxically quite relaxed and almost whimsical. I had struggled out to the waiting car with my bulging rucksack which had been packed for 24 hours and which I hadn't dare weigh – until this moment. As I waited by the car Laura ran inside to fetch the bathroom scales. My heart sank as the numbers on the dial registered that my pack weighed over 40 pounds. To a seasoned backpacker this is no doubt quite normal; but I had intended to whittle the weight down to around 30 pounds. Laura attempted to lift the pack and groaned under the strain muttering something like 'You must be mad!' A last kiss, a goodbye and I was off.

As the invisible umbilical cord linking me with Heather stretched further and further, my confused and transient thoughts began to crystallise into meaningful meditation. On the long scenic stretch of road between Dalwhinnie and Spean Bridge my mind began to settle into the task ahead. I thought back nine years to 1989 and the start of Scotwalk '89. Then I had driven with a friend and his dog to the Mull of Kintyre. There had been no heartfelt goodbyes, no niggling guilt complexes – in short there had been no wife and no family to think about. My domestic circumstances had changed beyond all recognition since then, but I didn't regret it in the slightest. At 44 years of age some would say I was leaving it a bit late to be having a family – but then some would also say I was leaving it a bit late to be acting out boyish dreams. As far as I was concerned the time was just right. There is a saying 'The young aren't on to it and the old aren't up to it'. Middle age is the perfect time to do a lot of things – it is that time of life when you suddenly realise that there could be less years ahead than behind – a sobering observation.

As I neared Spean Bridge I was pleased to discover that the weather was remarkably similar to that at Dalwhinnie. More times than I can remember I have driven this stretch of road east to west, leaving Dalwhinnie in blue skies and sunshine and arriving at Spean Bridge with heavy dark clouds shrouding the summits and a constant drizzle accompanying the rhythmic click of the windscreen wipers. I had studied the weather forecast obsessively for the last few days but hadn't gained much more than that it was essentially to be a mixed bag of sun, showers and wind over the following week. As far as Skye goes this could mean anything. Skye is renowned for its own idiosyncratic weather patterns and the changeability ensures there is never a dull moment.

I love the climb north-west out of Spean Bridge as the canopy of trees gradually gives way to the wild mountainous terrain beyond the Great Glen. Looking back from the Commando Memorial, the great hulking brute of Ben Nevis was swathed in cloud, but many lower hills were dappled with flecks of sunlight as more sombre clouds shifted in from the west. Having lived in Fort Augustus at the southern end of Loch Ness for seven years, I knew this road well but never tired of the subtle nuances of colour and scenery produced by the mountains, lochs and trees.

As I approached Invergarry a quiet excitement began to ignite within me. Here the Great Glen is left behind and a left fork is taken which leads west to the highland and Hebridean heartland, where ocean and mountain clamour for attention, where sun-kissed rocky ridges and glittering sea lochs jostle and juxtapose to create that indefinable charisma which characterises Scotland's western Highlands and islands. Beyond Loch Garry the road climbs steadily with the summit revealing the Knoydart ridges beyond Loch Loyne. Here is the point of no return. The heart is captured, the landscape both lures and lulls, there is a scent of Skye, a whiff of the Winged Isle – within an hour I would be in sight of The Island.

I put a cassette tape into the radio/cassette player. Entitled 'Skye Mist', it was a self-made compilation of music which for me had close links with Skye and could be loosely filed under that generic title Celtic Rock. It included such diverse bands as Runrig, Capercaillie, Clannad and music from the film *Local Hero*, all of which perfectly accompanied windscreen images of highland scenery. Runrig originated from Skye and have been an endless source of inspiration (both musically and lyrically) over the years. Unlike mainstream rock bands whose music is essentially rooted in urban life, Runrig's music reflects rural values and landscape and is based on a Gaelic tradition going back hundreds of years. One track in particular, 'Going Home' from the 'Highland Connection' album, describes vividly the journey home to Skye from months in the big city and has become a regular piece on pilgrimages to the island. When this track flooded the car, tears welled up as I drove past Loch Cluanie and into the ever narrowing jaws of Glenshiel.

Favourite mountains queued up to greet me on either side of this scenic glen – the seven Munros of the South Cluanie Ridge strung out like pearls on the left, the 'brothers and sisters' ridge on the right with its five sisters of Kintail. I had cut my teeth on these hills way back in the late 70s and early 80s when I had been based in Fort Augustus, and every time I drive down Glenshiel memories of grand hill days come flooding back. Today was no exception.

The common climatic condition known as the 'Cluanie Curtain', a curtain of rain and mist drawn and driven up the glen, was thankfully absent and the mountains stood out proud against a blue sky dappled with wisps of cumulus cloud.

At Shiel Bridge I abandoned the hoards making for the Skye Bridge and turned left along the single-track road which climbs in a series of hairpin bends over the Mam Ratagan Pass to descend to the remote and idyllic little hamlet of Glenelg, a stone's throw from the Kylerhea Ferry. Just beyond the last of the hairpin bends is a large carpark where I invariably stop to soak up the glorious view of Loch Duich and the Five Sisters. Again, today was no exception. At 6.45pm, a shade less than four hours after leaving home in Perthshire, I arrived at my pre-booked Bed and Breakfast near Glenelg.

Expecting a spontaneous highland welcome I eagerly raced to the front door only to be greeted by a note stuck to the door saying 'Andew Dempster, Gone sheep shearing – back late afternoon'. A wry smile curled my lips – it was good to be back in the Highlands. I suppose 'late afternoon' in the Highlands in mid-summer can mean any time between 4.00pm and midnight! I rang the bell anyway, and within seconds my highland hostess Mrs Chisholm had opened the door and was apologising for the note stuck to the woodwork.

'Aye, we've been shearing all afternoon – it's the maggots ye see – gets into the fleece. Anyway come in, come in and have a cup of tea.' Soon I was esconsed in the kitchen and imbued with the warm and free heart of true highland hospitality, the enduring hallmark of the crofting community. I felt it ironic that crofters, who collectively had hated sheep when they were first introduced, now viewed them as the mainstay of their livelihood. Bed and Breakfast was certainly relatively lucrative for the Chisholms, but their real passion and earnings came from crofting.

Anxious as I was to continue our chat, hunger pangs had taken hold and after depositing my night bag in my room I drove the mile and a half to the Glenelg Inn for some evening refreshment. It was actually through making enquiries at the Inn a few weeks earlier that I was given the Chisholm's address by their daughter who worked there. I had originally intended to spend this night at the Inn but the price was rather daunting!

In the Scottish Highlands and Islands there is a distinct lack of really good pubs. Most drinking and eating establishments range from the dismally standard hotel cocktail or lounge bars normally hoaching with tourists, to spartan public bars selling cold fizzy beer to gutsy locals. Alas, my preferred view of a really good pub is tainted with South of the Border characteristics and includes such notions as real ale, log fires, old-fashioned appeal and a pleasant mix of locals and tourists. The Glenelg Inn is such a place. The fact that it calls itself an Inn and not a hotel is a strong clue. When you walk into the Glenelg Inn you do not find yourself in a hotel reception type lobby but in the public bar. There is no lounge bar – or if there is, I've never been in it.

I ordered salmon quiche and salad and a pint of Gillespies stout – rather similar to Guinness but sweeter. 'Just pull up a fishbox and sit where you want' exclaimed the kilted owner. In the bar most of the seats are fishboxes, of the old wooden variety, and most of the tables are wooden beer barrels. The massive stone fireplace was fireless on this balmy summer evening, but the bar was buzzing with bullish youth, benign elders and everything in between.

I finished my meal and joined in a game of pool with a gang of youngsters (younger than me anyway!) who were a mixture of locals and mountain-bikers. One of the locals was a forestry worker, another worked on a fishfarm and a third was a deep sea diver on an oilrig. Apart from the more obvious jobs such as shop and hotel work and the ubiquitous crofting, these types of jobs form the core of employment opportunities in the Western Highlands. Forestry and fishfarming are essentially new areas of employment in the sense that they did not exist 50 years ago. Despite the whining of so-called conservationists who complain bitterly about forestry and fishfarms, they are bringing people back to once peopled areas. Of course wildlife matters, but surely people matter more. If only one thing is learned from the troubled past of the Highlands it is unquestionably this.

Much as I would have liked to remain in the cosy atmosphere of the Glenelg Inn, the walk began tomorrow and an early start was advisable – besides, I was driving, and I also wished to continue chatting with the Chisholms. I would not see the Inn for another month. It seemed a lifetime away. On the short drive back the imposing Bernera Barracks stood out proudly against a backdrop of speckled Skye hills across the placid waters of Glenelg Bay. The Barracks were part of a network of garrisons built by the government across the Highlands in the wake of the 1715 Jacobite rebellion; the idea was to use the army to hold in check and crush the spirit of the 'rebellious' highland clans.

On arrival back at the B&B I showered and sorted out some gear before going down for another very welcome cup of tea. I was informed by Mrs Chisholm that a lone walker by the name of Brian Lawrence was also staying overnight. He was tackling the highland drove route from Glenbrittle in Skye to Crieff in Perthshire, a distance of some 200 miles. Every autumn for centuries hardy Highlanders would tramp this mountainous route with hundreds of heads of cattle to Crieff and other Lowland cattle markets. In 1981 this epic trek was recreated with 29 Highland bullocks (and a cow called Matilda) and the story is splendidly told in Irvine Butterfield's *The Famous Highland Drove Walk* (Grey Stone Books). I suspected that Brian had probably read this book and had been inspired to attempt the route for himself. I looked forward to meeting him, as I could see we were likely to be kindred spirits.

I learned that walkers regularly stayed at the Chisholm's B&B but none so ambitious as one a few years ago who had walked around the entire coastline of Britain! I knew that this extraordinary feat had been accomplished by the long-distance walker John Merrill in 1978 but I had not realised that the trip had been repeated. The reported figure of 7,000 miles for this route made my paltry 366 miles round Skye seem like a stroll in the park. However, as far as I was aware no-one else had ever attempted a Skye coastal walk – or if they had then they kept quiet about it, though I did know that John Merrill had walked the coastline of

7

Mull, another large Scottish island. Being first or fastest has never been important to me and was not a factor in the answering of the question 'Why walk the coastline of Skye?'

The evening's discussion provided me with an insight into the Chisholm's way of life and the general problems of crofting in the Highlands. Like the majority of crofters, the Chisholms own their house but rent their land from the local landowner – in this case Lord Burton of Dochfour Estates. It is interesting to note that it is only since 1976 that a crofter has been entitled to purchase his croft land if he desires, but legal protection and security of tenure were secured in 1886. The Chisholm's croft has been in their family since the 1700s yet the absurd and almost obscene situation exists that Mr Chisholm cannot fish legally in the local river! I was also informed of the existence of a substantial New Age settlement close to the Pictish broch towers in Glen Beag near Glenelg. These travelling folk live in teepees and pay no rates yet the Chisholms pay rates for two unoccupied caravans on their rented land. Further, the powers-that-be from Skye and Lochalsh District Council have decreed that the caravans cannot be permanently occupied and must be stored away over the winter! Just where does one store a caravan? The Chisholms refused to comply with this second regulation.

Our discussion moved on to another landowner, Lord Dulverton, whose estate includes Sandaig beach, better known as Camusfearna, the setting for Gavin Maxwell's *Ring of Bright Water*. Having visited that magical spot on a previous holiday with no access problems I was confounded on a subsequent visit to be confronted with a sign saying 'No access to beach today'. As my intention on that occasion had not been to visit the beach, it did not affect me on a practical level, but the fact that it existed and with all the hallmarks of permanency, had gnawed away at me ever since. It turned out that between my visits Lord Dulverton had bought the estate and erected these signs – which really signified Lord Dulverton's intention that he was denying people access to the beach today, and every day.

The evening's chat with the Chisholms convinced me even

more that the landownership issue in the Highlands is in dire need of sweeping reforms, and that persecution of normal law-abiding people still continues albeit to a lesser extent than a century ago. The farcical situation of a foreign fat-cat buying huge tracts of the Highlands with the only prerequisite being a fat cheque-book; and a potential crofter having to run the gauntlet of regulations and petty red tape in order to secure a few acres of croft (with no guarantee of success) – is in short an absurd and unscrupulous state of affairs.

However, as I said my good-nights and retired to my room I didn't dwell on these matters for too long. Ahead of me lay four weeks of walking, a whole month to fulfil a long cherished dream. In my mind's eye I had visualised every section of the walk, and each bay, peninsula, sea loch and other features now formed a mental map in my mind. No amount of preparation and vision however could ever compare with reality. There would be new sights to see, different sounds and smells, fresh faces, off-beat occurrences, humorous moments, adventures and misadventures, highs and lows – a lifetime in miniature. I felt like a child on Christmas Eve. As I lay in bed my thoughts turned again to my highland hosts, so welcoming and genuine. After so many years of persecution such warmth could only be from the heart.

CHAPTER 2

A Walk round the Garden

(Tuesday 7 July – Thursday 9 July)

Glenelg to Ord

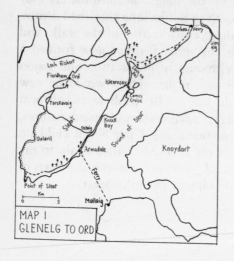

MAP I
GLENELG TO ORD

I WOKE EARLY. In normal circumstances I always do but often turn over and go back to sleep again. Today was different. The time was 6.20am and my mind was open and receptive. I drew back the curtain and glanced outside, anxious that the weather would allow me a reasonably dry first day's walking. It was cloudy but at least it wasn't raining. To have a continuous deluge on the commencement of the trek would be a miserable and lack-lustre beginning, though I knew there could be other such days.

I washed, dressed and pottered about the room, in a state of overwrought fidgety restlessness – I needed to be walking. Somewhere in the distance a cockerel crowed and a lamb bleated. Shortly after 7.30 I decided to wander downstairs and check out the breakfast situation. The table was fully laid complete with cereals and orange juice but no one was about. A delicious smell of fried bacon wafted through from the kitchen as I sat down to the first of what would be many excellent B&B breakfasts over the course of the next four weeks. Probably like most people, I do not normally eat a cooked breakfast as my appetite isn't up to it – unless it is cooked for me! With the energy expenditure of a month's walking I knew that a full cooked breakfast was a solid foundation for the day ahead and that I didn't need to worry about gaining weight.

Within minutes Mrs Chisholm appeared, abandoning her bacon in the kitchen, with a cheery hello and 'Aye, it's a fine day for the start of your walk'. She informed me that drove-route walker, Brian Lawrence, would be down shortly and he appeared a few seconds later. Mrs Chisholm had obviously spoken to Brian about me, as she had to me about him, and when we were introduced there was no embarrassing ice-breaking, just frank and direct discussion of each other's chosen treks. Brian was a teacher, like I am, and was spending three weeks of his summer break on the drove route from Skye to Crieff. He had taken three days to reach Glenelg from Glenbrittle and was indulging in his first rest day today. He seemed genuinely impressed with my intended objective and obviously viewed me as a more serious walker than himself. Astonishment crossed his face when I told him that a large proportion of the route was totally pathless and that I would be carrying a full pack. Astonishment, in turn, crossed my face when he told me that he had sent his pack by post from Glenbrittle to Glenelg and was worried because it had not yet turned up. Much as I admire the postal service, I can't imagine trusting all my worldly walking/cooking/sleeping gear to the post on a regular basis. Yet this is exactly what he intended to do for the duration of his walk. A short time later he was thankful to discover that his pack was safe at the Glenelg Post Office.

It was well after 9.00am when I reluctantly pulled myself away from conversation with Brian and began last minute packing of personal items into my rucksack. The Chisholms had kindly given me permission to leave my car in their field for the duration of the walk and for this I was immensely grateful. Brian, impressed by the size of my pack, offered to take a setting-off photograph of me. A pet lamb, probably the one I had heard earlier, seemed anxious to be included in the photo then suddenly scuttled off through the buttercups in the field. Just as I was about to go, there was a shout from Mr Chisholm telling me that I had left behind my telescopic trekking pole at the side of the car. Over the last few years I have become used to walking with a pole and this modern-day equivalent of the wooden walking stick has become a common sight in the hills and glens. Some bright spark has calculated that through reduced wear and tear on knee joints and the like, the use of a trekking pole can add five years to a hillwalker's hill time. Some even brighter spark has suggested that the use of two poles should give an extra ten years!

As the saying goes, it was now time to 'stop the talking and do the walking' with or without two poles. The actual departure was quick but poignant. I wished Brian all the best for the rest of his walk and hoped to meet up with him again on a future occasion. Emotional goodbyes were made with the Chisholms, a last wave and I was off.

I felt an infinity away from the endless deliberations on ethics, advance planning, pack problems, accommodation decisions and general organisation. Now there was only the pure enjoyment of the walk itself, the ethereal realm which all walkers and back-packers aim for, the real reason we embark on such ventures. The start of a long walk is a deliverance into this realm.

In a sense, of course, the walk had not yet strictly begun. I had to walk the mile and a half to the ferry crossing before setting foot on Skye. This proved to be an ideal warm-up period when all I had to do was put one foot in front of the other on a pleasant single-track road and try to free my mind and focus on the task ahead. The road makes a sweeping arc round the sandy Bernera Bay where a motley collection of caravans gives the impression of being washed up and stranded at high tide. A couple of collies careered up to me, barking in that half-welcoming and half-warning fashion, and I was glad of the security of a walking pole. A dishevelled figure emerged from behind one of the caravans and shouted something in a North of England twang, at which point the dogs meekly and obediently turned tail to rejoin their master. As I approached him we exchanged a few words. He had been coming here for years, usually staying for most of the summer. Whether the land owner extracted any rent from these long-term trippers wasn't clear but I suspected there had to be some monetary gain for someone.

Leaving the Bay, the road climbs steadily and curls round the final headland before descending to the jetty and ferry. I stopped momentarily and gazed across the Kylerhea Narrows to the delicate greens and browns of The Island and my intended route hugging the lower slopes of Ben Aslak – I could see no sign of a path from this range. At the final hairpin bend sits a picturesque white cottage built in 1690, once the Old Ferry Inn and now home to Roddy Macleod, the present operator of the oldest ferry to Skye. James Boswell and Dr Johnson stayed here during their famous highland tour in 1773 but found little satisfaction, there being 'no meat, no milk, no bread, no eggs, no wine ... Whisky we might have, and ... At last they caught a fowl and killed it.'

On reaching the cottage, I saw that the ferry was already loaded with its full quota of six cars and appeared to be on the point of departure. Not wishing to appear too anxious to any interested onlookers, I briskly walked, rather than ran, the short distance to the jetty but found myself breaking into an ungainly lope for the last 50 yards – I needn't have bothered. Roddy Macleod's well-trained eye had spotted me long before. 'Aye, there's no rush', he casually uttered, as he began unwinding the thick hawser rope from the capstan. I realised there is never any rush to do anything in the Highlands – life proceeds at a more leisurely pace. I took heed.

My feet made their last contact with mainland Scotland for a whole month. The adventure had really begun. If my impending odyssey could be compared to a lifetime in miniature, then the Kylerhea crossing was the birth. The currents in Kyle Rhea are some of the strongest and most violent on the West Coast of Scotland, running up to eight knots in a spring tide and increasing to twelve knots with a following wind. Hugh Miller describes navigating through the Straits under sail in the 1940s:

'Never, except perhaps in a Highland river big in flood, have I seen such a tide. It danced and wheeled and came boiling in huge masses from the bottom; and now our bows heaved abruptly round in one direction, and now they jerked as suddenly round in another; and though there blew a moderate breeze at the time, the helm failed to keep the sails steadily full. But whether our sheets bellied out, or flopped right in the wind's eye, on we swept in the tideway, like a cork caught during a thunder shower in one of the rapids of the High Street.'

On the basis of all this, it is quite remarkable that every year for hundreds of years, 8,000 cattle swam across these same powerful rip tides with only minor losses. Normally six beasts at a time struggled across, roped together head to tail. Not surprisingly, many cattle became hysterical, some biting the tail of the beast in front, causing a frenzied chain reaction. Others, seemingly desperate to relieve their misery, rolled over on their backs to drown themselves.

The five-minute crossing seemed contrarily benign on this calm day and labour pains were absent as I was delivered safely into the welcoming and protective arms of Skye's motherly influence. Roddy's bearded and weather-beaten face was a picture when I told him my four week plan. As the cars rolled off the ramp onto the Kylerhea jetty, full of satisfied customers, I thought back to the remarks of a prominent public figure who declared that the Kylerhea ferry would die in the wake of the Skye Bridge. In fact, it was now flourishing better than ever. I strolled down the ramp as Roddy and his son manhandled the sturdy turntable and prepared for another busy day. 'See you in a month' I shouted, my feet on Skye soil.

A few hundred yards up the road I stopped to look back at the ferry waiting for its return complement of vehicles. Beyond the jetty the tree-clad hillside marked what would be the final stage of my route in four weeks' time. Whilst on the ferry, I had seen the line of electricity pylons marching across the hill and over to the mainland. Beneath them I noticed a new forestry track which was unmarked on my map and I made a mental note of this.

On a long distance walk I prefer the first day to be relatively easy in order to ease the body and mind into the more demanding rigours of subsequent days. A recognised coastal path connects Kylerhea with the Kinloch Lodge Hotel which was fairly close to my intended first night stopover point at Isle Ornsay. The distance was around twelve miles.

Less than a quarter of a mile from the ferry a dirt track leads off to the left and a gate displays the encouraging sign 'Footpath to Kinloch Lodge'. I opened the gate which was one of the newer, longer-lasting metal variety designed in such a way as to cause the maximum amount of noise, inevitably inducing canine commotion from neighbouring farms. Today, however, the metallic clanging of the spring bolt fell on deaf ears and I wandered in silence past the few whitewashed stone cottages which comprise the crofting township of Kylerhea. The name Kylerhea derives from the words Caol (Kyle), meaning a narrow strait, and Readh, a fictitious Fingalian giant who attempted to jump across to the mainland.

In the muggy, windless weather fine wisps of smoke crawled skywards from a couple of cottages with a stack of peat piled neatly against the wall of one. Some of the gardens were beautifully tended and one in particular was a kaleidoscope of colour with fuschia, lupins, delphiniums and dozens of other delights which I couldn't name.

At the end of the track the coastal path goes off to the left just before a cottage. A wooden bridge crosses the Kylerhea River and I crossed this before passing through a small coppice of young trees. At this point the path forked, and had I studied my map carefully I would probably not have gone straight ahead to an area of peat cuttings. After much floundering in deep heather and ankle-sucking bog I regained the path and tried to gain some kind of rhythm.

The majority of Skye is covered by just two Ordnance Survey maps (32 and 33) but rather annoyingly the 'heel' of Skye containing Kylerhea is lumped in with 'Lochalsh and Glenshiel' (sheet 33). Not wishing to carry this map all round Skye, I had simply cut out the relevant section, folded it and inserted it in a small plastic credit card wallet which was handily kept in my shirt pocket.

I sat on an elevated rocky outcrop to study the features on the map and already I was aware of beads of sweat forming on my fore-head – it was going to be a sticky, clammy day.

The path ranged from a well-defined stony thoroughfare to a vague, boggy, hit-and- miss furrow in the heather and at various places I was sure the path had deserted me totally. After a couple of miles I had made a slow rising traverse to a naturally wooded area of oak, birch, hazel and rowan above the lonely little bay of Port Aslaig. Stopping to wipe the sweat from my brow, I felt the sun strong at my back and gazed out across the sparkling sea to Sandaig. Meadow pipits and chiff chaffs chirped and flitted in a thicket ahead of me, while the subtle fragrance of bog myrtle arrested my senses. A startled deer appeared, then disappeared as quickly in a flash of white rump. For a moment I was lost in myself and at total peace with the world. It was at that point that the walk really began – in a spiritual sense.

The sheltered southern peninsula of Skye in which I was now walking is known as Sleat (pronounced slate) and is often labelled 'the Garden of Skye' on account of its low, green, partially-wooded hills and lush vegetation. Its complex geology has resulted in an area which delights with surprises, such as sudden patches of wild flowers in the middle of open moorland and unexpected corners teeming with naturally growing trees. Sleat is unique in the whole of Skye. It is only in the last few centuries that trees on Skye have become 'as rare as a horse in Venice' as Dr Johnson remarked. When red deer and sheep were introduced to 'improve' the Highlands, natural woodland was relegated to death row through lack of regeneration, and in most of Skye (and most of the Highlands) trees are extremely scarce. In Sleat, however, the last vestiges have survived thanks to the underlying geology which helps them to grow faster.

My dreamy moment amidst the trees above Port Aslaig was rudely cut short by the appearance of the ubiquitous highland midge – or rather clouds of them. These pirhanas of the insect world are by far the biggest hindrance to be taken into account when planning a walking holiday in the Highlands. In large numbers they can induce frenzied derangement in normally sane individuals. Midges are insatiable and have an apparently quenchless appetite for human blood – Skye midges in particular have a notoriety which is legendary. Needless to say, I wasn't long in moving off. In preparation I had packed Jungle Formula lotion and a mosquito/midge hood to wear over my head, neither of which were used to any great extent. Smoke is reckoned to be high on the midges' list of pet hates so I had also taken a pack of mosquito coils, slow burning coils producing a smoky aroma which midges allegedly abhor. These are ideal for placing outside the entrance to a tent. I had even brought along a few packets of cigars if everything else failed! I smoke the odd cigar anyway.

Within minutes of my escape from the midges I had lost the path in a mass of deep bracken, regaining it some distance on. A couple of jets screamed like banshees across the sky, ripping asunder the tranquillity of this sheltered corner. I dropped down through heather to cross the Allt Cailte – translated as 'lost' or 'ruined burn' – with the path plainly visible on the other side snaking its way up through gentle folds of hillside.

As I passed through a gap, I lost sight of the sea, the constant companion who would comfort me, cajole me and connect with me in countless ways over the coming month. There would be human companions, but at the moment there was only a fusion of landscape, seascape and mindscape, a fruitful threesome which would ultimately yield a grand harvest of memories to dwell on in the ripeness of time. As William Hazlitt deftly put it: 'Out of doors, nature is company enough for me. I am then never less alone than when alone. I cannot see the wit of walking and talking at the same time.' I cannot recall the number of people who asked questions such as 'Who are you going with?' or 'You're not going on your own are you?' when discussing the planned walk round Skye. My defensive reply was invariably tinged with a dose of almost embarrassed ignominy. 'Oh no, not for the whole time – I've got friends joining me for a week and someone else for a few days.' It was virtually paramount to admitting that lone walking was somehow a sad and pitiable form of activity not to be boasted about. To be perfectly honest, I enjoy walking alone and I enjoy walking with company, and both have advantages and disadvantages. Alone I am more receptive to what the landscape has to offer. Beyond the sights, sounds and colours which any camcorder can record, is the feeling, the heart, the spiritual fabric of the surroundings, which only exist through interaction with these surroundings. It is the constant interplay and fusion of landscape and mindscape which renders the reality we perceive.

Walking companions generally increase the difficulty of forming this personal communion with the natural world but in some instances they can enhance the communion by 'tuning in to the same wavelength' or by being knowledgeable on aspects of the landscape. Human characteristics such as humour and togetherness are major morale-boosters on low points of a walk and this one was to be no exception. I was determined to enjoy every second of this walk – with or without company.

As I descended to cross the Allt Thuill, a great swathe of coniferous plantation lay ahead – as different from the natural wood of half an hour ago as a sterile electric bar heater is from a natural log fire. Forestry plantations have a habit of obliterating old paths, and although the map declared a dotted line marching dauntlessly through green, my experience led me to adopt a more pessimistic frame of mind. The path reached the forest boundary at a purpose-built wooden stile crossing the high deer fence – an encouraging sign I thought. I duly negotiated the stile, noticing the dead weight of my bulging rucksack. Beyond the fence was tussocky grass with the treeline still 50 metres downhill. I now found myself playing hide-and-seek with the path which disappeared intermittently into acres of spongy sphagnum moss and bog. At least I appeared to be heading in generally the right direction and things could only get better...

Within half and hour I reached a wide firebreak with a choked burn wriggling a tortuous path between overgrown vegetation and scattered semi-rotten pine wood. I had the distinct feeling that no one had been here in years, especially since the path seemed to have won the game of hide-and-seek. I staggered like a drunkard some way down the break and almost miraculously regained the path as it continued along another firebreak traversing the side of the hill. According to my map a forestry track ran parallel to the path I was now on but 300 yards downhill through thick sitka spruce forest. I thought about making a beeline for this track but resisted the temptation, continuing to stagger and squelch my weary way along a gradually fading footpath. The tussocks and moss soon gave way to blanket bog and the path became a figment of my imagination. Even the firebreak had petered out and I found myself hemmed in under a canopy of larch, birch, alder and oak – at least the sitka spruce was absent.

In seconds I made the decision to head hell for leather downhill, knowing that I would have to hit the forestry track at some point. As I descended, the noise of my footfalls on dry snapping twigs and my rucksack brushing past foliage disturbed a *gaggle* of grouse which exploded skywards in a crescendo of bad-tempered machine-gun retorts of 'go-bak, go-bak, go-bak'. I was sure I got a bigger fright than they did. I soon found myself waist deep, then shoulder deep in thick bracken which gradually opened out to a broad treeless area containing the first example of what there would be many of during the walk – the sad abandoned ruins of a once thriving village. The map only indicated a single square with the word 'ruin' but behind that innocent label lay a mournful fund of forgotten lives, destined to grow old and die in the New World far 'from the lone shieling of the misty island'. I subsequently discovered that the deserted village was known as Leitirfura, literally meaning a welcome place at the side of the hill, and was once the home of a large MacInnes family. About the only thing that Leitirfura welcomed now was the choking hold of bracken and the intermittent chatter of bird life. The once proud people who lived here were reduced to disclaimed, disowned pawns in a dispassionate 'game' called the Clearances a century and a half ago. To the landowners of that time the Clearances were more than a game, they were a matter of life and death – usually a better life for them and a valueless existence leading to premature death for many of their tenants.

Just beyond these ruins I stumbled on a stony track which

gradually ascended the hillside in a rising traverse. The track appeared relatively recently constructed and wasn't shown on my map – I had still seen no sign of a forestry track. I subsequently learned that this was a newish Forest Enterprise track and it was like a motorway compared to what it had been before. As it levelled out higher up, I began to feel that I had broken the back of the first day's walking though I knew there must be a fair distance to go yet. At several points there were breaks in the trees and I could look out across Loch na Dal to my destination – Isle Ornsay, with its island and lighthouse only 3 kilometres away but still 8 kilometres by foot.

As I rounded a bend in the track I met my first person since the start of the walk; not another walker but a woodcutter clad in bright orange overalls. We exchanged nods and continued with our respective tasks. The sound of his chainsaw was soon replaced by a distant grinding, grating and low rumbling interspersed with high-pitched regular pulses of sound. This vexatious din was in the direction I was going and I soon realised there must be some heavy construction work happening some distance ahead. The whole complexion of the day had been transformed from a tranquil coastal walk to a hubbub of noise and distraction – such is the nature of long distance walking.

Finally the track began to descend to reach the forest boundary and shortly beyond I met the main forestry track which contoured round the lower hillside. At this point the source of the noise was clearly visible – the well-used A851 Broadford to Armadale Road was in the process of being upgraded from single to double-track. The part of road which was visible was a clutter of JCB diggers and dumper trucks scurrying around like a team of worker ants – I did not relish the roadwalk to come.

A short distance further on a sign indicated the track leading to the Kinloch Lodge Hotel, home of Lord and Lady MacDonald, the latter being Claire MacDonald, the author of several cookery books and a fairly distinguished culinary expert. Included in the A851 upgrade was an overhaul of the Kinloch Lodge Hotel approach road. There are, in fact, two approach roads and the one

I had planned on following crossed a bridge near the outflow of the *Abhainn Ceann-locha* (river at the loch-head). There was a problem in that the old bridge was no longer in existence and a new one was in the early stages of construction. Following this road would entail a river crossing which I had not anticipated, but it turned out to be a routine hop across a few stepping stones in very shallow water and did not, thankfully, involve getting my feet wet. Ten minutes later I reached the bustling thoroughfare of the A851, painfully aware of the raucous ruction of mechanical giants and the steady stream of tourist traffic – I was back in 'civilisation'.

Until the 1800s, the only roads in Skye were nebulous tracks following the routes of cattle and drovers on their journey to the southern markets. In 1786 John Knox wrote 'It is hardly agreed upon by travellers which is the line of road, everyone making one for himself. Even sheep follow better routes, understanding levels better and selecting better gradients.' In 1801 Thomas Telford was appointed to make a feasibility study of the problem, resulting in the Act of 1803 which marked the beginning of serious road building in Skye. Between then and 1826 over 100 miles of road were built in Skye at a cost of around £400 per mile. I guessed that for the section of road I was privileged to observe being constructed today that figure could probably be multiplied by 1,000.

It is surprising that such a prominent and well-used section of road had resisted the onslaught of modern engineering advances and remained single-track with passing places for so long. As I walked along the side of this old road I gained an appreciation of the monumental effort involved in modern road-building. Chunks of rock, the size of coffee tables, were being shifted by a massive JCB, while huge loads of aggregate were dumped into the appropriate spot with a deafening roar. The high-pitched squealing I had heard an hour before was the sound of heavy-duty vehicles reversing. A completely new road was gradually but surely being constructed alongside the old single-track wavy hummocky route, which in its time was no doubt an engineering marvel, especially since its original construction would have involved nothing but human toil, sweat and tears.

I was experiencing human toil and sweat at this moment as I trudged wearily along the last few miles of tarmac towards my evening's destination. The combination of humidity, hard ground and heavy pack were ganging up mercilessly on me, seemingly in an effort to prevent me completing the day's objective. The last few hours of any day's walk with a large pack are usually the hardest, especially during the early stages of a multi-day back-pack. The body has not yet become attuned to the daily routine of heavy-duty walking and feet have not hardened sufficiently for the miles ahead. The mind has also to adjust to this rhythm and I find at least three days is needed before the walking becomes a way of life.

After a few miles I passed the last of the road-building detritus and entered a deeply wooded section of road, a welcome contrast, were it not for the endless traffic, but this was progressively thinning out as the day wore on. I passed the scattered hamlet of Duisdale, graced with a fine hotel, an old school and a church originally dedicated to St Columba. This area was once the stronghold of a large family of Mackinnons, who were standard bearers to the MacDonalds. Beyond Duisdale I left the trees and enjoyed a fine view out across green fields to Ornsay Island. The hotel was plainly visible and conjured up visions of beer and home cooking.

Turning down the little road signposted Camus Croise which led to the hotel, I began to search out possible camping spots but with little success. Just before the road crossed a river, I noticed a possible site near the river but decided it best and more diplomatic to make initial enquiries at the hotel. As I approached the Isleornsay Hotel I sympathised with the 19th-century Skye bardess, Mairi Mhor nan Oran, who remarked: 'When I reached Eilean Iarmain the furrows departed from my brow.' Eilean Iarmain is the Gaelic name for Isle Ornsay which literally means ebb tide island, the Norse name for an island which is joined to the mainland at low tide. There are dozens of Ornsays or Oronsay Islands on the West coast of Scotland, including another one in Skye at Loch Bracadale which was still a couple of weeks' walking away. Isle Ornsay was once the centre of the fishing industry of Skye and a writer in the parish in 1794 wrote of having counted over 100 sailing boats in the bay, many having come all the way from the Baltic.

At the hotel I was glad to relieve myself of the burden of the pack and I dumped it near the village hall by the quay, once the old salt store. It was then that I noticed a shop to the right of the hotel, which I hadn't taken into account in my plans – the tin of ravioli in my rucksack had made an unnecessary journey. Within seconds I was in the shop purchasing fresh milk and a can of chilled fizzy drink. I asked about camping but was kindly pointed in the direction of the hotel. Further enquiries there were not particularly encouraging and I was told that I couldn't pitch in the immediate vicinity but I might try the minor road to Camus Croise and 'ask someone there'. Reluctantly I yanked on the pack and limped off in the direction indicated, partially refreshed by the canned juice.

The island (Isle Ornsay) itself was a possibility for camping which I had previously considered, but the combination of its inaccessibility and my weariness suggested finding a site quickly, even if not in a perfect spot. Camus Croise (Bay of the Cross) is a straggle of crofts, holiday cottages and retirement homes, each with its own well-tended private patch of ground. I soon realised that there was a distinct lack of suitable places to pitch a tent and decided to return to the spot by the river which I had noticed earlier. My only doubt was that this location was visible from the road and that I would be told to move.

Half an hour later saw the tent erected by the river, a brew on the go and a carton of fresh milk ready and waiting. I lay back on my sleeping bag and grabbed a lazy few minutes while the water boiled. As I sipped hot sweet tea and munched shortbread I felt my whole body unwind and relax into that soothing state of solace which is only experienced after a long day's tramp. As it was still relatively early and I had a furious appetite, I reached for the tiny army issue tin-opener and opened the can of ravioli, knowing that I would no doubt indulge in a bar meal at the hotel later, besides, there was no point in carrying the can for another day.

Any ideas I had of exploring Isle Ornsay were now fading faster than my appetite. My more pedantic, fussy side indicated that I should make an attempt to reach the lighthouse on the island, as I was walking the coastline. My relaxed and laid-back half argued (successfully) that I had already had a hard enough day. I read somewhere that the lighthouse was built in 1857 by Robert Louis Stevenson's father and that the lighthouse cottage was one of the homes of Gavin Maxwell during his long study of otters.

It wasn't long before the lure of the hotel bar and its alcoholic refreshments beckoned me from my cramped tent and I headed in that direction. En route I stopped at the telephone box to 'phone Heather but there was no reply. Minutes later I was happily ensconced in the congenial atmosphere of the hotel public bar, sipping on a pint of Murphy's Irish Stout and contemplating the culinary choices on the bar supper menu. The bar had the look of very recent refurbishment with natural wood the overriding theme. I ordered fish and chips, which were quickly prepared and quickly eaten and washed down with a second pint of the other Irish black stuff. I lit a cigar and indulged in some people-watching.

At the bar a couple of 'smart but casual' young men were engaged in an intellectual conversation about university degrees, courses and academia. Just as their discussion was becoming interesting, they suddenly sprang into Gaelic mode, speaking it with a fluency and confidence which suggested they were native speakers. They were probably either students or lecturers at the local Skye College of Sabhal Mor Ostaig (the Big Barn of Ostaig). This remarkable institution was the brainchild of Sir Iain Noble, the local landlord who owns the northern part of Sleat. In 1973 the disused buildings on the site of an old farm steading took on a new lease of life as a Gaelic College. Since then, Iain Noble's acute vision, inspiration and insatiable enthusiasm for Gaelic language and culture have ensured that Sabhal Mor Ostaig has become an educational success story. The college is now a unique fully-accredited institution of higher education, equipping students through the medium of Gaelic in such diverse disciplines as business studies, local historical studies, information technology and musical studies. A commendable hallmark of the college is the significant number of students who secure permanent posts in the Highlands after graduation – a buoyant sign signifying a reversal in the number of young people leaving Skye and the Highlands.

Much as I would have loved to order a third pint and coax myself into their conversation, I felt weariness beginning to overwhelm me. The first eventful day of Skyewalk was taking its toll. A second telephone call to Heather was successful and we exchanged fervent pleasantries, with both of us agreeing that the day and a half since I left seemed like a lifetime. Yet the walk had barely begun. Would I last the course? Would she likewise? These thoughts turned over in my mind as I snuggled into my sleeping bag – then I rolled over and heavy sleep engulfed me.

* * *

A soft highland rain rustled and murmured on the flysheet of my tent like a thousand soothing whispering voices. They seemed to be cajoling me, coaxing me to extricate myself from my intimate nylon cocoon. It was early – only half past six, but the sighing sounds of Scotch mist had wakened me. I poked my head outside to find a sluggish solemn landscape and a grey emptiness out to sea. A couple of quarrelling herring gulls squawked in staccato shrieks to shatter the stillness of the early hour.

I lay back for a few minutes and dwelled on the relatively long day ahead. A distance of some fifteen miles of mostly road-walking would take me to Point of Sleat, the southernmost tip of Skye, where I intended to make camp. A sudden buzzing near my ear indicated that even in the short space of time that my head was outside the tent, midges had homed in on a potential feed. This was the signal to spring into action. I lit some mosquito coils and began boiling water for tea and porridge. A sachet of Quaker's Honey Bran Quick and Hearty porridge went down a treat and this, together with tea and shortbread, constituted a fairly nutritious breakfast. As I set about striking camp, the exertions of yesterday made themselves felt in a general stiffness and aching, especially around my lower back – perhaps I was getting too old for this sort of thing.

By 7.30am I was ready to roll, fully prepared for wet weather with gaiters, overtrousers and waterproof jacket. The rain had now worsened to a steady downpour and I had the feeling that it was on for the day. My planned objective was to follow the minor road to Camus Croise where the road ended and then stick to the coast for three miles to Knock Bay where the main road is joined. A few hundred yards down this road convinced me that this was highly optimistic given the prevailing conditions. The alternative was to back-track to the main road and content myself with an extended road walk. This, regretfully, was the decision I made and already, on the second day of the walk, I was slipping into the snare of soft options. A long coastal walk teases with temptations and the first seed of temptation was now planted. I hoped it was in sterile ground.

As I reached the main road a stiff breeze transformed the rain into a string of sporadic squalls, each stronger than the last. It was simply a case of head down, hood up, grit the teeth and adopt an unfaltering, unflagging approach through relentless, driving rain. The road gained in height gradually and even at only 50 metres above sea-level was fading into a murky curtain of mist creeping down in a leaden stifling pall from the dreary hillside above. My world was reduced to the ever dwindling rain-drenched strip of tarmac directly ahead. The only disturbance of this mono-dimensional existence was the passing of a vehicle causing a surging swell of airborne spray to add to the already saturated surroundings.

I squelched doggedly on past the sombre brooding mass of Loch nan Dubhrachan and saw the signpost indicating the minor road to Ord, tomorrow night's destination. The distance by road from here was only 7 kilometres yet my route round 'the Garden of Skye' following the coast was still another 40 kilometres. The sheer folly, the irrational absurdity of my coastal walk suddenly hit me square between the eyes. For an instant I thought the unthinkable – how easy it would be to tramp the short distance to a warm bed and a welcoming haven at Ord. In a second instant the rashness of this thought hit even harder. Wholly omitting an entire major peninsula on a walk of this nature was tantamount to a dereliction of duty, an abdication of my intended aim. Come wind and high water I was committed to a venture of my own design. For the foreseeable future I would be shackled to the shoreline, invisibly harnessed to Hebridean horizons. Yet here I was already forsaking three miles of coastline because of a bit of rain and low cloud. I felt the Winged Isle, the great bird itself, was subjecting me to a test to prove my worthiness for such prolonged intimacy.

Some assemblance of self-esteem was restored as I reached the coast again at Knock Bay. A short distance along the shoreline lay the ancient ruin of Knock Castle or Caisteal Chamuis, a MacDonald stronghold which today betrays its presence only by a name on the map. I read that the castle commanded a magnificent outlook over the Sound of Sleat to the Knoydart hills beyond – weather permitting. Having been in this area previously, I could vouch for this, but it would have required much imagination that day to conjure up the image. Just over a mile further along the road is Kilmore, from the Gaelic Cill Mhor (Great Chapel), where in 1681 a church was built on the site of an ancient chapel. This was burnt down by the MacLeods, destroying also a whole congregation of MacIntyres who had taken sanctuary there after losing a battle! The present church built in 1876 has been gracefully renovated and the interior walls carry many monumental plaques of important Clan Donald members. Below Cill Mhor is the stone of Saint Columba where, according to tradition, Saint Columba landed and consecrated the ground on which the early church was built.

None of these historical snippets had any immediate bearing on my present damp, discouraged and depressed disposition however. I was sinking into a vortex of despair and gloom which I knew could be fatal on a walk of this magnitude. My diary for that evening contained the phrase 'Feeling at a very low ebb; morale rock bottom', which neatly summed up my state of mind.

Here I was tramping miserably along the sole of Skye's great foot, only a day and a half into the venture with nearly 350 miles of walking to come. Ahead, Skye's tortuous crenellated coast hung haunting, spectre-like. The whole of Skye hung heavy above me, a catalogue of commitment stretching a full four weeks into the future. There was simply too much invested in the venture to violate it in any serious way, not to mention throwing in the towel – the thought had crossed my mind.

Of all the days of the walk, this was the one that I really craved the company of a walking companion. I desperately needed someone to shake me out of my gloom, or at least to sympathise with my feelings. I thought of Heather and home. I thought of a warm welcome at Ord tomorrow night. I thought of reunions with friends in the weeks to come, and I refused to allow the incessant downpour to drown these daydreams.

At Armadale Castle – now better known as the Clan Donald Visitor Centre – I began to feel I was making progress. Armadale Castle was re-vamped on the proceeds of the kelp industry, a labour-intensive and highly unpleasant task which involved immersion in icy seawater by the cutters. Kelp is the long oar-shaped seaweed which grows in abundance around the Hebridean shores and was an source of natural alkali used in the glass and soap-making industries. After cutting, it had to be dragged ashore, dried and burned to produce the ash which was the basic raw material. In the early 1800s, Lord Macdonald could make as much as £20 from each ton of kelp produced – the people who froze, toiled and sweated to provide him with it were lucky to receive a meagre tenth of that amount.

In 1972 the Castle had fallen into total disrepair and was bought, together with surrounding buildings and 20,000 acres of sheep moorland, by the Clan Donald's Lands Trust which eventually established a worldwide award-winning clan visitor centre. Today the complex hosts the Museum of the Isles, audio-visual exhibitions, a restaurant, gift shops, restored woodland gardens and Countryside Ranger events – in short, it is one of Skye's major tourist attractions. Even on a dismal day like today there was an endless stream of tourists to this cultural highlight – I wasn't one of them. I didn't class myself as a tourist. A traveller, a backpacker, yes – but not a tourist.

The tourists were left behind at Armadale, the ancestral home of the Macdonalds and the terminal for the Mallaig car ferry. From this busy bottleneck I continued along the coast road to the pretty little township of Ardvasar where previous travels had shown there to be a grocer's shop. As I removed my pack outside the shop my true state of dampness made its presence felt. Despite gaiters, overtrousers and Goretex jacket, I felt I had been totally immersed in water like a kelp cutter. I sympathised with prominent Skyeman, Alexander Nicholson, who wrote:

If you are a delicate man
And of wetting your skin are shy
I'd have you know, before you go
You'd better not think of Skye.

There is a story of two old Skye characters having a dram and a blether in a bar. Part of their conversation went something like this – 'Aye Hamish, it's been raining since June'. The dry reply was 'Aye, which June would that be?'

I entered the shop like a drowned rat and purchased a newspaper and my evening meal – a tin of spaghetti bolognaise and a tin of sweetcorn. I have never been a great believer in freeze-dried dehydrated mush, reasoning that the extra weight of cans is more than compensated for by fuller taste and nourishment.

'From Ardvasar it is an up-and-down road all the way to the Aird of Sleat ... I have lit my fire on that glamorous road that leads to the end of everything.' These words were written by T Ratcliffe Barnett in his 1946 book *Autumns in Skye, Ross and Sutherland* and played with my own sentiments – to a certain degree. It is an up-and-down road and it certainly gave the impression of leading to the end of everything today. However, any fire within me was well and truly doused by the dreich and dreary conditions which, if anything, had got worse. The three-and-a-half squally, squelching, switchback miles to the crofting township of Aird of Sleat were amongst the longest of the whole walk. My hunched and 'drookit' body was longing for rest, dryness and a hot drink. Dreams of company and chat were replaced by more immediate visions of curling up in a warm sleeping bag with a mug of tea.

At Aird of Sleat the strip of twisting tarmac is replaced by an equally twisting straggling land-rover track stretching two miles to the sea north of Point of Sleat. A large stone cottage proclaiming Bed and Breakfast at the start of this track threw up a last temptation but was resisted on the basis that there were only another two miles to go. Two miles which are described in the tourist literature as a 'popular and beautiful walk' were today a bleak and lonely trudge. Nearing the end of the track I was surprised to see one or two occupied dwellings and I began to scout about for possible camping spots. On the other side of a fence I noticed a roofless ruined cottage and decided to deposit the rucksack there before setting off on the last rough mile to the lighthouse at Point of Sleat. My original intention had been to camp at the Point but the miserable weather had wiped this notion clean away.

At the very end of the track sits an occupied cottage almost totally surrounded by trees, owned by someone who obviously values his privacy above all else. A gate displayed a sign indicating that the path went straight on beyond it and not left. This was very strange. My os map showed the path to the Point of Sleat breaking off south (left). I carried straight on and reached a small rocky natural harbour with a boat and bothy and a quickly fading path. Realising that there was no path to the Point here I returned to the gate and struck off in the general direction indicated by the dotted line on the map. Within seconds I found myself on a fairly distinct track of gravel and rock steps – the real path to the lighthouse. Why the sign on the gate? Some small-minded land snatcher obviously took offence at people walking to the Point. Yet the route was a recognised right of way.

The complexity of Sleat's geology is immediately apparent on the final push to Skye's southernmost extremity. It has been remarked that in Sleat it is possible to stand with one foot on the oldest rocks in Britain and the other on some of the youngest – an age difference of some 500 million years. The Moine Thrust, the prominent geological fault of Scotland's west coast, stretches rather indefinitely down the Sleat peninsula from Isleornsay to Aird and separates the sandstones and limestone of the west side from the much older Lewisian gneiss of the past where I was now walking. Lewisian gneiss has been dated at about 3,000 million years, which is 1,000 million years before primitive life began to develop. Thin bands of black basalt have forced themselves up through the gneiss producing the contorted hummocky landscape which characterises this corner of Skye.

The path meandered through the gnarled convolutions of rock scoured knolls, boggy moorland and heather choked gullies. I had the feeling I was going nowhere. Then, quite suddenly, the light-house appeared – a whitewashed shy sentinel standing purpose-fully but at the same time unobtrusively at the land's last lurch before it relinquished itself to the ocean's grasp. Between me and the lighthouse there appeared to be two great clefts to negotiate before the ribbon of path led to journey's end. The descent into the first cleft was made simpler by a series of man-made concrete steps leading down to a natural rocky harbour. Beyond, the path weaved its way over a heathery, bracken speckled knoll before opening out on a shingle and seaweed covered mini-bay. As I made my way up the sheep-shorn grass above the bay another similar shingle beach appeared on the opposite side. It was as if the sea was squeezing the last piece of land by the neck, forcing it into island status. This narrow neck of land was the second cleft. It would have made an ideal camping spot had the weather been better.

Minutes later I sat huddled in the leeward side of the light-house, eating a Snickers bar and staring forlornly out to the grey churning mass of ocean. Normally this would have been a fine viewpoint for the Small Isles of Eigg and Rum. Today the only fea-tures were the momentary white horses playing restlessly on the heaving swell and the occasional flutter of sea birds whirling and wavering in the wind.

The lighthouse at Point of Sleat was a symbolic turning-point of the walk. Like a cairn on the summit of a mountain, this beacon at the end of the land represented a crux, a pivotal point, about which past and future could be viewed in a clearer perspective. This far-flung but familiar mark of man on the landscape, a watchtower of hope to those at peril on the sea, seemed to become my personal beacon of belief. It was the eye of the storm – its feeble, faint light consoled and comforted, reassuring and strengthening my withering resolve. Between here and Skye's northern tip at Rubha Hunish, 250 convoluted miles of coastline lay within three weeks of walking. It seemed like a lifetime distant. In relative terms it was. The life that had its delivery at Kylerhea Ferry was already assuming its own character from fledgling to coming of age.

I abandoned my damp and draughty perch beneath the light-house and walked briskly back to the rucksack by the ruin. I erected the tent on a suitable spot behind the ruin and began the customary tasks which should eventually result in immersion in a warm dry sleeping bag with a mug of hot tea. Collecting water, laying out Karrimat and sleeping bag, removing wet clothing, putting on dry clothing, lighting stove, wringing out socks. It was during all this activity that I discovered the unthinkable – the lower two thirds of my sleeping bag were soaking. The golden rule of camping is that your sleeping bag should remain dry at all times. A dry sleeping bag and a waterproof tent are the barriers between cosy warmth and chilling dampness, between health and hypothermia – in extreme conditions between life and death. How had it happened? I immediately blamed my new rucksack, bought especially for the walk. The sleeping bag had been carefully packed in a lower zipped compartment and an elasticated water-proof cover had completely enclosed the whole pack. A fact about rucksacks is that they are very rarely waterproof – even with waterproof covers – and it is necessary to rely on a polythene inner bag which is usually bought separately. My old rucksack had its own nylon waterproof inner which I was using with the new sack – unfortunately, the sleeping bag, being in a lower zipped compartment, was outside the benefit of this inner. And to cap it all I had also stupidly packed a section of wet tent in the same compartment. I was to live with the consequences that night.

The final straw of that doleful day, came with a sudden call outside the tent: 'Hello, anyone at home?' I unzipped the inner tent and flysheet to see a man brandishing a fearsome looking walking stick. In an arrogant, objectionable, pompous, top-drawer English accent he uttered: 'Do you know you're committing a criminal offence?' He continued: 'Despite what the press says, all land in Scotland is owned by someone – did you not see the signs?' I confessed that I hadn't seen any signs disallowing walkers or campers. Before I even had a chance to point out that wild camping and walking were generally approved of in remote areas and that there was a long-standing tradition of this in Scotland, he condescendingly 'allowed' me to stay for one night only. He then disappeared as suddenly as he had arrived. Not one civil word was spoken, such as what I was doing or where I was going. I felt numbed, besmirched, dispossessed of my own native land, like an evicted crofter in the Clearances. So incensed I was by this intolerant, heavy-handed, English buffoon that I wrote the following note and left it in a plastic pocket under a rock by the camp spot early the next morning, where I knew he would find it.

1. I am not committing a criminal offence; at the very most (and that is debatable) a civil offence. The law of trespass in Scotland is a civil one, not a criminal one.
2. Most 'landowners' respect the moral right and long standing tradition to walk and camp on wild land.
3. Please have the courtesy to indicate the path to Point of Sleat and to talk civilly to walkers and campers.
4. I detest having an Englishman telling a Scotsman where he can or cannot camp in his own native country.
5. Skye has a lamentable history of hideous land ownership and persecution of crofters. Please do not perpetrate the situation.

My remarks in Point 3 followed the palpable assumption that this same individual was responsible for misdirecting walkers to the lighthouse, which turned out to be correct – the 'landowner' lived in the cottage surrounded by trees which I had seen earlier.

As I salvaged what warmth I could from the upper third of my sleeping bag that night, I was aware of the rain finally relenting. Perhaps tomorrow would be dry, perhaps tomorrow would be enjoyable. One thing was certain – if conditions deteriorated further, if morale sunk lower than today, Skyewalk was on a very fragile footing. Things could only get better.

* * *

I woke early to the rhythmic surge of sea and shingle. At 4.30am the pale yellow morning light had already entered my eiderdown domain. I had a sense that the tide was turning, both in a nautical and metaphorical sense. Wide awake, I unzipped the flysheet to be greeted by the tangle of the Isles, the briny bouquet of the ever present sea. This heady island intoxication was breakfast enough for my soul. A herring gull looked out to sea from his craggy perch, feathers faintly ruffling in a balmy breeze. I followed his gaze out over the swell to hopeful horizons. The nonsensical notion of owning this land and seascape was glaringly apparent.

By six I lifted pack onto shoulders and took the first steps of what I believed would be a long hard day's tramping. This south-western corner of Sleat displays a rugged, ragged pathless coastline to the restless sea, unlike the clean-cut, cliff-girt edges of north Skye. At least eight miles of this type of terrain would take me to Tarskavaig Bay, followed by another four or so to pre-booked accommodation at Ord. Twelve miles didn't sound a great deal but I was acutely aware of the nature of those first eight miles, especially with the burden on my back.

Almost immediately I was forced to the water's edge, scrambling over seaweed covered rocks in order to avoid a steep craggy bluff. As I reached dry land beyond, I was rewarded by the sight of a beautiful cluster of pinky white saxifrage lining a crack of a lichen covered crag. A short distance further on I disturbed a skylark from its earthly slumber, sending it soaring skywards in a sylvan symphony of song. There was a buoyant optimism to this early hour, hard-won from yesterday's pessimism, especially in the first light of morning when all things seem possible.

Within half an hour of setting off I passed the first of many black house remains which I would see that day. A sad collection of angular stones and patches of nettles betrayed the previous presence of man. The walking was rough. Rarely could any sense of rhythm be found but interest abounded. Grass, heather, bog, rock, tussocks, streams; all were negotiated. Now and again I stumbled on sheep and animal tracks and possibly even the relics of ancient man-made paths but these appeared and disappeared with infuriating regularity. I brought the map out mainly to check how far I had actually travelled; I was making disturbingly slow (but steady) progress. A couple of ring contours on the map – a hillock recognised on the ground; a wriggling blue line on the map – a swollen torrent to be crossed; each symbol had its manifestation in real life and there was a marvellous satisfaction in recognising and negotiating each successive feature.

At one point I gazed northwards across the sea to the tip of the Elgol peninsula beyond which the unmistakable twin-summited craggy profile of Sgurr na Stri had shredded its cloud mantle. Smoking tendrils of frayed cloud flayed the leaden flanks of the Black Cuillin Ridge which was to remain shrouded and shy for some time yet. It would be three days before I would be treading in the dark shadow of Sgurr na Stri's gabbro engraved lower slopes at Camasunary. This was to become a pastime – looking across sea lochs to prospective peninsulas, to future forays, to experiences still days or even weeks ahead. The same would soon apply in reverse of course – days from now I would look back to previous peninsulas, to already unfolded experiences.

At Rubha Caradal I searched around for an ancient Dun, marked on the map, but to no avail. A man-made path led me down a rocky staircase through a wooded stance of birch, alder and rowan into a bracken infested glen – Glean Caradal. Here I discovered the poignant remains of a fairly substantial settlement. Caradal Village was cleared in about 1880 and looked as though it must have been a constricted and difficult place to forge a living.

The burn of the Bealach na Ceardaich tumbles down a narrow gorge in the hillside with scattered remains of black houses occupying every conceivable flattish area.

Wandering through a maze of 'paths' in waist-high bracken, I stumbled upon a slightly better preserved relic of this not-so-distant past. As I stepped over the fallen lintel to enter the shell, the empty epitaph to once proud lives, I was engulfed in the disturbingly familiar brooding sentiments accompanying all such visits to Clearance settlements. The stone hearth was still intact, where homely peaty flames were in an instant doused by the tenants' bowls of milk and replaced by the flames of the roof thatch crackling from the evictors' torches – roof thatch of dried heather, which was once prohibited by the landowner from being cut from the moor for fear of jeopardising their grouse sport. For a few moments I gazed through a collapsed 'window to the west', the changeless framed view of generations. The essential despair and cruelty of the Clearances was plaintively summarised in the following passage written by a descendant of a cleared crofter:

'The hollowest epitaph to a man's life is the dereliction of the house which spawned him, the saddest of headstones to mark his being is a fallen lintel. The tomb which out-demeans a pauper's grave is the one sealed by the slump of timbers and the deranged slates of the roof which sustained a life. When the nettles stifle his hearth and overwhelm the bed where he sowed the seed of his sons and daughters, that summarises him. This was a life, it says, so lived that its legacy is too futile to count, too flimsy to brook continuity, a cup drained of hope.'

I dropped down through more bracken to cross the burn, with a watery sun attempting to bear aloft the indignities of this now-empty corner of Skye. Hardly a mile beyond, the steep heather-covered hillside gave way to the broad Strath of Dalavil, scene of further clearances and once the homelands of MacKinnons, MacGillivrays and Robertsons. Dalavil was cleared around the time of the Education Acts of the early 1870s on the pretence that 'it was for the children to get their schooling. It was cheaper to clear the crofters than to build a school there. It was quite isolated – there was no road to it, just a path over the hill.' Of course, the real reason was that the estate landowners and farmers wanted the best land, the broad grassy outflows for their sheep and the common grazings of hill land for so-called sport.

As I reached the broad outflow of the Allt a Ghlinne the results of yesterday's deluge were all too apparent – if the bridge marked on my map some distance upstream did not exist, then I was in for a major river crossing. I soon made the discovery that this indeed was the case. Reconnaissance upstream proved futile; the outflow from Loch a Ghlinne further up the glen was an unusually straight, fast-flowing and deep trench. I later discovered that this was Skye's only canal. The alternative was to head back downstream and attempt a crossing at the wider, shallower outflow to the ocean. A suitable island-studded area was deemed crossable with the help of walking pole and stepping stones – albeit with the majority submerged! The crossing was made with only one foot getting wet. With the crossing, I had completed a psychological first lap of the day and sat down on a rock for a major rest.

I glanced at my watch – 9.45am. I had completed 5 miles in 3 hours 45 minutes. This progress didn't even equate to one-and-a-half miles per hour (actually one-and-a-third). It hit me like a thunderclap how debilitatingly slow was pathless coastal walking with a substantial pack.

The weather was rapidly improving but the period between cloud and shine was laced by a bout of squally showers. These had now departed to leave in their wake an airy freshness and a translucent limpid light above the sparkling sea. A couple of white-faced cormorants stood motionless on a rock some distance away, while a flurry of oystercatchers took to the air in a dash of black and white plumage and red bills, their evocative 'kleep, kleep' calls the perfect sound accompaniment to the sprightly sunwashed scene. These common shore birds were to become an emblematic reminder of the walk, their customary presence a linking theme of Skyewalk.

I gorged myself on a Mars Bar, peanuts and wine gums while

absorbing the sun-soaked surroundings, content with my progress so far.

Reluctantly, I departed from my idyllic perch to begin the three-mile stint to Tarskavaig Bay and the second lap of the day. The map appeared to indicate that the hardest section of the day was over but I knew it was easy to be misled. This stretch began easily enough on a broad, grassy, sheep-shorn promenade but I was soon forced closer to the sea by bracken-choked knolls and chaotic contortions of scattered crags and boulders. The predominant blues and greens were colourfully interrupted by the partially bleached oranges, whites and other man-made tints of scattered plastic jetsam strewn everywhere. Much of this consisted of fish-boxes and bottles but there was a surprising number of orange rubber gloves and strange unidentifiable assorted detritus. There was an odd fascination in just sauntering along, searching out increasingly bizarre items. By far the majority of coastal plastic waste is refuse discarded from ocean-going vessels and it is all too common a sight round Britain's beaches. It adds colour and interest to beach stravaiging but is ultimately an eyesore.

An otter skulking around in the rushes between the tide limit and lower hillside provided entertaining distraction. Further on I spotted the first of many natural stone arches and couldn't resist 'threading the eye of the needle' by walking through it. For the final two miles before Tarskavaig Bay, an indented straggle of relatively low cliffs forced me to abandon the shoreline and join the sheep on the grass and heather above the cliffs. I say relatively low because although I guessed them to be about 100 feet high, they were small fish compared to the 1,000 feet monster cliffs in the north of Skye.

Reaching Tarskavaig Bay was the highlight of the day. During the cliff top section, the weather had hit another 'downer', but when I first caught sight of the bay the sun had finally chased away the cloud. I felt like a child discovering his first sandy beach. I couldn't wait to get down there and walk across the golden sands. A blissful euphoria overtook me which was an infinity away from the depths of despondency I had experienced only 24 hours ago. I realised just how large a factor the weather would play in determining my mood over the coming few weeks.

If one weakness of Skye's coastline was to be made an issue of, it would be a lack of sandy beaches. The number could probably be counted on one hand. There are certainly no long strands of shining sand like on Coll or Tiree, but coming across the small pockets which do exist is a revelation, especially when the weather is in a favourable mood. As I strolled across the bay, I was aware of four other people; but I certainly wasn't complaining.

All too soon I tore myself away from the sublime surroundings of sand, sea and sun and took the tarmac trudge up the hillside to the village of Tarskavaig itself. Tarskavaig was planned in 1811 and was essentially peopled by crofters who had been evicted by the MacDonald estates from more fertile inland glens in order to work in the kelp industry. Today, Tarskavaig's claim to fame is its Skye terriers and bearded collies, bred on the shores of the bay and exported throughout the world. It is a thriving crofting township, its neat whitewashed stone cottages and modern bungalows fusing into a textbook compact crofting community. The presence of cars and satellite dishes, however, were stark reminders that this was 20th-century Skye.

The road north from Tarskavaig meanders inland past peaceful Loch Gauscavaig before descending through a delightfully wooded stretch of oak, hazel and alder to the tranquil bay of Ob Gauscavaig – also known paradoxically as Thor's Bay. I should have felt guilty at not staying with the coast between here and Tarskavaig Bay but I wasn't. At no point on this section of road was I more than a mile from the sea and I construed this to be within acceptable limits.

On the nothern promontory of Thor's Bay sits one of the oldest fortified ruins in the Hebrides – Dunsgaith Castle (pronounced doon-scaa), only a few minutes walk from the road. Being a popular tourist attraction, there were a few cars parked at the end of the track leading to the castle and the idea I had of dumping the pack here before visiting the ruin was abandoned; my rucksack was just too precious to leave to tempt an opportune thief.

Besides, I also had another idea of forsaking the road and following the coastline proper between Dunsgaith and Ord, which was shorter in distance, cutting out a dog leg.

The track to Dunsgaith passes an isolated, weather-worn, empty cottage of traditional Scottish variety: two up, two down, double dormer windows and double chimney stack. I stopped and stared at the forlorn facade of what I took to be a fairly recently inhabited house. The downstairs windows were boarded up but an upstairs dormer displayed a single pathetic net curtain. The roof slates were in good repair and the external walls reasonably sound but in dire need of cleaning and re-pointing. Wild roses had taken over much of the garden but, in essence, I felt a few weeks' hard work would stop the rot. Feelings of sadness were soon replaced by anger that the cottage had been allowed to reach such a state of disrepair, especially since it lay on the tourist track to Dunsgaith Castle. In Skye, the boundary between dereliction and hope is not wide.

Moments later I reached the ruins of the castle, its main bulk situated on an outlying crag separated from where I was standing by a moat-like ravine. Spanning this ravine were two arched walls which at one time would be bridged by hefty wooden planks – long since gone. On the inside of each wall was an 18-inch wide ledge which presumably supported these planks. I reasoned that one of these ledges could be used to gain access to the main castle.

A. Dempster

Dunsgaith Castle

Dunsyaith Castle

Discarding my pack, I carefully shuffled my way along the right-hand ledge whilst gripping the not-so-firm rocks at the top of the wall. I was painfully conscious of the consequences of falling backwards into the ravine. I was also aware that I would have to return the same way! A short flight of well-worn stone steps took me to a broad grassy platform, a delectable spot to while away some precious moments in an indisputably romantic corner of the Winged Isle. Directly north beyond the rocky skerry of Eilean Ruaridh, Loch Eishort and Loch Slapin poked watery fingers into the mountain fastness of Skye. Wispy gossamer shreds of cloud caressed Belig's summit ridge while Garbh-bheinn and Bla Bheinn to its left were submerged in thicker cloud. Away to the left the Small Isles of Rum and Canna were etched on the horizon. A cluster of shags were assembled on a nearby skerry and several gannets plummeted from great heights into the sparkling waters of Loch Eishort. What a wonderful spot this would be to observe a sunset.

As I edged my way back across the ravine I couldn't help feeling that if this same ruin was in the South of England there would be a Danger sign warning people not to attempt a crossing, or the place would be surrounded by a barbed wire fence. More likely, strong planks of wood would have been placed across the stone ledges and the castle would have been in a better state of preservation. It seemed only a matter of time before someone injured themselves and started a messy legal indictment.

My visit to Dunsgaith kindled an interest in its past and I later discovered there was more myth and legend associated with the castle than hard facts of history. The castle is supposedly named after Sgathach, an Amazon who founded a military college, one of whose pupils was the distinguished warrior Cuchillin who built the Dun in just one night! Dunsgaith was the ancestral home of the MacDonalds of Sleat until the late 16th century when they left for Duntulm in the north of Skye.

For the final two miles to Ord I opted for the road, passing through the straggle of crofts comprising Tokavaig. There is nothing Gaelic in the names of Tokavaig, Tarskavaig, Ostaig,

Gauscavaig and other such -aig ending names. As with many place names on Skye, they are all of Norse origin and reflect the many inlets which indent the coastline. The road dipped then climbed round a limestone gorge where Scottish Natural Heritage have undertaken a long-term scheme of regenerating the natural wood-land – a small but significant step. I later learned that this natural wood was known as Doire nan Druidhean, or the Grove of the Druids, which local tradition believed to be a sacred meeting place of the Druids.

That final half-mile descent to Ord was a re-discovery of the richness of Skye's landscape and heritage distilled in the recollec tions of the day's colourful experiences. My senses, numbed from yesterday's dispirited and downhearted perspective, were now reel-ing in the sheer beauty of this delightful corner of Skye, and in the joy of simply being alive. Ord is surely one of the most tranquil and scenic villages on the island with views to the Cuillin which are said to have brought tears to the eyes of many an exiled Scot. Someone who undoubtedly agreed with this sentiment was the poet and author, Alexander Smith, who wrote his best-selling *A Summer in Skye* in 1865 while staying at Ord House. 'What Scott did for the Trossachs was done for Skye by a man modestly named Smith', wrote Derek Cooper in his definitive guide *Skye*; and this was not an overstatement. Smith's book captures the true spirit of Skye in a way which no other book has ever done – although Jim Crumley's *The Heart of Skye* is a close contender. Its durability is reflected in the fact that it has been reprinted as a paperback; I was lucky enough to find an old 1907 edition. Interestingly, Alexander Smith made a marital Skye connection by marrying Miss Flora Macdonald of Ord, a descendant of 'the' Flora.

Until the 1970s, Ord House was one of Skye's legendary fam-ily hotels with renowned lavish cream teas served by the Nicolson sisters. In its walled garden is a cabbage palm tree, sent as seed from New Zealand in the 1860s by an emigrant Skyeman. On my 1989 OS map of South Skye (sheet 32) the word 'Hotel' is clearly marked at Ord. Evidently the map-makers did not know that Ord House had long since ceased to function as a hotel. Their error had also misled me in the planning stages of the walk but indirectly led me to one of the most wonderful Skye discoveries I had ever made – Fiordhem.

The Skye tourist information office in Portree had informed me that there was no hotel in Ord but gave me the telephone number of a guesthouse known as Fiordhem which apparently had had a very favourable write-up. I contacted the guesthouse and booked for one night. While on a reconnoitre of Skye with Heather a couple of months prior to the walk, we stayed at Fiordhem and were bowled over by the delectably peaceful atmosphere and warm welcome. Such is Fiordhem's renown that it is specifically signposted at the Ord turn-off road on the A581 and is strongly recommended in *Staying off the beaten track in Scotland*, an Arrow paperback.

Fiordhem is a Swedish name meaning 'house on the fiord', originating from the host's mother who emigrated from Sweden in 1917 and bought the ruined cottage in 1960 because it reminded her of her home country. Her son, Tony La Trobe and his wife, Bridget, refurbished it almost from scratch to the homely haven it is today.

Being enthusiastic walkers themselves, Tony and Bridget were particularly interested in my expedition and would be the first sympathetic ears to hear of my experiences so far. I hadn't had a 'proper' conversation with anyone since leaving Glenelg nearly three days ago. Suffice to say, I was eager to enjoy their company again and also Bridget's mouthwatering cooking. So keen had I been to reach Ord that the time was only 3.00pm – the 6.00am start had proved fruitful. I looked forward in anticipation to sinking into that luxurious decadence which is so relaxing after several days on the hoof.

Fiordhem – 'standing as it does, twenty feet from the edge of Loch Eishort, with the water lapping under the garden gate, commands breathtaking views of Cuillin Mountains and the beckoning islands of Canna and Rum and gives unparalleled opportunities for studying at close quarters the abundant bird life.' So goes the blurb on the Scottish Tourist Board flyer and, for once, this is no exaggeration. The house on the fiord not only lives up to any advertising blurb, it surpasses it beyond all expectations.

It came as something of a shock to find Fiordhem apparently hostless when I arrived. Ringing the doorbell produced no response, so I removed pack and boots and entered as if I were at home. Four doors, two vestibules and a couple of loud 'hellos' took me to the inner sanctum of the house – the kitchen – but still no welcoming response. I then noticed Tony snoozing peacefully in a chair in the next room. He woke with a start, responding to my unexpected presence with enthusiasm, tempered with the blunted effects of an afternoon siesta. I felt slightly awkward at having disturbed his tranquillity and invading his space.

However, within seconds Tony's amiable and placid nature came to the fore as he shook my hand and apologised for Bridget's absence, explaining that she was on a shopping expedition to Broadford but would be back soon. I offered reciprocal apologies for having disturbed his sleep before letting forth on the events of the last three days. Reclining on a soft chair with a cup of tea I chatted to Tony in the exquisite yet homely surroundings of the dining room.

The whole house is full of interesting and unusual articles, such as an ornately carved Swedish sofa-bed, a Victorian china footbath and a collection of Willow pattern plates over the open fire, to name just a few. Fine original pictures are everywhere, as are books, reflecting Tony and Bridget's love of landscape, walking and the outdoors. It is not so long ago that Tony offered guided walks to his guests where they competed fiercely for the titles of Plucky Plodder, Path Pounder and Peak Performer, any one of which I am sure could apply to me! The three guest bedrooms have wonderful sea views and have a gentle charm honed by the hand of Bridget. Fresh floral fabrics, fine chairs, comfortable beds and that undefinable homeliness which spring from warm-hearted home-loving people.

My bedroom that night was The Cabin, a charming downstairs room with an unusual bow window looking out over Loch Eishort to Blaven and the main Cuillin range. Within half an hour of moving in, the commodious splendour was a clutter of clothes, tentage, boots, camping accoutrements, maps, books and bits of food. Such was my concern for the weight of my pack that a good few pounds of gear were left behind at Fiordhem to be collected at the end of the walk including such diverse items as a wild-life book, a plate, deodorant, soap, coffee, cigars, swimming trunks, a kettle, a T-shirt, a headtorch and even a half-filled plastic bottle of whisky! The last item was consumed that evening so didn't really count. Normally, a headtorch is a must when camping or bothying but I had discovered that reasonable natural light extended well beyond 10.00pm, long after I had snuggled down, so the head-torch was deemed superfluous. It is only after I have begun a long backpacking trip that I realise just what are the really necessary items and what can be safely discarded. Deodorant is plain daft – an unnecessary luxury. After all, I only shared a tent with myself, so soap came under the same umbrella.

I showered at Fiordhem, and when Bridget returned she put wet, smelly clothes in the washing machine in time for them to catch the drying sea breeze in the garden. The sleeping bag was spread out in the airing cupboard to dry off while I dozed peace-fully on the dreamy double bed. Life was bliss.

Dressed in shorts, T-shirt and socks, I wandered outside several times to check the progress of my laundry. On one occasion, I rushed back inside to fetch the camera as the changeable condi-tions had produced a wonderful lighting effect. Directly above, the sky was deepest blue, but out over the glistening surface of Loch Eishort a layer of cloud was filtering the sun's rays into a stunning spectrum of superb effects. Blaven and nearer hills were in darkest shadow, but shifting shafts of sunlight were dragging their silken, silvery threads over the main Cuillin beyond. At one point, these threads joined forces to deliver a single dazzling silver sliver of light on one spot of Loch Eishort – a God-spot according to Heather. Fiordhem was living up to its reputation.

At 7.30 Bridget surpassed her reputation as a cook with an excellent traditional spread of roast lamb with mint sauce, roast potatoes, green beans, carrots, cauliflower, cabbage and gravy. This was followed by trifle and cheese and biscuits all liberally washed down with wine, coffee and my own contribution of uisge-beatha. I can say without a hint of exaggeration that this was the best meal of the entire walk.

Company that evening included a pleasant middle-aged Scottish couple from Greenock and a stereotypical flamboyant older couple from the USA. The distinctly portly American woman seemed obsessed and fascinated by sheep and expected me to know the answers to all her questions, such as: 'How do they (shepherds?) know whose sheep they are?' or 'Why are some sheared and others not?' Rather than 'pulling the wool' over her eyes by giving her half-baked answers, I discussed the more far-reaching notions of why so many sheep were in Scotland in the first instance, which led naturally to the Clearances and fundamental issues of human rights. She seemed genuinely concerned but more immediately worried about her hotel booking in Ullapool for the following evening.

I managed to see the weather forecast for the next few days and my heart sank. Wet, wet, wet would be a suitable description. Thoughts drifted back to the second day and gloom engulfed me, though somewhat mitigated by wine and whisky. According to my schedule the next six nights involved camping. I felt compelled to book into a hotel or guesthouse for at least one of these nights. Back at Glenelg the drove walker, Brian Lawrence, had informed me that Strathaird House on the Elgol peninsula had given him a satisfying stay and on his recommendation I telephoned and made a booking for two nights hence. The peace of mind in knowing that even if the next two days were total wash-outs, I would have a warm, welcoming and dry haven for the second night, was absolutely necessary in the light of past experiences.

In the last three days the child that was Skyewalker had progressed through adolescence to adulthood. As I flopped into bed at 10.00pm, I felt that the walk was fusing together into something which would eventually be greater than the sum of its parts; the various disparate threads of experience were now joining, ultimately to be woven into a colourful and rich tapestry which would dwell in the memory for a lifetime.

Route Summary: Glenelg to Ord

Day 1: Glenelg – Kylerhea – Isleorsnay (12 miles – 19 km)

From Glenelg follow the single-track road to the ferry point (sign-posted) and take the ferry to Kylerhea. There is a minimal charge of about 50p for passengers. Turn left along the road and go through a gate with the sign 'Footpath to Kinloch Lodge'. A recognised right of way extends for seven miles from here to the Kinloch Lodge Hotel, although it can become quite indistinct in places through lack of use. From the area of the hotel reach the main Broadford to Armadale road (A851) by way of a good track/minor road. Follow this road south for about three miles until the turn-off for Isleornsay and the Isleornsay hotel.

Day 2: Isleornsay – Point of Sleat (15 miles – 24 km)

From Isleornsay a literal following of the coastline involves walk-ing through the small settlement of Camus Croise before three miles of rough pathless walking to Knock Bay and A851. Alternatively, adhere to the A851 which heads slightly inland to a maximum of one and a half miles from the coast. From Knock Bay continue on tarmac road for nearly nine miles to Aird of Sleat. From Aird of Sleat a rough land-rover track followed by a path leads to the lighthouse at Point of Sleat (the southernmost tip of Skye).

Day 3: Point of Sleat – Ord (13 miles – 21 km)

From Point of Sleat follow the coastline for eight miles to Tarskavaig Bay. This involves wild trackless walking on rough ground with a major river crossing at Dalavil. It is the hardest sec-tion of the walk so far. From Tarskavaig a good minor road leads to Ord in a little over 4 miles though not literally following the coastline. Determined coastal walkers will probably walk out to Tarskavaig Point and follow the coastline from there. Whatever option is chosen, an excursion out to Dunsgaith Castle (GR 595122) is a must.

Accommodation and other information

Glenelg:	Hotel and B&Bs. For camping, enquire at hotel.
Kinloch Lodge:	Excellent food (Lady Claire MacDonald) but pricey.
Isleornsay:	Hotel. Camping restricted but enquire at hotel. Small grocery shop.
Ardvasar:	Good grocery shop.
Aird of Sleat:	B&B at end of tarmac road.
Point of Sleat:	Wonderfully wild (but exposed) camping.
Ord:	Fiordhem guesthouse (not to be missed – but pre-booking essential).

CHAPTER 3

In the Shadow of the Cuillin

(Friday 10 July – Monday 13 July)
Ord to Glenbrittle

Far, far distant, far on a horizon,
I see the rocking of the antlered Cuillin,
Beyond the seas of sorrow, beyond the morass of agony,
I see the white felicity of the high-towered mountains.

Sorley Maclean

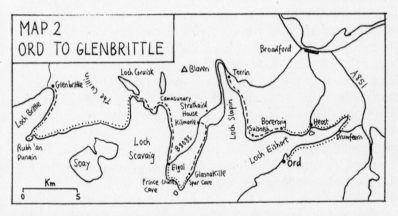

I ROSE AT 8.30AM but had been awake long before, jumping out of bed to confirm the miserable weather forecast of the previous night. The Cuillin were obliterated totally, as if they never existed. Less than two miles across the grey lifeless waters of Loch Eishort, the stark cliffs and muted greens of Boreraig and Suisnish – tonight's destination – looked dismally uninviting. Yet I felt ready and refreshed, eager to cope with the challenges of the day; more so after a double dose of sausage, bacon, tomato, egg and fried bread, washed down with lashings of tea and orange juice. The house on the fiord had been a halcyon haven of warmth and spiritual and bodily renewal.

Packing was slow and deliberate. A pre-packed cache of food was partially used but still seemed incredibly heavy, though lighter than the plastic bag full of assorted items left at Fiordhem. By 10.15 I struggled through the house with a fully laden rucksack and deposited it at the front door. Heartfelt goodbyes, a promise to keep Tony and Bridget informed of my progress, and a few farewell photos before stepping out on the sea-borne stage.

There was a rawness to the morning induced by the harshness of the wind, the ocean's restless surge, and a gut feeling that rain wasn't far away. A tarmac private road took me up the hill past Ord House and several new houses. A land-rover track skirted the side of the hill before dropping down to a boggy glen where a large isolated white house stood facing out to sea. From here until tonight's camp spot was completely pathless coastal walking round the hooked head of Loch Eishort, my first major sea loch circuit of the trip. Tony and Bridget had informed me that they had taken four hours to reach the road end at Drumfearn (some four miles further on) on one of their many local walks and this with only light day-packs. This fact alone spoke volumes about the rugged nature of the coast. Just how long would I take with a full pack? The more immediate concerns of putting one foot in front of the other, maintaining a steady rhythm and positive outlook were foremost in my mind however. It wasn't raining, I was dry and I felt on top of the morning.

Beyond the end of the track the walking was characterised by sheep tracks (one thing sheep are good for), bogs, tussocky hillside contouring and tricky gorge crossings. At one point I spotted two otters snaking warily through the heather and grass, intent on remaining anonymous, which they evidently were not! These shy mammals are scarce in other parts of Britain but abundant in Skye, feeding on the coastal fringes, but also venturing inland along rivers and sometimes even visiting hill lochs.

High upon the western slopes of Sgiath-bheinn an Uird – probably one of the most neglected ridges on Skye – I noticed a line of deciduous trees, which I knew from the map descended to sea level a mile further on. A cascading burn had carved out a deep gash in the hillside shortly before this and a long lush finger of forest clothed this gorge directly along my proposed line of attack. I gradually descended and crossed the gorge lower down from where relatively easy hill contouring led to the main mass of alder, birch and oak woods further on. This next section was to prove the most difficult of the day – a 'nightmare' as I recorded in my diary that evening.

Negotiating tactics were spontaneous and erratic. One minute I was bush-whacking my way through thick foliage, the next I was slipping and scrambling on seaweed-covered rocks on the shoreline. When one option became unbearable I switched to the other and so on in a frustratingly futile attempt to ease the capricious nature of the walking. On the rocky shoreline I soon learned the art of wedging my feet in a hollow on slippery rocks, so avoiding tumbles. At one point I found myself hemmed in by a line of low cliffs. Above was a thick mass of impenetrable foliage, below a narrow platform of treacherously slippery seaweed-covered rocks with no guarantee of their continuation beyond the next headland. I opted for the low-level alternative, wondering if the tide was going out or coming in.

As I slid and stumbled onwards I glanced the half-mile or so across the sea loch to Eilean Heast and imagined an observer watching my slow progress with wide-eyed incredulity. I felt sure that if a boat appeared and offered me a lift I would have gladly accepted – though, of course, it never did. A lazy canoeist attempting a circumnavigation of Skye's coastline may well have cut across at this point, so omitting the last two miles to the head of Loch Eishort. The corresponding shortcut for the walker would be to cut across a land peninsula rather than a 'sea peninsula'. Thus, the heads of sea-lochs were unavoidable for landlubber circumnavigators of Skye, while the heads of peninsulas were unavoidable for sea-going circumnavigators.

These frivolous thoughts idled in my mind as I turned the headland and made the welcome discovery that a wide gravel and rock beach had replaced the slippery shackles of the last half-mile. Within half-an-hour I had cleared the last vestiges of forest, Drumfearn only a mile distant. I was pleased with my progress so far. It was on this last stretch to Drumfearn that I noticed a small boat disturbing the placid waters of Loch Eishort. Suddenly, a flare shot skywards and the boat turned, appearing to head in my direction. I promptly made the rash assumption that this was a teaching colleague who had informed me that she and her husband were sailing round Skye in the summer and might meet up with me at some point. Being a home economics teacher, she was sure to have some succulent delicacy on the go for supper and, more to the point, they were bound to ferry me across the loch thus saving a few hours trudge. My hopes were dashed, however. The vessel in question belonged to the Drumfearn Mussel Farm, though the use of a flare remained a mystery.

I carefully negotiated three awkward barbed wire fences before I finally reached the end of the track at Dumfearn, where the Drumfearn Mussel Farm land rover was parked. Here I unloaded the pack and flopped down for a well earned breather and bite to eat. The time was only twenty to two – just over three hours from Ord and considerably less than Tony and Bridget's forecast. I was justifiably chuffed. And the rain still hadn't made an appearance either.

Gazing out across the sea loch, the opposite shoreline seemed tantalisingly close. The water surface was studded with floating black barrel-type objects from which, apparently, hung underwater ropes to which mussels adhered in their hundreds. The boat spotted earlier seemed to be in the process of removing these mussels. I had had no idea of the existence of mussel farms but there obviously was a livelihood to be made from the business.

Beyond this point, Loch Eishort narrows considerably before widening once again to the tidal shallows and the outflow of the Abhainn Ceann. The narrowest section is barely a couple of hundred yards across but the opposite point is still a frustrating rough walk of two miles. One last awkward boggy area with trees was finally negotiated before I reached the oozing mass of seaweed, sand and mud which formed the head of the loch. At least the tide was out and I figured that a crossing of this, with possible wet feet, was preferable to rigidly sticking to the shoreline.

As I searched the moisture-laden mire for a suitable line of attack, I was alerted by the distant sounds of machinery and vehicular movement. It struck me that I was less than a mile and a half from the A851 Broadford to Armadale Road and the roadworks encountered on the first day of the walk. Once again, the irrationality of what I was doing crystallised in my mind, only to melt and vaporise with the vivid memories of the last few days. Coastal walking wasn't logical. Like dozens of other outdoor activities, it had no rationale other than simple enjoyment, escapism and keeping in touch with natural rhythms and inner harmonies.

My chosen crossing point proved easier and drier than imagined and I managed to maintain a route where the deepest part was only a few inches. A herd of cows on the opposite side looked on with a curiosity almost verging on concern for my imagined predicament. For no reason, I erupted into fits of laughter, the assembled bovine beasts' incredulous expressions further feeding my euphoria. Here I was, standing in several inches of sea-water and mud at the head of a Skye sea loch watched by an audience of cattle and enjoying life to the full. My soul was singing to the symphony that is Skye.

Reaching the opposite side it dawned on me that I was now, for the first time in the day, actually walking in the direction of my nightly destination at Boreraig, still five rough miles distant. I had also forsaken the garden of Skye and was now walking in the shadow of the Cuillin, in a metaphorical sense. The walking was easier than the last few hours but care was still required with tussocks, bog and the odd hidden trench. I dropped down onto a picturesque shingle bay opposite Drumfearn, the scrunching of my boots accompanied by the loud yelping of redshanks and the kleep-kleep of oystercatchers. Beyond here I tried to stay with the immediate shoreline but was soon forced onto the rough and undulating grass and heather above. The coast made a broad curving sweep into sheltered Loch an Eilean and the road and tiny township of Heast (pronounced Haste). The only sign of life was a lone figure pottering about on a floating fish farm platform out to sea. This was the first time I had ever been to Heast, although a road winds it way north for five miles over the Druim Bhain to connect with Broadford on the other side of Skye. No part of Skye is more than five miles from the sea.

Anxious to reach Boreraig, I quickly donned waterproofs at Heast as a steady drizzle had begun and struck off on the last two and a half rugged miles. This final barren stretch was enlivened by the sudden appearance of another backpacker, walking in the opposite direction to myself. He assured me that he wasn't another Skye coastal walker but a geology student from Bristol University and part of a larger group. His task was to analyse a square kilometre of land a day by taking rock samples and studying rock types. Further on I met three of his colleagues who informed me that the area was principally basalt with sandstone, plus gabbro and granite intrusions with the odd pocket of limestone. I bowed to their superior knowledge, clinging boldly to the fact that Skye's geology is so complex and diverse that much research is still required to fill in many details.

Nearing Boreraig, I noticed a long thin ribbon of white water plunging vertically over a basalt crag to shore level. Beyond, gentle swathes of sheep-shorn meadow rolled in run-rig folds to the broad protective hand of Boreraig Bay. Sprinklings of speckled stones linked by crooked crumbling lines of drystane dykes betrayed the presence of a once thriving settlement. The peaceful green expanse was backed by the steep scarp slopes of Beinn Bhuidhe plummeting into the sea beyond the bay in a contorted band of dark friable cliffs. In the immediate vicinity, pock-marked crystalline rocks topped with yellow lichen stood among acres of sea-smoothed rounded stones in a myriad muted tints, the ocean caressing and moulding their mottled forms as it had done for tens of thousands of years.

In brightening skies I stumbled along the rocky shoreline, the weight of my pack now of prime concern. At the waterfall I climbed up a steep path overgrown with bushes and bracken to emerge on springy turf and acres of homeland stolen from the people and given over to sheep for nothing but profit for those 'masters of shame'. Boreraig and neighbouring Suishnish are particularly remembered among all the Skye Clearances as being the most brutal and the saddest display of insincerity, deceit and hollow lies. In 1854, when the land was stripped of its very life blood, a circular was put out defending the inhumanity on the basis that Lord MacDonald had been 'prompted by motives of benevolence, piety and humanity ... because they (the people) were too far from the church'.

The innocent crofters in Boreraig and Suishnish would not leave their homes voluntarily and were ruthlessly driven out by a body of constables. Three men resisted and were imprisoned in Portree before being marched on foot to Inverness for trial. A verdict of not guilty was returned but this did not stop the families of the accused from being evicted the following Christmas.

As I searched around for a suitable camp spot, I felt like an intruder in this domain, inhabited now only by wandering sheep, oblivious to everything but the few square inches of grass in front of them. At least they did provide acres of flat green carpet ideal for pitching and I was spoilt for choice. I eventually chose the middle of a broad green expanse surrounded by the haphazard remains of numerous shielings and drystane dykes and a narrow, swiftly-flowing burn. In the now strengthening sunlight, I erected the tent, gazing out across the steely grey waters of Loch Eishort to the conspicuous collection of whitewashed houses at Ord, and wondered if Tony or Bridget were watching me through a pair of binoculars – they had said they would look out for me. I subsequently discovered that they had, in fact, spotted a figure and a tent!

By now the weather was perfect for camping – sun and a gently drying breeze. The pitch and outlook could not be bettered and, without a doubt, Boreraig was the finest camp site so far. Lying on my sleeping bag with that first mug of sweet tea was sheer bliss, all the more so due to the elemental simplicity of situation and circumstance; the absence of people, noise and distraction. The faint rustle of the wind in the flysheet, the odd bleat of a sheep high on the hillside and the intermittent plaintive cry of a curlew – these were the sounds of silence, the calls of the wild.

The families who lived here a century and a half ago knew and understood this wildness. They lived by its rules, rising with the sun and retiring to peat-smoke blackened homesteads as darkness fell. Their entire lives were bound up in this natural protective amphitheatre which provided all their simple needs. They had no desire for, and indeed no conception of, a 'better' life in Nova Scotia or anywhere else. For most, the promise of jobs, success and wealth in far off bustling cities was replaced by the cold reality of banishment, homesickness beyond belief, death of loved ones en route to the New World and even the lack of a will to live.

As I looked out of my tent to the patchwork of greens and browns, the scattered lines of stones, the corduroy corrugations of distant run-rigs below the sheep-studded slopes of Beinn Bhuidhe, I realised that this was the view that would have been seen by families for scores of years – minus the sheep, and framed by a lintel-topped square of stones. In 1854, dozens of families were uprooted

A ruin at Boreraig

and torn away from the view, the life that had sustained them since birth; torn away from the briny air, the oystercatcher, the curlew, the otter and the endless surge of the ocean.

The most profoundly moving first-hand account of eviction was that of the eminent geologist, Sir Archibald Geikie, in 1851, when he described the clearance of Suishnish. One afternoon as he returned from a ramble 'a strange wailing sound reached my ears at intervals on the breeze from the west' and he describes 'a long and motley procession winding along the road that led north from Suishnish'. He goes on to describe 'old men and women, too feeble to walk, who were placed in carts; the younger members of the community on foot were carrying their bundles of clothes and household effects, while the children with looks of alarm, walked alongside'. Finally, he wistfully remarks, 'Everyone was in tears; each wished to clasp the hands that had so often befriended them and it seemed as if they could not tear themselves away. When they went forth once more, a cry of grief went up to heaven, the long plaintive wail, like a funeral coronach, was resumed and after the last of the emigrants had disappeared behind the hill, the sound seemed to re-echo through the whole wide valley of Strath in one prolonged note of desolation.'

As the last of the light faded on that summer evening in Skye and the echoing cry of a lone curlew split the silence, I began to appreciate the true depth of these sentiments.

* * * * *

At 4.15am I lay awake listening to the chatter of a bird of unknown identity. A faint light was already filtering through the tent walls and the pitter-patter of raindrops urged me back to sleep. By 7.30 I was tuned in to a pattern of sunny intervals and squally showers and aimed to rise and strike camp in the space of a sunny window in the weather. There is always the temptation in these conditions to leave the tent up as long as possible in order to dry thoroughly from the previous squall. The drawback is, of course, that the next squall may come sooner than expected and wet the tent once again in the mad rush of dismantling and packing.

However, everything went to plan and I was walking by 8.40 in brilliant sun, following the marked scenic path below the loose and vegetated cliffs of Carn Dearg. This path is completely hemmed in between cliff and sea and, in several sections, I found it difficult to believe that any sort of track could possibly have been constructed. At one point I passed a 100-foot high waterfall which the decreased volume of water had reduced to a lacy feathery veil bouncing and cascading off the numerous ledges of the dark basalt and andesite cliff. The fall was perfectly framed with trees on either side and the cliff itself was a mass of green vegetation.

After a mile or so, the path rose steeply for nearly 300 feet and as I climbed up several sheep scuttled off into the thick bracken on either side. Towards the top the path steepened and narrowed to a trench of sandy clay, the right side rearing up in a series of sculptured sandstone outcrops. I imagined life here a century and a half ago, picturing a lurching line of crofters and cattle making their way up here en route from Boreraig to Suishnish. Barefooted, mud-caked children, hunched weather-beaten women with creels and peats on their backs – the image in my mind seemed real enough to be true. At the top I removed the pack and rested on a wonderfully exposed overhanging outcrop topped with a layer of sheep-shorn grass. Clusters of sea-thrift and starry saxifrage poked their heads out from rocky nooks. Looking back, the curving line of water-streaked cliffs dropped down to bracken and a boulder strewn beach, the path hardly visible. To the right, the grey-blue expanse of Loch Eishort reflected the sun in a blinding glitter of blazing brilliance.

From this point, the character of the day altered significantly. The path followed the cliff top for a short distance before gradually turning north over heathery moor to Suishnish. The watery finger of Loch Eishort was finally forsaken for Loch Slapin, another long sea finger poking deep into Skye's hill country. But it was one hill, or rather mountain, which totally dominated the scene for the next few hours – the grand Cuillin outlier of Bla Bheinn (Blaven) which translates as 'blue hill'. Sheriff Alexander Nicolson, a Skyeman and an early mountaineering pioneer of the Cuillin range, suggested Blaven was the finest mountain on the island and I found it hard to disagree.

As I descended to Suishnish, the craggy pinnacled crest of the Blaven-Clach Glas ridge was clear of cloud and the numerous gullies and scree fans were visible, dropping a thousand feet down the grape blue verticalities of this impressive mountain. Blaven was a perfect backdrop to the vivid sunlit green of grass and bracken sweeping across the Suishnish hillside. Within the low stone dykes and scattered ruins I was surprised to find a relatively recent half-painted green wooden shack with rusted corrugated iron shelter. Further on, behind a straggle of wind-stunted trees was a stone bothy with a bright orange-red roof. I subsequently discovered that the Board of Agriculture had briefly re-crofted Suishnish after the Great War and I guessed that the bothy, at least, was erected then.

The constantly shifting pattern of sunshine and squalls had continued since Boreraig and was producing some stunning lighting effects. One minute Blaven stood proudly in sun-sculptured splendour and the next it had faded to a flat washed-out grey mass. As I approached the bothy a transient, half-hearted rainbow flickered briefly above the trees, only to drown in an ocean of ominous wind-tossed cloud. Great sheaths of sunlit landscape appeared and disappeared as the vaporous mass sporadically eclipsed the sun. True to form, I had to change camera film in the middle of this Skye light show, just as the next squally shower made its unwelcome entrance on the shifting stage.

I sheltered in the gloomy bothy with its stench of sheep droppings. The only sign of any human having recently entered this rancid shrine of decay and neglect was a half-worn leather walking boot sitting forlornly on the window sill. Not relishing the thought of hanging about, I left the bothy before the spongy clouds had fully wrung out their rations of rain. This proved to be the clearing-up shower, however, and gradually the sky oozed acres of translucent blue, clouds being chased away in that marvellously refreshing post-rain breeze.

The next couple of miles were the highlight of the day. Sun, cooling breeze, an excellent track and glorious sun-dappled views across Loch Slapin to Blaven and the Red Cuillin. High above, scattered squadrons of cumulus threw shifting shadows across the speckled green slopes and screes of the Slapin hills, endowing the whole range with a dynamic three-dimensionality. Closer to home, a tangle of bracken and heather lined the track, with the odd cluster of deep pink foxgloves adding colour to the blue-green sheep-studded scene.

All too soon I reached the gently curving bay of Camas Malag – and the inevitable signs of civilisation in the form of parked vehicles and people. Tourists are as much a part of a Skye summer as are midges; up until now I hadn't seen much of either. Several cows wandered about on the shingly beach adding to the general atmosphere of highland tranquillity. At the other end of the bay, the track heads inland to the picturesque township of Torrin. At this point I left the track and stuck with the coastline until the next sandy bay less than a mile further on. Finding a suitable rock, I settled down for a spot of lunch relishing the solitude and sun-washed seascape. I began to wish that I hadn't booked accommodation at Strathaird House that night with the weather now on a turn for the better. So much for the forecast of a few days ago.

Beyond the bay a dense cloak of deciduous trees appeared to block the route and I made a quick decision to head up to Torrin via a grassy path enclosed by bushes and overhanging trees. Torrin translates as 'little hill' and provides the perfect picture postcard setting for the view of Blaven, rising 3,000 feet above the head of Loch Slapin. It has also been the site of habitation for many centuries, boasting two duns and the standing stone of Clach na h-Annait.

The single-track road beyond Torrin literally hugs the coastline in a loop around the head of Loch Slapin. I passed the quarry where Skye Marble is excavated and made into chips before being exported to places near and far. It is said to have been used in the building of the Vatican and the Palace of Versailles as well as the altar of Iona Abbey and Armadale Castle. One of my photographs of Blaven shows Loch Slapin tinged with green from the quarried marble.

As I trudged the hot tarmac, I was aware of a seagull swooping and diving at me. Seconds later I noticed a chick scurrying about in the grass and realised it was protecting its young. Rounding the head of the loch, it occurred to me that I was now only about four miles from Strathaird House and I began dreaming of ice-cool pints of lager and lime. In the sheltered nooks and crannies of Loch Slapin the sun was a demon, and this, together with a heavy pack and the regular rhythm of hard road walking, was producing sweat on my brow and sore feet. Beyond the Narrows, the road climbed, gradually leaving the coastline and swinging across open moor before descending to the tiny hamlet of Kilmarie. Shortly before Kilmarie I turned off along an old disused muddy track which led to Strathaird House. On the right I passed the newly opened Hayloft Restaurant (Kirkibost Steading) which has been tastefully converted from little more than a barn. Strathaird House itself was built about 150 years ago by MacAllisters and is joined to a much older MacKinnon farmhouse, renovated to provide comfortable accommodation.

It certainly had that warm, welcoming feel of an old country house as I stepped into the gracious interior. An incongruous Australian drawl of 'Hi there, you must be Andrew Dempster' came from the lips of Laura, daughter of the owners, John and Jenny Kubale. Leaving my weighty pack in the hallway, I was shown my bedroom before being conducted on a guided tour of the guests' sitting room/library and washing/drying/ironing room, both of which were well used in the following few hours.

Minutes later I was comfortably ensconced in the sitting room, the dreamed-of pint now a reality. I was touched to discover a well-thumbed copy of my first book *Classic Mountain Scrambles in Scotland* and duly signed it. I whetted my appetite on coastal delights yet to come as I flicked through a copy of Ralph Storer's *Fifty Walks in Skye and Raasay*.

The remainder of the afternoon and early evening was spent pottering at the personal chores of the long-distance walker – showering, washing and drying clothes, postcard and diary writing, posting off slide films and, of course, 'phoning home. I drooled over a tasty seafood meal at the Hayloft Restaurant before wandering down to Kilmarie to pay a visit to Alan Morgan, an old friend who had transported gear by land rover on our many trips to Camasunary Lodge, just over the hill. Alan is employed by Strathaird Estate as an odd job man, a Jack of all Trades, one of which was to keep an eye on the bothy and lodge at Camasunary Bay. Originally from the North of England, he presents a bearded, powerfully built profile with a character to match. Once Alan is engaged in conversation it is almost impossible to get a word in edgeways. His main thrust that evening was the tangled bureaucratic intricacies of his attempt to buy The Steading, where I had just enjoyed my evening meal. The story was long and involved and there was obviously deep personal resentment that he hadn't secured the deal. He had the look of a caged lion as he poured me another dram. Alan didn't join me, being teetotal. On a brighter note, our chat turned to some interesting Lillian Beckwith-type characters living near Elgol, one of whom owns an untaxed car with only one gear. Living in Glasnakille, he drives the mile and a half to Elgol daily, but backwards – the only working gear in the car is reverse!

The conversation swung to land ownership issues and in particular the John Muir Trust, which has recently bought this area, including Blaven. Strathaird was once in the hands of Ian Anderson, frontman of the successful rock act, JethroTull, and was sold by him a few years back to the Trust whose prime concern is conservation – not only of wildlife but of the indigenous population. I was taken aback, therefore, to discover that Alan possessed a deep mistrust of the motives of the J.M.T. and I never managed to tease out the real reasons behind this, though I suspected that his non-purchase of The Steading played a large part.

I finished my second dram, politely declining a third, before farewells and a final stroll in the gloaming back up the hill to a soft bed and dreams at Strathaird House. With five days down and over 60 miles done, I had less than 300 miles still to go. Skyewalk was gradually maturing into a fine malt.

* * * * *

The following morning I enjoyed what was to be the finest breakfast of the walk. Whether I was just hungrier than usual I don't know, but the cereal with banana, full cooked fry-up with all the trimmings and a whole jug of coffee hit the spot. I chatted with two English couples, both genuinely interested in my month's itinerary. In a further attempt to reduce pack weight, I left two long-sleeved shirts at Strathaird House, believing tee-shirts and a fleece to be ample. Most of my walking up until now had been in these last two items and I saw no reason for circumstances to change radically.

By 9.40am I had stepped out into the sultry, windless morning, acutely aware that this could be the day when the midges struck with a vengeance -and I had planned to camp at Loch Coruisk that night! Today's route would take me round the Strathaird Peninsula and into the very heart of the Cuillin. The second part of this route, from Elgol onwards, was a classic coastal walk in its own right and one with which I was well acquainted.

I turned off the Elgol road near the bridge at Kilmarie and followed the old graveyard road to rejoin the coast beyond the river. The small section of coastline containing Dun Ringill had been omitted but I could live with this. Below the main Elgol road a series of footpaths, tracks and roads loosely follows the coastline connecting a string of crofts, culminating in the more substantial township of Glasnakille. This was my proposed route and provided an ideal warm-up for the more demanding rigours which lay ahead. As I sauntered blissfully along, my gaze drifted out across the watery expanse to the undulating line of the Sleat peninsula and my route of three days ago. Already I felt the walk was taking shape and evolving into an overall experience with its own distinctive character.

Before leaving Ord, Tony and Bridget at Fiordhem had asked me to look out for an old friend of theirs who lived at Glasnakille. I was told he resided in a house named, oddly, Rajput Cottage, one of the last buildings on the right-hand side of the road through Glasnakille. While looking for this, I noticed the sign pointing the way to Spar Cave, a 'celebrated cavern' noted for its stalagmites and stalactites and very popular during the last century when a toll was levied for entry. Access requires low tide and a torch, but since neither of these was available and time was at a premium, I felt little guilt at leaving this excursion for some future occasion. Skye's coastline is indented with scores of caves, many only accessible by boat. Now there was an idea for a sea-loving adventurer – a complete sea circumnavigation of Skye, exploring all the caves ... *Classic Caves of Skye* could be the resulting book ... But I was dreaming...

I soon discovered Rajput Cottage and decided to go and introduce myself to Tony and Bridget's friend, Tony Cousins. I had been knocking on the door of the glass vestibule for some time when a man in a dressing gown appeared, leaning out of a dormer window above. I had hardly mentioned Tony and Bridget LaTrobe when he shouted down in a cultured English accent, 'Go in and sit down'. I entered the vestibule, removed my pack and made myself comfortable. Tony and Bridget had informed me that Tony Cousins' wife had died recently and that he would be glad of company. He duly appeared and over a couple of long, cool glasses of refreshing orange juice, we spent half-an-hour in stimulating conversation.

Tony had obviously led a full and very interesting life, his occupations ranging from coffee plantation owner to private detective for Quantas Airlines and Singapore stockbroker. It made my teaching career seem like watching paint dry! The name Rajput was an Indian regiment which he had been in during the Second World War, his father having been in the same regiment during the Great War.

Time was pressing and much as I would have liked to continue conversing with this fascinating character, it was time to resume my travels. We shook hands and I departed, continuing along the track to the last house. Surrounding it was a rather unwelcome electric fence but two gates led me down a path to a small sheltered bay, my way apparently blocked by cliffs beyond. I cut off to the right, crossing a stream before scrambling up through choking heather and bracken and crossing a deer fence. The way now seemed clear to the southern tip of the Strathaird peninsula just half-a-mile beyond.

Port an Luig Mhoir, or 'haven of the black hollow', is a rocky bay nearby with an historical claim to fame. Bonnie Prince Charlie spent his last night on Skye in the cave which is marked on the map in this bay. This was where I had originally intended to spend the night had I not booked into Strathaird House (camping in the bay as opposed to sleeping in a cave!). Many highland maps show caves allegedly having been slept in by Bonnie Prince Charlie but the majority of these are miles away from his five-month route and could not possibly have been used by him. However, historical records showed that there was no doubting this one and I was keen to find it.

Much of the romanticism of Skye is due to this anti-hero and had he been able to sail directly to France in the wake of the Culloden catastrophe, it is doubtful in the extreme if he would have been shrouded in the romantic fervour that he is today. During his five months as an outlaw, of which only six days were spent on Skye, he built up a cult following out of all proportion to his previous following as a leader of men. Time and time again he came within a hair's breadth of capture, but the loyalty of good friends never forsook him, despite the promise of £30,000 for his capture, which was untold wealth in those days. One such friend was the legendary Flora Macdonald, the Skye lass who guided him on Skye for three days with Charlie dressed as her serving-maid.

At the bay in question I found a suitable rock, dumped my pack and went off in search of Charlie's cave. I was impressed by a grotesque, indented limestone cliff, a bizarre battle-zone of gnarled flakes, cracks and overhangs. My scrambling/rock-climbing side had me surmising possible routes and I wondered if anyone had ever attempted a climb here. Beyond this cliff I boulder- and rock-hopped my way along the rocky shoreline, revelling in my packless state. Rum's unmistakable profile floated on the horizon like some great lumbering leviathan. I noticed several small caves in the limestone cliffs, any one of which could have provided refuge for a prince with a price on his head. I returned to the pack and climbed up above the cliffs before resting on a massive, flat limestone slab offering superb views north to the scattered cottages of Elgol and Blaven's soaring south ridge rising in a single clean sweep from sea to summit. Nearby was the promontory of Suidhe Biorach (The Sharp Seat) where, legend has it, childless married women sat in the highly optimistic hope of achieving fertility.

Midges soon had me on the move again and by two o'clock I reached Elgol, on the shores of Loch Scavaig, a familiar haunt. Elgol takes its name from the warrior, Aella, who fought a battle against the Picts and Scots at this place. Despite Elgol's far-flung location at the end of a long single-track road from Broadford, it sees plenty of tourists and today was no exception. Apart from the fact that a motor-boat takes tourists to Loch Coruisk from here, the view of the Cuillin from Elgol is something of a classic and has been described by some, including A.W. Wainwright, as the best view in Britain. Having seen the Cuillin from Ord in Sleat, I would now disagree but nevertheless it is still highly impressive.

Slowly, I eased my sluggish frame up the steep hill, panting in the sultry conditions. Near the top of the twisting tarmac road I resisted the temptation to spend half-an-hour in the little seasonal tea room which was choked full of tourists anyway. A little way beyond, I left the road and took the well-trodden footpath which would lead, in three spectacularly scenic miles, to the idyllic bay of Camasunary. No matter how many times I walk this route (which is quite a few) I never tire of the interplay of mountain and seascape which has made this one of the most popular coastal walks on the island. For a first taste of Skye-walking it has no equal and will undoubtedly whet the appetite for the succulent delicacies of the Cuillin ridge. The Cuillin draw the eye like a magnet on this walk but there is one peak in particular which the eye seems more irresistibly drawn to – that of Sgurr na Stri (Peak of Conflict) which, although it barely makes 1,600 ft above sea level, affords the finest ringside view of the Cuillin at close hand. Sgurr na Stri literally rises out of the sea in one explosive upthrust of gabbro and effectively forms a barrier between Camsunary and Loch Coruisk.

As I strode along the path which clung precariously to the

steep western slopes of Ben Cleat, I became aware of a distant chug-chugging drone and distinctive vocal tones on a tannoy system. Far below on my left the *Bella Jane* was ploughing a furrow in the otherwise unruffled expanse of Loch Scavaig, heading to Loch Coruisk with its cargo of paying passengers. I was glad to be walking and seeing and not talking and fleeing.

Halfway between Elgol and Camasunary the path descends to sea level at the 'pretty stony beach' of Cladach A' Ghlinne. A couple of other walkers were pottering about on the rocky shoreline. This is always a tempting, remote spot to while away a lazy half-hour but today I kept on the move, anxious to reach Camasunary by late afternoon. The following half-mile of path is a superbly exposed sheep track hugging steep grassy slopes with some grand situations. At one point the path becomes a trench, tangled in a mass of small stunted trees and bushes, only to reappear slightly further up the hill, after apparently ending in a sheer drop. Once clear of the trees, the final run to the 'bay of the white shieling' is presented, the white gable-end of the latter normally a welcoming haven below the vastness of Blaven's south ridge. It seemed odd to be arriving at Camasunary with the knowledge that I would not be staying there.

However, as I approached the bay, the familiarity and warmth exuded by the grand surroundings and the fond memories of precious times, swaddled me in a cocoon of cogent potency. Within seconds I knew I wouldn't be camping at Loch Coruisk that night. If I couldn't stay at Camasunary Lodge then I would spend the night at the bothy further along the beach. This was where I had my first real introduction to the charms of this spot back on Hogmanay 1985/86 with a group of kindred spirits. Then, as on numerous occasions since, we had stumbled over the Am-Mam track loaded to the gunnels with food, fuel (in the form of coal) and plenty of whisky. Two years later we repeated the expedition before eventually graduating to the more up-market residence half-a-mile away for Hogmanay '92/'93 and '94/'95.

Approaching the lodge, I noticed a new extension was in the process of being constructed, in the form of a boat shed and indoor toilets. Alan Morgan had informed me that the next lot of residents would not be appearing until the next day, having delayed their entry date by two days. The mainstay of this group was an old teaching colleague of mine whom I had introduced to Camasunary in July 1992 and who had never looked back since. I was sorry that I had missed him by only a day, especially with the possibility of a free bed!

Thoughts of kipping down in the new boat shed were soon abandoned and I wandered along the springy machair to the bothy, surprised but pleased to find it deserted – unusual for mid-July. Unlike the lodge, the bothy is a much more modest and humble affair, offering free bedspace on stone floors, an open fire and resident mice. Like scores of other bothies in Scotland, it is owned by the local estate but maintained by the Mountain Bothies Association, an organisation which is dedicated to those who enjoy 'the wild and lonely places'. Having been a member of the MBA for many years and greatly respecting their admirable and monumental efforts in securing the use of many previously ruinous cottages for hill gangrels such as myself, I feel the MBA has, perhaps, reached over-saturation point in becoming too big for its own good. A recent policy of not publishing the grid references of bothies, because of fear of vandalism (a common problem for some bothies), seems a shade counter-productive to their own ethos that bothies are there for anyone to use – non-MBA members included. It would be sad to see this organisation degenerate into a secret society. I have personally been rebuked by the MBA for over-publicising Camasunary bothy in a previous book – a claim with which I totally disagree – and I refuse to accept that extolling the merits of a bothy in a book which will only be read by serious hill-lovers can possibly contribute to further vandalism. Making the location of bothies more secret will not cure casual vandalism – the problems runs much deeper, involving education and society at large. However, I digress.

In the bothy, I had the freedom to slowly unpack and unwind from the physical rigours of the day, spreading gear about the room I had chosen to sleep in and in the front room where I settled down with a mug of tea, some shortbread and my diary. The hushed sound of surf on seashore filtered through the bothy walls, oystercatchers called, a sheep bleated somewhere in the distance. Life was bliss. I wandered outside and drifted along the tideline, accompanied by dancing displays of ringed plovers flitting over the small wavelets breaking at my feet, their liquid 'too-i-too-i' calls singing the special song that is Camasunary. Now and again a single high-pitched 'pheet' betrayed the presence of an elusive rock pipit; its call struck at the very core of wildness and crystallised the sense of place emanating from this sacred spot. As always, I felt a spiritual re-seeding, a breathing of life back in to fill the pocket of emptiness created by my prolonged absence from the bay of the white shieling. I turned round and ambled back to the bothy, my gaze arrested by the all-embracing, mottled, craggy face of Sgurr na Stri, standing guard over the bay.

Back inside I sat by the table preparing a tin of curry and Uncle Ben's rice. Whilst leafing through the bothy book containing visitors' comments, I was disconcerted to find an insert from five obviously very annoyed backpackers who had been visited by a tall, brash, bearded individual who had informed them in no uncertain terms that Camasunary bothy was for emergency use only and that the normal bothy code did not apply here. They also had written that he had become very abusive when they had attempted to reason with him, saying that he would return with a party of 'heavies' and forcibly evict anyone still at the bothy! It was patently obvious to me that the bearded heavy in question was Alan Morgan, with whom I had spoken the previous night. It seemed that he took his job of keeping an eye on the bothy in a rather over-the-top manner, which was possibly another reason he had fallen out with the John Muir Trust.

Just as I began to expect to be on my own that evening, I heard voices outside and saw two people passing the side window. The latch bolt shifted noisily and the door creaked open to reveal a young couple with huge packs. Their friendly 'Hi there', followed by 'Is it O.K. if we stay here?' immediately gave them away as Americans. I replied in the affirmative (not expecting Alan Morgan that evening) and duly explained that this was an open bothy, a foreign notion in the USA. They had walked from Sligachan via Glen Sligachan and were obviously glad of shelter as rain was now falling steadily. Skye weather was returning to normal.

My unexpected visitors, Daniel and Miriam, were delightful company and for the remainder of the evening we engaged in sparkling conversation revolving mainly around the differences between hiking in America and in Scotland. They queried the lack of tree cover in the Highlands and especially Skye, and this inevitably led to the Clearances and Scotland's troubled history. Throughout our cosy chat, they graciously shared their Whyte and Mackay whisky and memories flooded back from Hogmanay '85/'86. With light rapidly fading and the last drop of whisky squeezed from the bottle, we departed to our respective rooms, saying our farewells as I expected to be up and away by 6 o'clock. Tomorrow would be a long hard day.

* * * * *

A soft, subdued light played on the musty bothy walls as I lay in my sleeping bag, listening to shifting, scratching sounds of

Camasunary

unknown source. The time was barely 5.00 a.m. Surely Daniel and Miriam were not up at this early hour? I rose quickly and soon traced the noises to a mouse in the log basket of the other front room. By 6 o'clock I had breakfasted, packed and was ready to meet the challenges of the day, which I guessed could be considerable. I had already extended the day's walking by almost three miles by not continuing to Loch Coruisk yesterday. Hence the early start.

Today's route would take me round the rough coastal path to Loch Coruisk via the infamous Bad Step, a route with which I was thoroughly acquainted but which never palled. From there it was completely pathless, walking around the brutally steep slopes of Gars-bheinn, the butt end of the Cuillin Ridge which plunges inexorably into Loch Scavaig. A long meander would take me out to Rubh' an Dunain at the entrance to Loch Brittle where I had arranged to meet up with a friend who would accompany me for the remaining four miles to the camp site at the head of Loch Brittle.

There was a gloomy, sombre feel to the weather as I stepped outside. Low, black clouds hung like dead weights above Marsco's crouching form. I had a deep sense of foreboding, like an omen of some impending doom. I took heed and mentally prepared myself for what lay ahead. The first problem of the day lay only yards from the bothy in the form of the river which flowed into the bay and must be crossed in order to reach the coastal path. When I first visited Camasunary in the early 1980s, a rickety foot suspension bridge crossed the river. Several years later, on my next visit (Hogmanay '85), the bridge had been washed away leaving only the remains of the stanchions and it has never been replaced. Further upstream, stepping stones exist but often these are partially or wholly submerged and other tactics must be used. Over the years we have used an imaginative variety of methods such as fastening bin bags to feet and legs; using one pair of wellington boots in a group by throwing them over the river for the next person to use, then concealing them until we returned later, or just removing boots and socks and wading across barefoot. Today I was lucky. Despite last night's heavy rain, the tide was out and I managed to negotiate the stepping stones dry-shod with the help of my trekking pole.

The path from here switchbacks along the base of Sgurr na Stri, rarely more than a stone's throw from the sea at any point. It encapsulates the essence of truly wild walking in a sense which I have never experienced anywhere else in Scotland, so much so that it is common knowledge amongst close friends and family that I would like my ashes scattered somewhere near Rubha Ban, the point from which the bay of Camas Fhionnairigh is just visible before turning towards the heart of the Cuillin at Loch Coruisk.

As I neared this point, I noticed a brightening of the sky out to sea and the Island of Eigg seemed to float on the horizon like a layer of thin cloud. Gars-bheinn was grim and grey – what I could see of it – and, as always, there was a sense of entering the core, the kernel of the Cuillin domain, the crepuscular cauldron of mountain and cloud looming and luring, like entering the land of Mordor in Tolkien's *Lord of the Rings*. And, like Mount Doom in Mordor, this rugged route threw out obstacles to thwart the unwary, in the form of 'the Bad Step', an unavoidable steep slab of gabbro which plunges into the sea, totally blocking the path. The Bad Step is negotiated by a narrow crack/shelf system which scramblers will take in their stride but which many walkers have found very unnerving. On one occasion, a female member of our party was reduced to a tearful, quivering wreck whilst halfway along this crack and much reassurance and gentle persuasion was required before her hands could be unfrozen from the rock and she could be coaxed into the final moves to freedom. I had crossed the Bad Step countless times but never with a fully laden rucksack, but the Crack of Doom proved straightforward with a steady head and steady hand.

Beyond the Bad Step the path winds its way through a jumble of huge angular blocks and boulders to the tiny sheltered bay at the head of Loch nan Leachd, or loch of the slabs. From here the path can be quite difficult to follow and despite my familiarity with this area, I stupidly wandered too high and ended up extricating myself from the clutches of deceptively smooth gabbro slabs which were partially covered in a lethal layer of water. A slip here could easily have put an unceremonious end to the venture – and possibly my life. Another warning sign. Again, I took heed.

Whilst high on these slabs I noticed the mast of a yacht in the natural harbour in Loch na Cuilce just beyond, and wondered if I would finally meet up with my teaching colleague who was sailing round Skye. Minutes later I reached Loch Coruisk or Coire Uisge (the water corrie), the jewel in the crown of the surrounding Cuillin and the most dramatic mountain loch in Great Britain.

Today, it was cloaked in sombre gloomy mood but was as atmospheric as ever. Sir Walter Scott visited Coruisk in 1814 and such was the profound impression it made that he was inspired to verse:

Rarely human eye has known
A scene so stern as that dread lake;
With its dark ledge of barren stone
...
For all is rocks at random thrown,
Black waves, bare crags and banks of stone
As if were here denied
The summer sun, the spring's sweet dew,
That clothe with many a varied hue
The bleakest mountain-side.

I sympathised with these emotions as I stared out across the brooding expanse to the grim gaunt walls of gabbro beyond.

The Scavaig river connecting Loch Coruisk with the sea must be one of the shortest rivers in Scotland, a mere few hundred yards. I crossed the stepping stones easily and walked the short distance to the flat grassy area near the Coruisk Memorial Hut belonging to the Scottish Mountaineering Club. The yacht I had spied earlier was not my colleague's. I sat down on a rock to eat an orange and watched the yacht owners pottering about in preparation for the day ahead. My eyes wandered to the head of Loch na Cuilce and the disturbing sight of steep gabbro slabs plunging directly into the water – this was my intended route. The alternative was a 300-foot climb and descent of the crag above, which I didn't relish. Anxious to check this out at close quarters, I quickly finished my orange and wandered along to the slabs. My original view had been partly foreshortened and from the side they didn't appear as steep. However, a few tricky moves were unavoidable and the added handicap of a large pack was somewhat disconcerting.

I crossed the Allt a' Chaoich or Mad Burn, which wasn't too much in spate, and continued, keeping fairly low down near the water's edge. I had remembered seeing what appeared to be a massive gabbro crag running down the steep hillside like a projecting rib of some vast dead creature. From the other side of the sea loch it appeared to bar all passage and I seriously worried if I would tease out a route. I soon came upon the rib in question and negotiated my way onto it with little or no problem. However, as often happens, pride came before a fall and I suddenly slipped on wet rock, both feet plunging into a rock pool. Again, I took the slip as a signal to slow down and take care. I was tired and this would turn out to be the longest, hardest day yet. A marker cairn stood at the top of an easy grassy gully which led down to a deceptively tricky drop. I made several unsuccessful attempts to descend the drop but found that the weight of my pack was unbalancing me. I knew I could descend easily without the pack, but then what? Patience won out over panic, however, and a solution materialised. To the right of the descent route a crystalline convex slab sloped down to a ledge which I knew I could reach from the bottom. Carefully, I inched my way partly down the slab and placed the pack as low as I could, allowing the friction of gabbro to hold the pack. A strap dangled down to within grasping distance from the ledge. I then climbed down easily before clambering onto the ledge to retrieve the pack.

This extended maneouvre had my adrenalin going and the discovery of a reasonable unmarked path beyond here gave me a high which put wind in my flagging sails. The weather was improving too, with squadrons of fluffy cumulus floating by in a freshening breeze. A gang of noisy gulls wheeled and cavorted overhead. The day was looking up. My new found path clung desperately to the steep hillside and several places required delicate footwork in order to avoid a potentially fatal tumble. Beyond Rubh' a' Gheodha Bhuidhe, loosely translated as 'point of the yellow cove', the path was less distinct and eventually disappeared altogether.

Seaward views were now dominated by the offshore island of Soay (pronounced Soy) which is almost two separate islands due to two opposing narrow sea lochs, the northerly one a fine natural harbour. Soay's rich and varied history is out of all proportion to its size. Before 1823 only one family lived there but the island was given a new lease of life during the Clearances when scores of evicted families from Skye settled there. Within 30 years the population rose to 120 and a school with 40 pupils opened. If only one good thing came out of the Clearances, then it was the re-population of Soay. The inhabitants were basically self-supporting but much had still to be imported. However, in prolonged periods of bad weather this was impossible. Islanders returning from shopping in Skye had to light a fire on the shore at Elgol, the nearest road connection, to signal for a boat to come over and pick them up. In 1946, the author, Gavin Maxwell, bought the island and started a basking shark fishery, building a slipway and small factory. Three years later this folded, due to lack of demand for shark oil, but was revived briefly by Maxwell's harpooner, Tex Geddes. Then, in June 1953, shades of the St Kilda evacuation were recreated when, on a glorious summer day, all of Soay's inhabitants, except Geddes and his family, left in a blaze of publicity aboard the SS Hebrides to be resettled on Mull. This was entirely their own decision, as they had had enough of the hardship and deprivation of life on a small island. Since then, a steady stream of new settlers, including an Australian family, came to seek the quiet life and responded to the challenge of small island living with the result that, against all the odds, Soay is now a thriving community.

I hope one day to visit Soay but today I was contented enough to be at the closest point to it from Skye – less than a mile across Soay Sound at Ulfhart Point. My diary for that night records

'Beyond Ulfhart Point the going becomes horrendous with bracken, trees, gullies and bogs'. Even this negative remark was probably an understatement written in the serenity of a cosy tent. What really depressed me at this stage was the view ahead of apparently endless headlands and cliffs stretching for over five miles to Rubh' an Dunain. I was also making dismal progress, not even managing a paltry one-and-a-half miles per hour.

The tumbling gurgling waters of the Allt Coir nan Laogh dropping down from rocky Cuillin heights marked a turning point in the day. The crossing of this was no less cumbersome than the previous couple of hours, but beyond, the terrain became less impervious to the passage of a weary walker. Still, it could not be described as rhythmic walking by any stretch of the imagination. I was no longer contouring along steep bracken and tree choked slopes but stumbling over undulating hillocks clothed in deep heather, sometimes lucky to find faint furrows of sheep and deer tracks. Another major stream crossing at Allt na Meacnaish led up on to a pleasant cliff top section but I was becoming too tired to enjoy the fine exposed situations. My body was rebelling. A week of rough walking with a full pack was taking its toll, both physically and mentally.

Conscious of the fact that I was meant to be meeting up with Ken Black any time now, I began scouring the hillside for signs of him. As is often the case in situations like this, my mind began to play tricks. I was sure I could see a figure on a hill top silhouetted against the sky and heard a shout from that direction. However, this wasn't Ken's way; far more likely that we would just stumble on each other almost by accident. The reality was that we almost missed each other. Somewhere around Slochd Dubh (black hollow) in an area of grassy hillocks, I heard a shout from behind. I swung round and there was Ken. There was an immense sense of relief and emotional release as we shook hands and exchanged greetings. It was a wonderful feeling to be back in the bosom of an old friend. We settled down in the lee of a drystane dyke, had a bite to eat and chatted, though the conversation was a rather one-sided account of my adventures over the past week.

Ken had already been out to the 'point' of Rubh' an Dunain (point of the fort) and he kindly offered to carry my pack while I took his small day-pack. I would visit the point and then catch up with him later on the path to Glenbrittle. During my many stays at the campsite in Glenbrittle, the towering Cuillin had been the magnet and I felt ashamed that I had never walked the four miles to Rubh' an Dunain. I was sure there couldn't be many people who on their first visit to this majestically wild spot had walked round the coast from Camasunary.

The headland itself is a historic goldmine, containing ruins of old black houses, a chambered cairn, one of the best preserved examples of a galleried dun in Skye and even a canal of sorts, connecting the sea to the inland Loch na h-Airde. The MacAskills dominated this small area for generations, acting as coastguards for the MacLeods who had driven away the violent Norse invaders who had settled in Skye in 1293. The MacAskills had also been guardians of Dunsgaith Castle in Sleat where I had visited four days ago. Not finding a suitable anchorage for their boats, they constructed the canal which, though only a few hundred yards long, was an extraordinary feat for the time.

The absence of a heavy pack gave wind to my sails as I made a clockwise circuit of Loch na h-Airde, visiting the Iron Age Dun, now only a segment of wall on the landward side remaining, but on a beautifully exposed rocky spur. Skye native, Martin Martin, wrote in 1703: 'All these forts stand upon eminences, and are so disposed, that there is not one of them, which is not in view of some other, and by this means when a fire is made upon a beacon, in any one fort, it's in a few moments after communicated to all the rest, and this hath been always observed upon sight of any number of foreign vessels, or boats approaching the coast'. There are about 60 such defensive structures strung along Skye's coastline, all in a fairly ruinous state.

Despite my packless state, exhaustion wasn't far away and I didn't do complete justice to this primitive wind-scoured place on the edge of the land. I vowed I would return from Glenbrittle some time in the future. As I caught up with Ken, I thought about tomorrow. Weather permitting, I had planned to climb Sgurr Alasdair, the highest peak in the Cuillin, with Ken. Being well acquainted with this range of mountains and something of a

The Cuillin from Glen Brittle

Cuillin junkie, it would be my eleventh ascent of this peak, but Ken's first. Despite my ample previous experience, it would still require the same expenditure of energy and I wondered if I would be up to it after seven hard days' back-packing – and it was to be a rest day!

Re-united with Ken, I retrieved my weighty pack and we sauntered slowly along the track on the eastern shore of Loch Brittle, on the last lap of a very long day. Over the years I have grown to respect Ken not only as a valued friend, but as an ideal walking companion. Like me, he recognises the need for physical and mental space whilst walking and rarely do we walk shoulder to shoulder engaged in deep con-versation. Gazing across the grey mass of Loch Brittle, the vast cliffs of Minginish plunging sheer into the sea presented a foretaste of delights to come and a tempting trailer to the main feature of Duirinish coastal highlights, still a week's walking away. The track to Glenbrittle seemed endless and for a disturbing while the tiny sprinkling of oranges, blues and whites marking the tents at the campsite seemed no closer. Finally, at five o'clock, eleven hours after leaving the bothy at Camasunary, I hobbled into the camp-site.

Within half-an-hour the tent was up and I had changed into a light pair of Rohans and my Skyewalk tee-shirt, with a fistful of notes in my zipped pocket. I may have been tired but I was more than ready for a meal and a few pints in the Old Inn at Carbost, the nearest pub to the campsite, but still a nine-mile drive away along a single track road. Needless to say, Ken was driving. Another half-hour and we were ensconced in the convivial atmosphere of the Old Inn, wolfing down soup, steak and chips, and a sweet which I couldn't finish – all washed down with a copious quantity of beer. Replacing lost calories and fluids was a wonderful experience. No doubt Ken and I would be back here again tomorrow (Tuesday) after our Cuillin climb. Wednesday night I would be camped out in some wild spot between Loch Eynort and Talisker Bay. Carbost was on my itinerary for Thursday night, when I would be meeting up with two other friends.

As I lay in my tent that night, the first stirrings of an idea began to form in my mind which would profoundly affect the nature of the entire walk from here on. Perversely, I hoped tomorrow would be dull and wet, for then the idea could materialise.

Route Summary: Ord to Glenbrittle

Day 1: Ord – Boreraig (12 miles – 19 km)

This is a particularly wild and mainly pathless section around the head of Loch Eishort. Much variation is possible on the southern shore of the loch, from low-level seaweed and rock bashing to high-level heather bashing. The northern shore of the loch provides easier going on more amenable terrain, with traces of a path in the latter section leading to Boreraig, an old Clearance settlement with an abundance of superb camping spots.

Day 2: Boreraig – Strathaird House (11 miles – 18 km)

An easy day with magnificent scenery. An excellent shoreline path continues west of Boreraig before climbing and curving north to Suisnish, another famous Clearance settlement. From Suisnish an excellent land-rover track follows the east shore of Loch Slapin with magnificent views of Blaven. Beyond Camas Malag, cut off to Torrin or stay with the coastline, joining the A881 road north of Torrin. Follow the road as it loops round the head of Loch Slapin and finally in four miles reaches Strathaird House. Dun Ringill is worth a visit from here.

Day 3: Strathaird House – Camasunary (11 miles – 18 km)

A superb day's walking with the latter part providing breathtaking seaward views of the Cuillin Range. Note that the entire Elgol peninsula could be bypassed by using the Am Mam track to Camasunary. At Kilmarie, take the old graveyard road and follow the coastal trail on single-track road and land-rover track to Glasnakille. From here, cross country to the tip of the peninsula and swing round to Port an Luig Mhoir where Bonnie Prince Charlie left Skye. From here, follow the coast round to Elgol where there is a tea-room and a classic view of the Cuillin. From Elgol a magnificent coastal path heads northwards for just over three miles to the idyllic bay of Camasunary where there is an open bothy. It is also possible to camp near the bothy. Note that a second night could be spent at Strathaird House using the Am Mam track. This would be a fine circular trip.

Day 4: Camasunary – Glenbrittle (16 miles – 26 km)

Possibly the most demanding day of the entire trek – wild, rocky and mainly pathless. Cross the river on stepping stones and follow the shoreline path round the lower slopes of Sgurr na Stri. In two miles this leads to 'The Bad Step', an unavoidable slab of gabbro which can be negotiated by a crack and shelf lower down (easy scramble). Continue to Loch Coruisk (the heart of the Cuillin) on a vague path. Swing round the head of Loch na Cuilce on tricky crags of gabbro (keeping to the water's edge) and continue south on a vague path which negotiates one particularly tricky rock section. Completely pathless and awkward terrain leads all the way south and west to Rubh' an Dunain, a wild and windswept spot containing historical remains. Follow the south-eastern shore of Loch Brittle to Glenbrittle. Much of this is by land-rover track.

Accommodation and other information

Heast:	Possible B&B but wild camping only at Boreraig
Strathaird House:	Fine food and accommodation
Camasunary:	Bothy (MBA) or camping
Glenbrittle:	Campsite, Youth Hostel and small grocery shop on campsite

CHAPTER 4

Minginish Interlude

(Tuesday 14 July – Thursday 16 July)

Glenbrittle to Carbost

WAKING UP HAS LESS appeal in a campsite than when wild camping. Even at the early hour of 6.30am, murmuring voices, clinking

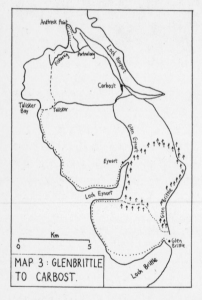

MAP 3 : GLENBRITTLE TO CARBOST.

cutlery and tent-pegs, low hissing of stoves, rustling of plastic bags and other sounds of early risers were magnified in the still morning air. I poked my head out to a fine drizzle and a grey clag clamped firm on the Coire Lagan skyline. It didn't look like a day for tackling Sgurr Alasdair. I lay back and in my mind fleshed out the idea of the night before.

Rather than climb Alasdair, Ken and I could tackle the next stage of the walk from Glenbrittle to Loch Eynort and return to Glenbrittle via Bealach Brittle, a fine circular route but, more importantly, without carrying a heavy pack. The following day Ken was due to return to his home in Golspie but, before doing so, I reasoned that he could give me a lift over to the Old Inn at Carbost where I could dump the pack, having booked accommodation for that night. He could then run me down Glen Eynort to the head of

Loch Eynort where I could resume the walk from where we had reached the previous day. I would then follow the coast round to Talisker Bay, Fiskavaig and into Loch Harport to Carbost, again without the burden of a full pack. This second day was an enormous undertaking, even with a light pack, but the compensation was a full rest day on Thursday at the Old Inn. If today had been bright and sunny, then my planned ascent of Sgurr Alasdair would probably have gone ahead and my reformulated walk plans gone astray – but it wasn't and I didn't feel, therefore, that I was conning Ken out of his first major Cuillin expedition. Nevertheless, I was worried about his reaction to the sudden change of plan.

I needn't have worried. Pottering over breakfast an hour or so later I put the idea directly to him. 'That's no problem, Andy, it would be good to do part of the walk with you', he calmly replied with not a hint of dissatisfaction or regret. That was Ken all over – he took life as he found it and rarely found cause to complain. I was elated. The plan was taking off and would soon affect more than just the next two days.

By ten o'clock the weather had perversely taken a turn for the better with the cloud beginning to shift and shuffle uneasily around the ridge, momentarily revealing the stark faces and buttresses of individual peaks. The drizzle had relented and there could be no getting away from the fact that it was clearing up. However, the decision had been made and we shouldered our light day packs and set off in the direction of the river Brittle which we crossed by a shaky pedestrian suspension bridge. A vague path wandered off to the left, passing a lone cottage. This we followed, before making a gradual rising traverse up the tussocky hillside forming the north western boundary of Loch Brittle. Between here and Loch Eynort is a compact little stretch of wild sheep country punctuated by several small hills such as Beinn an Eoin (Hill of the Bird), Truagh Mheall (Miserable Hill) and An Cruachan (The Stack), none of which I had ever ascended due to their lack of stature and unfortunate location next to the hypnotic cirque of Cuillin peaks across the glen. Their ascent involves the classic Catch 22 situation of never wanting to climb them on a bright day for fear of wasting a grand Cuillin climb and never wanting to climb them on a poor day for the lack of views to the Cuillin – hence they are never visited! A long-term plan of mine is to ascend all Scottish island summits over 1,000 feet so perhaps they won't remain virgin peaks for too long.

As we climbed higher, majestic seaward views to Rum and the other small isles opened up, whilst the scattered collection of coloured dots marking the camp site were dwarfed by the gargantuan Kingdom of Gabbro behind, still partially shrouded in curling tongues of moisture-laden mist. As the angle of ascent relaxed we wandered further inland across watery bog and sphagnum moss, the surrounding silence pierced intermittently with the plaintive liquid call of a golden plover, the perfect ornithological embodiment of the wild scene.

We came within striking distance of the coast again just short of the deep gorge which slashed deeply into the hillside beyond Dunan Thearna Sgurr (rocky sloping heap). An extensive inland detour was required in order to cross the Allt Mor (Big Stream), before ascending a grassy sheep-shorn hillside infested with rabbit burrows to regain the clifftop further on. Scurrying rabbits zig-zagged across our path as we reached the highest point on the cliff at over 200 metres above the unbroken blue ocean. These were the highest cliffs yet encountered on the walk and I felt the stage was being set, the appetite being whetted, for the monsters to come at Duirinish and Dunvegan Head. Even from here, I could gaze ahead over tomorrow's impressive array beyond Loch Eynort, to the hazy blue finger of Skye's rugged north-western peninsula jutting far out on the horizon. Beyond Duirinish, almost floating on the horizon, were the whispered brush strokes of North Uist and Benbecula. Closer to home, the natural arch of Stac an Tuill (stack of the torrent) drew the eye far below where a multitude of gannets, gulls and guilliemots were competing for cliff space, their raucous cries reverberating in the still air. Ken assured me that he had seen several storm petrels, small dark birds with a conspicuous white rump and Britain's smallest seabird.

The walking was easy and fast on close-cropped grass and sheep tracks but slowed down with inevitable photo-stops and standing-and-staring interludes to just soak up the stunning cliff-scape and allow the scene to speak to the soul. The contrast between now and yesterday was profound. I felt I was walking on air.

Beyond Stac an Tuill we gradually descended, as the cliffs dropped in height, but the interest was maintained by a series of craggy inlets giving further opportunities for photography. At the entrance to Loch Eynort we discovered a well-preserved dun with a substantial part of the wall still remaining. Below this, but a few thousands years ahead in history, were the heart-rending ruinous remains of a small settlement of black houses. Keeping low on sheep tracks we followed steep bracken-covered hillside for a mile to the abandoned cottage of Kraiknish. Across the half-mile of Loch Eynort, dozens of caves were visible dotted along the opposite craggy shoreline, many only accessible from the sea. Tomorrow I would be negotiating my way somewhere above the level of these caves. But that was another day.

Cuillin lover, B.H. humble, in his fine little book *Tramping in Skye* (1st edition 1933), describes arriving at Kraiknish from Carbost and makes the comment: 'From here the map shows a path winding over the hills to Loch Brittle. We were able to follow it for a short distance and then, as paths have a habit of doing in Skye, it disappeared, leaving us marooned on the moorland.' The situation today was almost the complete opposite with swathes of new forestry and a plethora of marked tracks and paths. The chunk of land north of Bealach Brittle is almost totally surrounded by forestry plantations with only one small break on the Bealach itself, just south of the little peak of Beinn Staic.

We followed forestry tracks to the Bealach but then cut off south as the track curled back north away from the campsite. After some bog and heather bashing we stumbled on Ben Humble's Path which we took to be an old drovers' route. A final steep descent by the edge of the forest using an eroded trench-like path led back to the bridge and campsite, ending a thoroughly recommended circular walk, ideal for the many occasions when the Cuillin are out of bounds because of poor weather.

A lazy hour or two was spent brewing, washing, changing and festering before the drive to the Old Inn for a second night of pub food, drink and chat. Halfway back to the campsite from Carbost the previous night, we had both suddenly realised that we had forgotten to pay for the meal, so tonight we apologised to the barmaid and coughed up our dues. She was so astounded by our honesty that she promptly gave us pints on the house. Getting a free pint of beer for forgetting to pay for our meal was West Highland logic at its best!

I had enjoyed my short interlude with Ken. Tomorrow he would be returning to his wife, Morag, and their guesthouse in Golspie. I would be back on my own again – but not for long. I had already booked into the Old Inn for the following night and the next day I would be meeting up with two other friends who were joining me for a week. Another night would be spent at the Old Inn on Thursday before the three of us set off on Friday. The Old Inn at Carbost was becoming the focal point of this Minginish Interlude. The character of the walk was radically changing.

* * * * *

I woke early the next morning, conscious of the long day ahead, but didn't rise. I was in the frustrating position of being totally dependant on Ken running me to Carbost to dump the pack, then down Glen Eynort to resume the walk. When we both did emerge from our tents, I had the feeling that Ken didn't fully gauge the urgency of my situation. By 8.30 I was packed and ready to go, while Ken was only just returning from a wash, his tent still up. I sat in the passenger seat of his car studying the map while he methodically folded his tent, still apparently sensing no pressing need to be up and away. All around, bleary-eyed campers were making the first moves of the day, while bright-eyed climbers tinkered with hardware contemplating first moves on gabbro crags high above. The campsite at Glenbrittle has become the main centre of Cuillin climbing over the years and is undoubtedly the finest and most scenic site on Skye.

The day was bright with a freshening breeze and the ridge was clear of cloud. Part of me wanted to wander up the well-worn track to Coire Lagan and Cuillin dreams, but most of me was anxious to continue my dream of walking the coastline, a dream that was slowly becoming a reality.

At ten past nine we drove out of the campsite in a trail of dust and I sat back and revelled in half-an-hour of comfort before the walking day began. The main pack was duly dumped at the Old Inn before we drove the five miles down to the end of the public road in Glen Eynort and the start of the day's walk. I was well aware that two miles of forest track had been effectively omitted, but I could live with the fact that this short section from Kraiknish to the road end was a gap in the walk and broke the continuity. The thought of walking to Kraiknish from the road-end in Glen Eynort and then returning before beginning the main walk was basically that – a thought – and a very brief one!

It was ten o'clock when Ken and I said our farewells and I began the long coastal loop from Loch Eynort to Loch Harport. There was a very peaceful air about this secluded, sheltered corner of Skye. The first mile was delightful on a rough road and track, past an old church and cemetery. Out on the unruffled surface of the loch a lazy heron lurched its way into the cover of trees on the far side. The sun was already warm and the day held the promise of some marvellous walking. I wasn't to be disappointed.

Beyond the little peninsula of Faolainn any traces of a path were purely sheep-tracks and I found myself contouring round steep bracken-infested hillside riven with numerous deep gullies, making for a total absence of any kind of rhythmic walking. The steep slopes of Biod na Fionaich forced me to climb higher up the hillside where easier terrain and a small gorge led to the broad green expanse of the hanging valley of Tusdale, with its waterfall and an extraordinarily well-built drystone wall. Sheep were dotted about everywhere and there was an air of fertility and productiveness which seemed to indicate a former Clearance settlement. I could have stopped and rested here but the urge to move on was greater. Being harnessed to a schedule has its drawbacks.

I crossed the Tusdale Burn and continued on a natural wide grassy terrace enjoying dramatic views cross the mouth of Loch Eynort to yesterday's cliffs and sea-stacks. Another steep climb led up to a second terraced area just before Clen Caladale where I had originally intended to camp before plans changed. I stopped for a breather at the site of an old settlement, surrounded by scattered rocks, old lazy beds, pockets of bracken and dozens of scurrying rabbits enjoying the morning sun. High above, two mewing buzzards with broad wings clamped to the air like giant moths, surveyed the sun-washed scene for signs of food. I was sure rabbits would be high on their list of titbits. I changed the film and had a can of juice before continuing on past Glen Caladale where the walking really blossomed out into a full blown clifftop extravaganza for the next four miles. This was coastal walking at its very best. Close-cropped grass, easy sheep tracks and awesome situations characterised the next few hours.

The grassy topped sea-stack of Stac a'Mheadais gave the optical illusion of a sheep sitting on its top – unless sheep could swim across a few hundred yards of churning sea and climb sheer cliffs. Beyond here I crossed an immense gorge by following a fence and climbing steep grass, with an audience of sheep looking quizzically on, obviously unused to walkers. As I topped out on the high cliffs beyond this gorge, I could see a wide grassy strath ahead climbing up to another high point named Biod Ruadh (Red Cliff or Point). As I descended, following the line of the fence, I became aware of a large scattered herd of cattle all seemingly heading over in my direction from the lower slopes of Preshel Beg, a striking hill to my right. The basaltic fluted columns of this hill are similar to those found on the Island of Staffa, and Preshel Beg made an awe-inspiring backdrop to this huge natural amphitheatre. With mist now beginning to creep eerily around the hilltops and the lowing of cattle booming and echoing around, the place exuded a macabre but strangely uplifting atmosphere. I seemed to be chasing the sun to the north while simultaneously being chased by following cloud. When the cattle became too close for comfort, I opted to walk on the seaward side of the fence and soon realised why the fence was there at all – to stop the beasts plunging over the almost vertical cliffs just a few metres to my left.

By the time I reached the high point of Biod Ruadh the sun had chased away any following cloud and I had reached the spiritual high point of the day. Biod Ruadh is 280 metres above sea level and in places is an unbroken vertical drop to the ragged white-flecked edge of an ocean of the deepest blue. Looking north-west out beyond Talisker Bay, my gaze settled on Idrigill Point on the Duirnish Peninsula and the unmistakable profiles of Macleod's Maidens, the most striking sea-stacks off the coast of Skye.

The mile or so from here to Talisker Bay was a marvellous, pleasant, slow descent, the eye and heart captivated by the constantly changing seascape bathed in that special translucent light only found in the Western islands of Scotland and especially the Winged Isle. Just before Talisker Point I had to swing right at a steep rocky bluff, following the top of a crag where I could look directly down the few hundred feet to the bay itself. At least a dozen people were scattered along the sandy beach and others were on the track leading to the beach. I was abruptly back in civilisation again. Talisker Bay had a special place in my heart as Heather and I had visited there one sunny afternoon while honeymooning on Skye. We could have done without company then, but for different reasons from today! I descended the last steep heathery hillside to the track and rested.

It was now three o'clock; five hours had elapsed since I had left the head of Loch Eynort. I knew that the next section of coastline round to Carbost was longer than that which I had just completed and general tiredness and aching feet were an additional item to take into account. I had two options – rigidly staying with the coastline and hobbling into the Old Inn at some late hour in the evening and missing a meal; or compromising somewhere along the line and arriving at a reasonable hour. With both time and heels pressing, I decided to use the Huisgill track which cut directly through the hills to the road at Fiskavaig. This short-cut effectively meant I was omitting the section of grand cliff-girt coastline from Talisker Bay to Fiskavaig – some four miles, replaced by one and a half miles. Apart from the Camus Cross section in Sleat on the second day, this was the only relatively major chunk of coastline I had missed out so far. I knew I was steering a fine line between guilt and guile; between endurance and enjoyment. The guilt of knowing that I was breaking my self-induced rules was balanced precariously with the guile that perhaps I was just bending them. The fact that I had no rules to start with nullified both propositions. Whatever the case, the decision was made and I stuck to it.

I ambled eastwards along the Talisker track gazing up at Preshel Beg's twin brother of Preshel More, really the striking craggy shoulder of the higher but far less interesting Stockval. When I first set eyes on this impressive hill a few years ago I vowed I would climb it – it still remains virgin territory for me today, but is just an excuse to return to Skye, as if any was needed. The track turned gradually north beyond Talisker House, a tautology, as Talisker actually means 'the house at the rock'. Dr Johnson stayed here on his Skye journey and wrote:

'The place beyond all that I have seen from which the gay and the jovial seem utterly excluded, and where the hermit might expect to grow old in meditation, without possibility of disturbance or interruption. It is situated very near the sea, but upon a coast where no vessel lands, but when it is driven by a tempest on the rocks. Towards the land are lofty hills streaming with waterfalls. The garden is sheltered by firs, or pines, which grow there so prosperously that some, which the present inhabitants planted, are very high and thick.'

The 'present inhabitant' in the late 1700s was Colonel MacLeod, the house traditionally being in the possession of the son of the MacLeod Chief. Any self-respecting hermit today could not expect to dwell in Talisker Bay 'without possibility of disturbance or interruption' especially in high summer on a warm day like today.

Passing through a farmyard with a crowd of revellers enjoying a barbecue, I reached open hillside, a final cottage and steep zigzags leading up on to moorland heath, where the Huisgill track led directly north for just over a mile to the road at Fiskavaig. Two folk were on the track going the other way, a rare occurrence. Ahead, I had a fine view of the tidal island of Oronsay (not the Sleat one!) which I hoped to visit in a few days time. On the map I noticed a broch about half-a-mile off to the left where the track met the road, but didn't take the time to visit it. I later discovered it to have the remains of a narrow gallery, a roofless oval cell and a guard chamber – something else to check out at some future date.

At the road I suppose I should have headed directly north to the road-end and path leading out to Gob na h-Oa and made a literal hold on the coast to Fiskavaig Bay from there. Time and tiredness dictated otherwise. I plodded along the winding road through the scattered, straggling township of Fiskavaig with its interesting variety of houses: old and new, sold and for sale, half-constructed and semi-ruinous. The well tended gardens betrayed the presence of retired couples and escapees from city life. Many Skye locals complain that the steady influx of incomers to the island is grossly inflating house prices, leaving local newly-weds stranded with no home, or making do with a caravan. I could see their point. From the mid-19th century the population of Skye steadily declined from about 23,000 to around 8,000 in the mid-20th century. In the 60s and early 70s it declined still further but in the last two decades of the 20th century it saw a major influx of urban refugees with the population now standing at nearly 9,000.

Fiskavaig wanders imperceptibly into the next township of Portnalong (the port or harbour of the ships) where Heather and I had rented a small cottage for our week's honeymoon just a year before. Like most other villages on Skye, Portnalong suffered during the Clearances, but after the Great War a determined attempt was made to repopulate the area by settling a number of families from Lewis and Harris who gladly took up the challenge. Their indigenous skills of homespun tweed-making soon found a market, but is sadly now a thing of the past in Portnalong.

Between Fiskavaig and Portnalong a flat peninsula extends out to Ardtreck Point Lighthouse which I did not visit. However, I vowed that if my two friends arrived early enough tomorrow, I would persuade them to join me on a circuit of this. Just short of the T-junction in Portnalong was the old village school, now tastefully converted to the – wait for it – Skyewalker Independent Hostel and Cafe. With a name like that I had no option but to pop in for a cuppa. I was soon sitting in what had been the old technical block enjoying the most refreshing and welcome pot of tea I think I have ever tasted. When I explained my Skyewalk to the homely tea lady she refused to allow me to pay, saying that would be her contribution to the walk. I was most taken aback but very grateful.

The tea was the ideal boost for the final three-and-a-half mile leg along the single-track road following the long blue ribbon of Loch Harport. With renewed vigour I strode purposefully along the gentle undulations of tarmac, my mind happily occupied by looking over the sea loch, mapping possible routes and noting potential hazards for the route in two days' time. Ahead, the sawtoothed outline of the Cuillin ridge made brief flickering appearances from behind bubbling masses of cloud, rising beyond green rolling moors dotted with white cottages. Loch Harport marked for me the division between South Skye and North Skye but, more profoundly in the context of Skyewalk, it marked the end of the first phase of the journey.

At 7 o'clock I reached the Old Inn, retrieved the pack and slunk off to my room in the modern annexe. I relished my first shower since Strathaird House, and the rest and relaxation which followed. But my mind was already working on the logistics of trying to remove load carrying from the next few days. The current plan was that two friends would be arriving by car tomorrow, leave the car at Carbost and walk with me to Stein in Waternish, arriving there a week later. They would then retrieve the car by fair means or foul (bus or hitch). My new idea was of a kind of leapfrog system which would ensure that the car and heavy gear always remained with us. The scheme relied on one volunteer willing to drive the car and kit to the next evening's destination and then perhaps walking back to meet the other two who were walking the whole way (one of whom had to be me). When I telephoned Mike, the car owner, that evening, my conversation was dominated by my idea but I had the distinct impression that Mike was a little taken aback by the suggestion, feeling that we should stay together and walk as a threesome. I could see his point and returned to my mental drawing board.

I spent a third indulgent evening lazily in the bar, eating, drinking and playing pool and generally unwinding from the physical rigours of the last nine days. My Skyewalk T-shirt provided the catalyst for conversation with a mixture of people, one of whom asked me if I was the person who wrote *Classic Mountain Scrambles in Scotland* and *The Munro Phenomenon*. This was only the second stranger I had ever met who admitted to having read my books (both were met in a pub!). Five pints later I drifted off to my room, the re-drafting of walking logistics put off until tomorrow.

* * * * *

Rest days on long-distance walks are very rarely that. There is always a multitude of details to attend to such as washing clothes, posting film, diary writing, organising and generally re-orientating mind and body for the next phase. Another high-fat, high-calorie cooked breakfast formed the foundation stone for these activities before I strolled outside with the vague notion of visiting the Talisker Distillery, the only whisky distillery on Skye. Situated in Carbost, just a few hundred yards down the road, I knew this was the ideal opportunity.

Classically and geographically, the Scottish Highlands produce two types of malt whisky, the Speyside malts and the Islay malts. Talisker, however, falls into neither category and the 'explosive golden spirit of Skye' is as distinctive and unique to whiskies as the Cuillin mountains are to other Scottish mountains. Its merits were celebrated as far back as 1875 when Robert Louis Stevenson mentioned it in the poem 'The Scotsman's Return from Abroad':

> 'The King o' drinks as I conceive it
> Talisker, Isla or Glenlivet'.

The distillery, founded in 1830 by the MacAskill brothers, caused much controversy and ill-feeling when it was first built, Skye being then a more parochial and church dominated place than it is today. A former parish minister, the Reverend Roderick Macleod, described Talisker's establishment as 'one of the greatest curses that, in the ordinary course of Providence, could befall any place'. It was a pity that his feelings could not have been directed at the MacAskill brothers for another reason. Blinded by the prospects of high profits, they acquired the Clearance mentality of the land-owning classes and evicted crofting families to turn land over to sheep farming. Since 1830 the distillery has changed hands many times, and is currently owned by United Distillers. What hasn't changed, however, is the distinctive flavour of Talisker, which has been described as 'intense, peppery, pungent, peaty, powerful, seaweedy, sweet-and-sour and building to a warming finish after initially exploding in the mouth'. I could only agree with all these heady descriptions and was about to rediscover them that evening in the Old Inn!

The next tour of the distillery was unfortunately not until the afternoon which was when my friends Mike and George would be arriving. I wandered back to the Inn for a bite of lunch. Mike and George arrived at 3 o'clock as I was in the process of airing my damp tent on railings outside the annexe. We exchanged greetings and I tried to keep the lid on my experiences, preferring to recount them later in the more relaxed surroundings of the bar. The main piece of news from the 'outside world' was that France had won the World Cup – such things were an infinity away from my Skye coastal commentary.

I gave Mike and George some time to unpack, unwind and settle into their room before the conversation inevitably settled on tomorrow's plans and logistics. Mike proposed a scheme which involved some very deep thinking and soul-searching as far as I was concerned. His plan was that we go to Glenelg to pick up my car, using his car to get there, and then use the two cars to initiate a leapfrog system where we would all be walking together and have a car at our nightly destination. The scheme seemed faultless but something about it niggled at me, gnawing uneasily at my purist ideals. To return to the starting point of the walk ten days down the line just didn't seem right. In a sense the continuity of the walk had already been severed over the last few days by the fact that Carbost had become a centre of one or two days of walking; but his scheme felt different, an unacceptable measure which I couldn't stomach. We had even made plans to put it into action when I explained my feelings to Mike, who, being the easy-going person he is, understood perfectly and the planning went back to square one. Besides, this now meant that the three of us could don boots and go off and attend to some unfinished business – the Ardtreck Peninsula which I had missed out yesterday.

After the cramped hours in a car, Mike and George were glad of the fresh air and to feel Skye soil under their boots. We drove to the end of the 'loop road' in Portalong and set off for Ardtreck Point lighthouse just over a mile distant, partly on tarmac and partly cross-country. It was good to be walking with company once again.

Mike and George are both some years older than I and had been determined to join me for a hefty chunk of the walk (over 100 miles). I had known Mike for many years and, like Ken Black, he was a regular gangrel on our many happy escapes to Camasunary. Rarely in a lifetime does one meet a totally dependable, salt-of-the-earth individual who can be described as a true friend. Mike is one such person. George is married to Mike's step-daughter and of a quieter and more reserved disposition than Mike. I had only met George briefly on a couple of occasions, but he turned out to be a solid and reliable walking companion. Mike's sharp and sensitive wit, together with his down-to-earth practical approach to life, were to bring a healthy new perspective to the walk over the next week.

As we descended a rocky bluff and strode the final few hundred yards out to the lighthouse, I cast my mind back to the Point of Sleat lighthouse. I had walked about 100 miles since then and over 120 miles since the start of the walk. Distance and time-wise I was a third of the way through the venture. Behind these bald

Dun Ardtreck

A. Dempster
Dun Ardtreck.

statistics, of course, lay a store of experiences which characterised phase one of Skyewalk. I hoped that the remaining two thirds of the walk would live up to those experiences, and somehow I knew I would not be disappointed.

Ardtreck lighthouse stood proud at the Point, a white guardian at the entrance to Loch Harport and only half-a-mile across the sea narrows from Bracadale Point. We took a few quick photographs before continuing round the coast to the real guardian of the loch, Dun Ardtreck, another historical site consisting of remains on top of a stack of rock rising 50 feet above the sea. Part of the landward facing walls were still intact and the door and traces of a gallery were evident. Total cloud cover made for rather flat photography but the view across to Ullinish Point and Oronsay with the distinctive flat-topped MacLeod's Tables beyond was certainly worth a shot.

We meandered back to the road and track looking out over Fiskavaig Bay, before completing the loop to the car. We made the observation that there appeared to be many bus-shelters on Skye but a distinct lack of buses. This proved to be another cul-de-sac in our search for a solution to the heavy pack problem. However, on arrival back at the Old Inn things began to look up when we discussed the situation at the bar. The barmaid had a brother who would apparently be willing to transport one of us to tomorrow night's destination while Mike would drive his car with the packs which would be left there. We would then return in the other car to Carbost and begin the day's walk. We met the brother later, agreed on some payment, bought him a pint and relaxed in the knowledge that for tomorrow at least, the situation was in hand. Taking one day at a time seemed to be the wisest outlook.

The fourth and final night at the Old Inn, Carbost, was full of good cheer and further enlivened for me by the heady anticipation of the fresh blood of Mike and George. They were poised expectantly on the brink of a week's walking on the Winged Isle. For George in particular, who had never set foot on Skye, this was adventure indeed. To Mike, having never walked in the north-west of Skye, it offered new territory and new horizons. For me, the supposed veteran walker, the evening marked the divide between South and North Skye, the start of a new chapter in the walk in which there would be much that was new to me as well. The 'explosive golden spirit' that was Talisker whispered the promise of golden days to come, and the magic of Minginish slowly surrendered to dreams of Duirinish. Three pints and many drams later, even the torrential downpour outside could not dampen our Winged Isle wanderlust.

Route Summary: Glenbrittle to Carbost

Day 1: Glenbrittle – Loch Eynort – Glenbrittle (10 miles – 16 km)

Cross the river Brittle by a small suspension bridge and traverse grassy slopes, gradually swinging northwards above grand cliff scenery. Several miles of fine cliff top walking lead to Loch Eynort where a forestry track from Kraiknish leads back over the Bealach Brittle. Strike off on a smaller drover's track to reach Glenbrittle. The return to Glenbrittle provides exceptional views of the South Cuillin ridge.

Those wishing to 'walk continuously' will opt to carry on walking round Loch Eynort and wild camp between here and Talisker Bay.

Day 2: Loch Eynort – Carbost (16 miles – 26 km)

Even adopting some shortcuts this is an exceptionally long day (a full coastal circuit would be in the order of 22 miles) and many walkers may prefer to spread this fine coastal loop over two days. A convenient halfway point is Talisker Bay where it is possible to wild camp near the beach. This is coastal walking at its best. Leave the road end at Loch Eynort and follow the track past the cemetery. The next three miles is rough trackless terrain before the grand cliff-top walking begins beyond Glen Caladale. At Talisker Bay it is possible to avoid the next four mile section of coastline by taking the Huisgill track through the hills ending at Fiskavaig. Follow the road to Fiskavaig Bay and take the loop road and path leading out to Dun Ardtreck and Ardtreck Point. Follow the road from Portnalong to Carbost, hugging the south-western shore of Loch Harport.

Accommodation and other information

Talisker House:	Expensive hotel, otherwise wild-camp
Fiskavaig and Portnalong:	Numerous B&Bs. Skyewalker Independent hostel
Carbost:	B&Bs. Old Inn (excellent food and drink – including Talisker whisky – distillery nearby)
	Shops in Portnalong and Carbost

CHAPTER 5

Duirinish Dreams

(Friday 17 July – Tuesday 21 July)

Carbost to Dunvegan

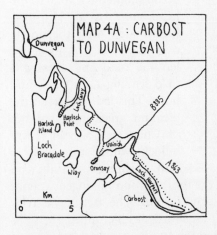

MAP 4A : CARBOST TO DUNVEGAN

All traces of the previous night's deluge had disappeared the next morning and there was a fresh, full-faced promise to the weather. Another cooked breakfast slid down all too easily before the day's gear was decanted into small daysacks. We each had our allotted tasks in the pre-walk plan: I would accompany our kind driver to Ullinish, our destination for that night, while Mike would follow in his car. George would wait outside the Inn guarding the daysacks until we returned. The waitress's brother duly arrived only a shade later than scheduled and I piled into his clapped-out vehicle, wondering if it would make the twelve road miles in one piece. The next twenty minutes on a bone-rattling switchback was suitably accompanied by the jarring anti-harmonics of acid-house rap muzak blaring out of a visibly vibrating car speaker. Conversation was out of the question. The return journey with Mike was a repeat performance but with the volume control a shade lower to allow some semblance of conversation.

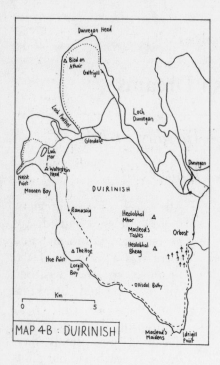

MAP 4B : DUIRINISH

Back at the Inn we joined George who was sitting contentedly on the wall soaking up the, by now, warm morning sun. We gave thanks and money to our rap-taxi man and made a start on the real task of the day, the gentle art of walking. The first couple of miles was an ideal warm-up on single-track road to the head of Loch Harport. Immediately after the bridge over the river Drynoch, we left the road and crossed a field leading to a track and farm. This led in turn to the pleasant green grassy slopes of Cnoc an t-Sithein (Fairy hillock) whose steep western flank (Braigh Coille na Droighniche – roughly 'Hill of the thorny wood') plunged straight into the glistening waters of Loch Harport. The ascent was relatively easy with light loads and on short, sheep-cropped grass. As we climbed, grand views opened up and we stopped, stared and snapped, breathing in the serenity and beauty of our surroundings. The surface of the loch was calm, save for a few ruffled ribbons induced by the light breeze. The opposite side was dominated by the white sun-reflected formality of the Talisker distillery and its attendant cottages and crofts scatterd along the lochside. Beyond and above, a rural patchwork of greens and ochres merged into the mottled tones of open heath and craggy skylines backed by a deep blue sky and tattered cumulus fragments.

Somewhere on the sun-warmed slopes of Uchd Mor (big breast) the three of us lay back blissfully, gorging ourselves on wine gums. I made the comment that we must have borne a strong resemblance to the three old codgers in the television situation comedy 'Last of the Summer Wine'. The comparison was poor from the age point of view but the image stuck for the remainder of the week. Beyond Uchd Mor we made a steep descent through bracken to the Meadale Burn where blackhouse ruins were dotted about in every conceivable nook and cranny. The map indicated a path following the coast, gradually traversing up the hillside and round into the next glen at Sumardale. However, the deep bracken had obliterated any sign of it and we opted for scrambling along the water's edge on the dry, lichen-covered rocks, happy as sand-boys. Within half an hour, however, our passage was barred by a craggy bluff, forcing us up through a clogging clump of prickly gorse bushes and eventually to a well-earned lunch spot high above the loch.

A pleasant level section with a drystone wall led to the delightfully peaceful Sumardale with its sprightly river and falls tumbling and twisting to the sea. Just before the steep descent to the river we stopped by a little hunched birch tree clinging to the slope which was a riot of phallic fox-gloves, providing a fine foreground to the grand seascape beyond. The unusual and un-named knoll on the protruding nose of land south of Gesto Bay formed part of this seascape, and far in the distance, the bleached green twins of Macleod's Tables stood proud against azure skies.

George and I, being landscape lovers, snapped happily away, while Mike, a more people-orientated person, photographed us photographing the landscape. We dropped down to cross the river by convenient stepping stones and swung round the coast to climb the little knoll near Gesto Bay. I was curious to see whether the top, being in a commanding position at the entrance to Loch Harport, would support any remains of a fortified structure such as a dun or broch. There were remains, though the map failed to indicate any; but some hundred metres higher the map showed Dun Taimh on the more substantial hill of Beinn Dubh.

Gesto Bay was an irresistible magnet of peacefulness and isolated charm. We dallied leisurely along the rocks and seaweed of the south shore, basking in the warm sunshine and tranquil atmosphere. At the head of the bay stood the ruin of a two-storey house and a few hundred yards to its left a white, newer house, which looked well kept and occupied. Both were set against a background of lush green meadow and trees in full summer foliage. An old drystone wall ran the full length of the bay head, separating the houses from the stony beach where George and I removed boots and socks to indulge in a paddle while Mike took photographs of us squealing and squirming on the sharp stony beach.

Mike then wandered up the beach to chat to a young man by the name of Harry Scott who was staying in the white house on holiday and who generously invited us all up for afternoon tea – exactly what we needed! We sat on the sturdy garden bench and a few minutes later Harry appeared with a tea tray. Harry had the looks, accent and general demeanour of an English army officer straight out of some 19th-century colonial outpost, although his brown corduroy trousers and heavy pullover somewhat detracted from this fanciful notion. 'Tea's up chaps', he announced in a military tone, and proceeded to pour the tea and give us some fascinating history of the immediate area.

Harry had been spending family holidays in the white house for years and his family history was closely tied up with it and the ruined Gesto House, the second oldest house on Skye. This fact made more impact when he narrated the story of an influential Macleod clan member who once lived in Gesto House where an uninvited guest picked a fight with him. Swords were crossed and the guest raised his sword high to bring a fatal blow down on Macleod. However, the low ceiling of the room was his downfall – the sword stuck firm in the wooden rafters and Macleod grabbed his chance with a swift stroke to the guest's heart.

Harry's family connections with Gesto House were fascinatingly and beautifully portrayed in a photograph album from 1891 which he showed to us. The photographer was a Jessie Scott, whom he reckoned was his great-great-grandmother. As the three of us sat contentedly on the garden bench, soaking up the sun, sipping tea and peering at black and white photos of a bygone age, I had the distinct feeling of being transported to some other time or plane of existence. That magical half-hour was a defining moment in the trek, a snippet of memory to savour and recall in the years to come. Reluctantly, we said our thanks and exchanged farewells with Harry, who said that he might just drop in and see us that evening at the Ullinish Lodge Hotel where we were camping.

We wandered up a short section of steep vegetated hillside to the main road and followed it round the next small headland into Loch Beag. This picturesque sea loch was a vibrant kaleidoscope of colour and movement. A stiff seaward breeze was whipping up white flecks on the surface and a few brightly-coloured fishing boats were bobbing and heaving in the heavy swell. The road swung round the head of the loch in a wide arc to the scattered townships of Bracadale, Struan and Struanmore. The name Bracadale, like many others in Skye, is a curious amalgam of Norse, Gaelic and English and also refers to Loch Bracadale, the extensive island-studded and loch-indented expanse of water which lies between Ullinish and Duirinish. Thomas Pennant, who visited the Hebrides in 1772, had strong feelings that a town should be established on Loch Bracadale, believing it to be 'the fittest place in the island for the forming of a Town' with an 'unspeakably secure' harbour. Looking at the map it is hard to disagree with him and one wonders whether, if he had got his way, Portree would have grown to become the island's capital.

At Struan we bought provisions before setting off on the last one-and-a-half miles to the Ullinish Lodge Hotel. It was only after the walk was finished that I discovered we had walked past Dun Beag, one of the best preserved brochs in Skye, standing a few hundred yards to the right of the main road at the point where the small road branches off to the hotel. According to Derek Cooper in his *Skye Guide*, a staircase still exists and 'the whole ruin is an eye-opener after the usual heap of rubble which marks the remains of most Skye brochs'. The map also showed Dun Mor, a fort to the north of Dun Beag, as well as a couple of chambered cairns and a souterrain in the area around the hotel.

By late afternoon we reached the hotel and made enquiries about camping. To our astonishment we were told that we could pitch tents on the lawn to the side of the hotel and use the hotel's washing facilities. We were in the process of erecting tents when the rain began with a vengeance. Having honed the technicalities of tent erection to a fine art, I was safe and dry in my shell before it really came down in sheets, leaving George and Mike unfankling wet guy-ropes and cursing the unfortunate timing. But guilt overcame guile and I donned waterproofs to give George a hand. Almost as soon as it had begun, the rain stopped and a watery sun sparkled on glistening nylon fly sheets – by this time we had retreated to the hotel for some welcome refreshment.

The Ullinish Lodge Hotel did not possess a bar, but the bistro/restaurant provided a reasonable meal before we decanted into the relaxing lounge with pints of Caffrey's Irish ale. Wishing to continue the walk in lightweight fashion, we made enquiries regarding transport to our next night's destination of Roag. The response was positive; the hotel's owner/chef could transport the gear in leapfrog fashion at 10 o'clock the following morning after he had completed breakfast duties. We were on a roll as far as our luck was concerned.

At 11 o'clock that evening, just as we had given up any expectations of our Gesto friend Harry Scott appearing, he did, complete with girlfriend. Striding into the lounge, he looked as if he had just come down off his charger: 'Hi chaps, how are you doing?' Harry and his girlfriend had just been out to the tidal island of Oronsay which we hoped to visit first thing the next morning. He insisted on buying us all a round of drinks and for the next half-hour we recounted the experiences of what had been a memorable day. George and Mike were only a day into the walk but were already basking in the rosy glow of Skye's magical spell.

* * * * *

Even at the early hour of 6am, the morning sun had turned the inside of my tent into an oven. Half-dead midges writhed and finally drowned in the condensation on the inner of the tent. I lay watching them with perverse satisfaction until I could stand the heat no longer. Outside in the still air, thousands more of the little blighters were forming a disorderly queue for a blood breakfast. George and Mike were soon up and about – midges in the morning are not conducive to a relaxed start to the day.

By 6.30 we had set off in the direction of Oronsay. A mile of walking on an initially dewy grassy path took us to Ullinish point where, at high tide, it is possible to walk across the narrow sandy spit to the island of Oronsay. The tide was well out and we strolled across the sand and shingle, bathed in the sunny peaceful Skye morning. Small wavelets surged and sang rhythmically, the sound magnified in the still air. This contrasted perfectly with the intermittent high pitched 'pheet' of rock pipits flitting and diving in the search for food, while the ubiquitous oystercatchers greeted the morning in their usual way.

Oronsay is about a kilometre long and rises up in a single sweep of green sward to vertical cliffs at its south-western extremity. Fifteen minutes saw us at the highest point, enjoying crystal clear views across deep blue Loch Bracadale with its family of small islands including Wiay (the largest) and the cliff-girt Turner Island and Harlosh Island. Breakfast called, however, and much as we would have liked to have lingered on this glorious spot we made a beeline back to the hotel for an 8 o'clock fry-up. George declined breakfast, possibly as a result of over-indulgence the previous evening!

The double car act was performed by Mike, myself and the owner-cum-chef with a rather embarrassing start. Lack of communication had resulted in him sitting waiting for us at the front of the hotel while we sat and waited at the side. As he was doing us a favour and his time was precious, we felt extremely ashamed. The arrangement was a carbon-copy of the morning before with George remaining at the hotel while Mike's car was deposited at Roag, further up the coast. On the return we listened to our driver as he told in broad Cockney twang of hideous London hotels and his ultimate escape to an island paradise. He only opened in summer and seemed to make enough then to survive the winter.

We paid and thanked him and set off on the main walk of the day. North of the hotel we followed the middle section of the loop road before branching off along a minor road/track past Eabost. The name ending, 'bost', is an Anglicisation of the Norse or Icelandic word bolstadhr, meaning homestead, farm or steading and is very common in Skye (Carbost, Braebost, Colbost, etc). We passed several steadings before we reached the end of the track and crossed open heath to Colbost Point. The low-lying fertile coastal strip known as machair was a sweeping carpet of lush green grass awash with wild flowers, mostly buttercups and daisies. Machair is much more common on the low-lying western fringes of the Outer Hebrides where long sandy beaches predominate.

A short distance further on we met an elderly Yorkshire couple who were wildflower enthusiasts and we had our eyes opened to the wealth and variety of botanical specimens at our feet. Buttercups and daisies were top of a very long list. Within a few moments we had seen the tiny white stars of Eye Bright, deep blue Gentians, yellow trailing St John's Wort, delicate yellow Birdsfoot Trefoil, Heath Spotted Orchid, tufted clusters of Thyme and dozens of other rare specimens. Some of these names were known to me and others rang distant bells from childhood excursions to the countryside when I had collected dried wild flowers in a scrapbook. It is a sad reflection on society that many of us lose touch with the gentle hand of nature when we grow up. There is a saying: 'Men never grow up, they just get older.' If that means they still possess a childish sense of wonder and playfulness in adulthood then I definitely don't want to grow up. Even marriage hadn't curtailed my 'childish' dream of walking Skye's coastline though I suspected that fatherhood would have more of a debilitating effect! As we lay sprawled on the springy machair, sunning our sprightly middle-aged frames, we were children at heart.

We swung round the coast to the cluster of crofts at Eabost West and followed a minor road back to the A863 and the tourist trail of traffic – a stark contrast to the peaceful machair of half-an-hour ago. Two miles of tarmac bashing took us to the head of Loch Caroy and the ruined St John's Chapel, built by a handful of Episcopalian families headed by MacLeod of Gesto. Apparently this same MacLeod had committed the sinful act of shooting a seal on a Sunday (presumably it is O.K. on any other day of the week) and his minister and congregation of the Wee Free Church at Struan disowned him. MacLeod and a few other supporters of Sunday seal shooting set about establishing the Caroy Church were they worshipped in the Episcopalean fashion.

Loch Caroy's western boundary is the Harlosh peninsula, an unavoidable dog-leg which must be tackled if we were truly following the coastline. We followed a pleasant minor coastal road down Loch Caroy's rocky shoreline, and stopped for a leisurely lunch and a refreshing dip of the feet. At the scattered hamlet of Balmore, where the road doubled back up the other side of the peninsula, we made a bid for Harlosh Point along a track and across open heath. En route we looked out for an old chapel marked on the map but failed to find any sign. The last of the land at Harlosh Point was mildly dramatic with minor 15-metre cliffs. A thin pencil-like sea stack made a fine focal point to a photograph of me on a cliff-edge.

Under more sombre skies we wandered back to Balmore and the continuation of the loop road, passing countless crofts, steadings and holiday homes. During these last few road miles, weariness was creeping up and I needed to be settled in a tent somewhere. A small section of main road followed by a mile of single-track took us finally to Roag and Mike's car. Exactly where and when the decision was made to drive to Dunvegan campsite I don't recall, but in the circumstances it seemed to make perfect sense. The original plan of camping on Roag Island was abandoned, partly because it would entail a good mile's trudge across the causeway with all the gear, plus the associated hassle of finding a site, but also because we had a car and Dunvegan campsite was only three miles away. The promise of a hot shower and a few pints at Dunvegan (without driving) may also have been an additional factor!

An hour later the three of us were well settled in Dunvegan campsite. I had showered and 'phoned Heather and was in the process of making a meal, fully revived by a mug of sweet tea and a couple of pieces of shortbread. The next phase of the walk had also been discussed and a fresh plan had emerged. The car would be left at the campsite for the next three days while we walked round the extensive Duirinish peninsula. First thing tomorrow morning, we would transport the heavy gear by car to the road end at Ramasaig where we planned to camp the following night. We would then drive back to Dunvegan, dump the car and complete the walk to Ramasaig. From there, the next day, we would continue on to Glendale with light packs, where a B&B had been booked. We would also check that the owner, or someone, would drive us back to Ramasaig to retrieve the heavy packs that evening. Finally, on the third day, we would leave heavy gear at the B&B and complete the coastal walk back to Dunvegan, round Dunvegan Head, driving back to the B&B to retrieve our packs in the evening. In this way, we would have completed the wildest, grandest, remotest section of coastal walking without the burden of full packs. The scheme seemed watertight; whether other things did remained to be seen.

Mike's culinary skills, or lack of them, made themselves obvious that evening when I noticed him with a large saucepan containing a brown watery substance which could have been soup. It turned out that he had been attempting to make a dehydrated meal using two large cupfuls of water instead of the prescribed 300ml. I offered him some spare pasta shells while he successfully opened a tin of beans (the dehydrated disaster was discarded) but he still required direction on how to cook the pasta! I had only ever observed the practical D.I.Y. side of Mike, who was a wizard at inventing, building and fixing things, but when it came to cooking he was a fish out of water. His wife, Eva, is a tremendous cook, which is probably just as well!

Later that evening the Dunvegan Hotel was the venue for three thirsty Skyewalkers where we indulged in heady conversation, cigars (unused midge repellent) and Red Cuillin Ale. The latter was the brainchild of two ex-Portree High School teachers who decided to abandon the chalk-face to open a brewery where they make Red Cuillin and Black Cuillin. Both are excellent ales and it has

▲ Blaven from Loch Slapin

The Cuillin from Elgol ▼

▲ The Cuillin from Elgol

Rum from the cliffs south of Eynort ▼

▲ Clifftop walking south of Loch Eynort

Clifftop walking in Duirinish ▼

▲ Neist Point, Skye's most westerly point

Rock formations at Neist Point ▼

▲ Approaching Dunvegan Head

Late evening in Stein ▼

▲ Rubha Hunish, Skye's northern tip

Rubha Hunish ▼

▲ A north Skye seascape, near Rubha Hunish

Portree ▼

▲ Ben Tianavaig and the Trotternish Ridge

On Ben Tianavaig ▼

always puzzled me that I have only discovered a few places on Skye where they are sold.

We returned, well oiled, to our respective tents, poised on the brink of what I imagined would be one of the most magnificent sections of the walk. I slept deep and dreamt Duirinish dreams.

* * * * *

I was rudely awakened at some unearthly hour by the screeching of gulls, then dozed until 7.30. A hazy, lazy sun was already throwing long shadows across the muggy midge-ridden morning. In my mind I was attempting to juggle three distinct lots of gear to be packed in separate bags. One daypack to carry, one large pack to leave at Ramasaig for this evening and one bag of night clothes to dump at tomorrow night's B&B. Trying to think ahead and take time to make decisions wasn't easy with the attention of hungry midges.

Finally Mike and I departed in the car to dump gear. It was luxury to sit back and let Skye drift by from a car window. Ten miles and twenty minutes later we reached the lonely outpost of Ramasaig – the end of the road – and the end of today's huge chunk of coastal walking. A suitable spot in the cover of a sitka spruce plantation was found to conceal the packs before we returned to Dunvegan via the B&B at Glendale to dump small bags of dry night clothes. Seeing a sneak preview of the next two days gave me a slightly unsettling feeling. Today was the thirteenth day of the walk but I am not superstitious.

We finally set off at the late hour of 10.30, leaving the car in the campsite at a suitably out-of-the-way spot approved by the Warden. The first three miles of road walking to Orbost was a pleasant start, a preparation for sterner stuff to come. I was conscious of the fact that we had missed out the small section of coastline containing Roag Island and the little headland East of Loch Bharcasaig but I refused to dwell on it. The rules of the game were to enjoy and minimise endurance.

Alexander Smith was very taken with Orbost in his *Summer in Skye* and he writes: 'I made up my mind that, had I the choice, I should rather live at Orbost than at any other house in Skye.' Yet he goes on to write that Orbost House is 'expressionless and familiar in the suburban districts of large cities, and ... quite out of keeping with the scenery and the spiritual atmosphere of the island'. He continues this assault for a full page, and one wonders how long he would have ranted had he seen the horrific new edifice that has been constructed here. This totally out-of-character modern villa sits high up to the right of the track and gives the impression that some inner-city council house has just been transplanted, warts and all, to Skye soil. We could not understand how such a monstrosity could ever have been allowed planning permission.

The track from Orbost meanders gently down to idyllic Loch Bharcasaig, a beautifully sheltered south-facing bay which marked the beginning of the seven-kilometre walk out to Idrigill Point and MacLeod's Maidens, one of the most celebrated coastal walks on the island. Despite its popularity we only met one couple in the forest section after the bay. Beyond the mile of forest, the track was replaced by a rough path which climbed gradually through heathery knolls to a bealach (pass) overlooking the vast bracken-choked amphitheatre containing Brandarsaig Bay, the site of another large Clearance settlement. The air had a sultry, oppressive feel and a soft smirry Scotch mist began to fog up my glasses. This unwelcome change in the weather continued but did not detract from the wild beauty of our surroundings. Another short ascent took us to further abandoned settlements and a pass between the little hillocks of Steineval and Ard Beag. Little was seen of Camas na h-Uamha (Bay of the Caves) but had we climbed Ard Beag, the view across the bay would have been 'exceptional' with caves, stacks and double arches, according to Ralph Storer in his *50 best routes on Skye and Raasay*. Between here and the Maidens, the cliff-girt coastline is littered with superb caves but all are only accessible from the sea.

In the vicinity of the Maidens, the path became less obvious in a plethora of sheep tracks and we cut across the moor in the general direction of our objective. Having ventured here previously I had a good idea of the ground and in minutes we were at the cliff edge peering across at the tallest Maiden, the Mother stack, with one of her 'children' looking out shyly from behind. From our precarious stance this highest sea-stack on Skye, at a shade over 200 feet, gave the impression of some crystallised frozen leviathan arching out of a restless sea, a stark verticality in a grey-blue world of horizontals, paradoxically harmonising with the wild surroundings. MacLeod's Maidens are traditionally the wife and daughters of a 14th-century MacLeod Chief who were shipwrecked and drowned on this spot while returning to Dunvegan from Harris where the Chief had been fatally wounded in a clan battle. In 1959 the Mother stack was first climbed by I.S. Clough and J. McLean, though reaching the base of the stack must have been a challenge in itself.

On the eroded cliff edge we found a semi-sheltered nook, partially in the lee of a freshening breeze and the rain that now had the feel of being on for the day. We munched lunch, donned waterproof jackets, and the rain continued unabated. Creeping cold and pressing time forced us into a quick departure and the start of what has been described as the finest clifftop coast walk in the British Isles – the seven switchback miles to Lorgill Bay. This was new territory for all of us, and little did I know that when I had visited the Maidens a few years back that the clifftop continuation which had lured me then would be accomplished as part of a 360-mile trek round Skye's coastline.

Initially we swung round the wide arc of Inbhir a'Gharraidh (Mouth of the Dyke). From the opposite side of this bay we enjoyed what is undoubtedly the best view of MacLeod's Maidens, where they can each be seen in profile. The Mother has an uncanny likeness to a statue of a seated Queen Victoria and I imagined her mouthing the oft-quoted 'We are not amused' to her cowering offspring off to the right.

Climbing higher on the south-western slopes of Ben Idrigill, the view ahead was a twisting line of sheer cliffs plunging vertically into a turbulent grey mass almost as far as the eye could see. In the worsening weather, sea and sky had merged to leave a horizonless void out to our left, and the landscape was transformed to an ethereal dreamscape. For a while we walked in utter silence, awed and humbled by the stunning surroundings.

A grand easy descent took us down to the burn in Glen Lorgasdal and a further gradual ascent led out to a stupendous crumbling clifftop viewpoint where we could look back to the Maidens. Nearby stacks, a natural arch and a lacy white ribbon of water plunging over the cliff edge added to the awesome scene. Camera always at the ready, I snapped away, the rain-washed muted green, blue and grey tones enlivened by the day-glo orange of Mike's £5 car-boot-sale nylon jacket. Passing Glen Ollisdal we could see a remote cottage sitting about half-a-mile further up the glen. This is an M.B.A. bothy (like Camasunary) and had been on my original itinerary for overnight accommodation before the logistical changes. I would have liked to visit the bothy but it was already late afternoon and the rain was now verging on torrential. This was the worst the weather had been since the second day of the walk back in the Sleat peninsula. Considering that the summer of 1998 was supposed to be wet, two wet days out of thirteen on Skye was pretty good.

MacLeod's Maidens

At Glen Dibidal we entered a deep gorge through which the Dibidal River tumbled in torrents to the sea via a massive waterfall. We dropped down and negotiated the rapids at the narrowest point before continuing on the last three-kilometre section to Glen Lorgill. This part of the walk contained myriad natural arches, stacks and caves but by this time the conditions had at last begun to dampen our appreciation of them. I was cursing myself that I had left waterproof overtrousers in the main pack, as rivulets of rain had run down my Goretex shell jacket completely soaking my walking breeches. Even with gaiters, my light Goretex boots had long since reached saturation point and my socks were soaking.

The crossing of the Scaladal Burn proved as tricky as Dibidal, and such was the ferocity of the wind-driven rain that a quick decision was made to sneak round the leeward side of aptly named Cnoc Fuar (Cold Hill) by a small lochan and drop down by its outflow into sheltered Lorgill Glen (the glen of the deer's cry). This was home to about ten families of crofters until a fateful summer's day in 1830 when 'life in Lorgill came to an end' as Derek Cooper put it. The callous indifference with which the Clearance of Lorgill came about is contained in the document read by the sheriff officer who was accompanied by the factor, the minister and four policemen on the day the news was imparted to the unfortunate families:

'To all the crofters in Lorgill. Take notice that you are hereby duly warned that you all be ready to leave Lorgill at twelve o'clock on the 4th August next with all your luggage but no stock and proceed to Loch Snizort, where you will board the ship Midlothian (Captain Morrison) that will take you to Nova-Scotia, where you are to receive a free grant of land from Her Majesty's Government. Take further notice that any crofter disobeying this order will be immediately arrested and taken to prison. All persons over seventy years of age and who have no relatives to look after them will be taken care of in the County Poorhouse. This order is final and no appeal to the Government will be considered. God save the Queen.'

The day before the departure, after singing the 100th Psalm, the children laid flowers on the family graves and returned home for their final night on Skye. On the 4th, they marched the long miles to Loch Snizort and set sail for the New World. According to local tradition nothing more was heard of them – ten crofting families effectively wiped off the face of the earth on the whim of a greedy landowner and in the full face of 'the great men of God who stood and watched it all go on'.

Nothing of this atrocity was known to me on that rain-lashed

July day, but I have since vowed to explore the area more intimately than was possible then. The clinical detachment of that
sheriff officer's document has haunted me and demands a return
to Lorgill on a sunnier day.

Any thoughts we had of climbing the steep slopes of The Hoe
in order to stick with the coast to Ramasaig were washed away in
the Duirinish deluge. We squelched our weary way along the
vague path through Lorgill Glen, crossing the river near an old
shepherd's bothy and sheep fank. From here a reasonable land-
rover track crossed the dreary Lon Ban (White Marsh) for the last
wet mile-and-a-half to the road end at Ramasaig. It was 7 o'clock
when we retrieved the rucksacks from the shelter of the trees.
Eight-and-a-half hours of rough walking had taken its toll and
we still had to find a suitable camping spot. After much humming
and hawing and to-ing and fro-ing, we eventually settled on a
reasonably flat green area by the un-named stream flowing into
Ramasaig Bay. The indecision continued, as George and I discussed
the pros and cons of two possible sites while driving wind and rain
made a mockery of the whole issue. Meanwhile, Mike and his tent
merged into a flapping, flailing flurry of nylon guy ropes and the
odd arm and leg, as he attempted to erect his tent. Finally George
and I decided on our respective spots and began the struggle of
creating a semi-dry temporary home in the surrounding morass.
With my years of experience I relished the challenge, and within
minutes my task was complete and I was giving Mike and George
a helping hand.

Eventually we had all settled into our private domains to
attend to the important matter of getting warm and dry. Literally
every stitch of my clothing was soaked apart from a breathable
T-shirt. Boots, socks, underpants, breeches were piled in a sodden
stinking mass in the tent porch before I slid snugly into a thankfully
dry sleeping bag. The combination of body heat and goose-down
soon produced a cosy glow and I lay back, snuggled in my private
warmth and thoughts. Outside, the maelstrom of rain and wind
was an unrelenting roaring blast mixed with the surging roar of
the, by now, swollen river. Any communication between the three

tents was hopeless, despite their relatively close proximity. I brewed up soup in the front porch of the tent, followed by a tin of chicken tikka masala, sweetcorn, and a packet of Uncle Ben's rice. A mug of hot sweet tea rounded off the meal perfectly. I am a firm believer in the merits of eating well during walking expeditions, especially in weather like this, and I was horrified to learn the following morning that Mike had only eaten a banana.

The end of my diary entry for that day was: 'Nice to be in here snug and warm. Pity about highlight day being a washout but it is the thirteenth day of the trip.' Amen.

* * * * *

At home, a ticking clock can keep me awake but the continual battering of rain and wind against the tent made only a vague impression on my subconscious that wild night. At 8.15am I made a reluctant move to brew tea and eat some shortbread, conscious of the fact that the rain was gradually lessening. During the night a puddle had formed in the porch and I wrung out socks for the second time before throwing all wet clothing into a plastic bag. The only dry items of clothing were the underclothes I had slept in, shorts, and already used unwashed socks.

Grunts and groans from the other tents indicated life and George's bleary-eyed unshaven face peeking out from his 'chrysalis' gave him the appearance of snail and shell. I grabbed the camera and captured the comical picture of him along with Mike dressed in only a shirt and cheesy grin, backed by the foaming peaty brown torrent of the stream and low cloud clearing off the hills. This set the scene for the rest of the morning, which was already beginning to clear up with a freshening drying breeze and a hint of sunshine. Less than half-an-hour later the whole area was engulfed in a limpid, lambent light lending a sparkling, invigorating freshness to land, sea and soul. Heady optimism pervaded our rising spirits and we set about the day's tasks with vigour.

The chaotic campsite strewn with items of gear and clothing drying in the sun gradually coalesced into six rucksacks, three heavy ones to be left out of sight under the trees (and picked up later) and three light daypacks for immediate use. It was 10.30 when we finally shifted into first gear and began the stiff climb up the deserted single-track road from Ramasaig in ever-brightening skies. George led the way, as he always did on hills, and soon left Mike and me puffing and panting in his wake. For the first couple of miles we had decided to follow the road, despite being about half-a-mile from the coast, then cut off to reach the prominent Waterstein Head overlooking Neist Point, Skye's most westerly extremity.

The much smaller freshwater namesake of Loch Eishort was passed en route, conjuring up memories of a week and a half ago. From this vantage point the lofty stratified ramparts of Waterstein Head soared up in one clean line from sea to summit, almost 1,000 feet above. To its left, the long bony finger of Neist poked out to the wind and water-lashed promontory containing the conspicuous white lighthouse and associated buildings. It would be a couple of hours before we reached there.

We abandoned the road at the highest point, donning gaiters before bog-trotting across open moor, now like a saturated sponge following last night's soaking. As we climbed higher, the sphagnum moss and heather gave way to firmer grass and we belted up the last few hundred feet to the triangulation pillar. Waterstein Head must be one of the finest, airiest viewpoints on Skye. It may not be quite the highest cliff on the island but it certainly offered the most dramatic and strategic vantage point anywhere on the walk so far. Neist Point – our next destination – jutted out into the ocean like the horny tail of some vast sea creature. A fence ran along between the edge of the cliff and triangulation point which I crossed by jumping off the pillar! Photos were taken before the relaxing wander down swathes of green grass following the edge of Waterstein Head's northern escarpment. This led naturally to the road north of Loch Mor (Big Loch) which we followed for just over a mile to the car park marking the start of the walk out to the Point.

At this juncture we had rejoined civilisation, with hordes of tourists armed with cameras and camcorders all set on bagging what could now be termed (with the advent of the Skye Bridge) the most westerly point in mainland Britain. Of course I, and most normal people, still class Skye as an island, despite its recent tenuous concrete link with the mainland, but Neist Point is now, like it or not, the most westerly point in Britain which can be reached without the use of boat or plane. In pre-bridge times this honour was bestowed on Land's End in England, beating Ardnamurchan Point in Scotland by only a few miles – so the ball is back firmly on Scottish soil unless English engineers build a twenty mile bridge to the Scilly Isles; though, doubtlessly, Scottish engineers would be required for a bridge of that length! Tongue out of cheek, Neist Point would have been my final destination had I stuck with my original summer plan of walking from Buchan Ness and thus completing the longest East to West crossing of Scotland – another dream to store up until the time is ripe.

Well-constructed steps led initially to a steep scarp section, followed by a tarmac path which swung round a hollow and on out to the lighthouse, built in 1909 and now fully automated. At the end of the path we were taken aback to discover a graveyard surrounded by a fence. Closer inspection revealed that the graveyard was not real but had been a set used in the film *Breaking the Waves* which won the Silver Medal in the 1996 Cannes Film Festival. A notice had been erected explaining this fact and that no offence was intended to churchgoers. I wondered how many people, churchgoers or not, would have taken offence at the fact that the mock graveyard had just been left in place to needlessly litter this isolated corner of Skye.

More surprises were in store when we walked down to the rocky coastline beyond the lighthouse. I noticed a couple of cairn-like constructions made from the numerous rocks strewn everywhere. Nothing exceptional about that, except that these were just the tip of a very large iceberg. Within minutes we were surrounded by a petrified forest of similar artificial creations, ranging from simple stone towers to elaborate labour-intensive edifices which must have taken the best part of a day to build. The bulk of these strange rock structures were constructed on the solid foundation of a natural highly indented rock pavement providing a wonderful scrambling playground. This forest of rock follies created a weird primordial Druidic atmosphere echoing Celtic symbolism and mythology. My initial reaction was 'Why?' Why were they constructed and by whom? Further information revealed that Neist Point was a gathering point and shrine for so-called New-Agers who met here at the Summer Solstice to create their Celtic cairns and no doubt indulge in other hallowed hippie activities.

We spent the best party of an hour just wandering round in awe and curiosity and nibbling lunch before heading back to the lighthouse. Yellow lichen splattered rocks and a clump of pink sea thrift made a fine foreground to the lighthouse perched high on a fulmar infested cliff with its attendant foghorn peering over the abyss and across the restless blue expanse of the Little Minch. Neist Point was another turning point of the trip, a crux from which to view past and future, now almost in equal measures. The half-way point of the walk was rapidly approaching both in time and distance. I reckoned 160 miles (260km) were up by Neist Point and by the end of tomorrow I would have completed about 180 miles and 15 days (the true central point). I had grown much and travelled far since my lonely storm-lashed seat, huddled beneath Point of Sleat lighthouse, trembling on the brink of an uncertain future which had now delivered me safely to this far-flung edge of the world.

Neist Point

On our return to the car park we set off to follow the crescent of clifftop which ends at Oisgill Bay. This grand circuit provided a dramatic retrospective aspect of the north-western craggy fringe of Neist Point culminating in the lighthouse, and is the view shown in most pictures of the Point. The highest point supports an old wartime lookout post in the shape of an unsightly concrete box, and was hastily bypassed. Time forced us to omit the three-mile coastal loop containing Biod Ban (White Cliff) and Lower Milovaig and we cut through a natural cleft in the hillside to rejoin the road at a cottage with a picturesque rock garden which we had admired en route to the Point. A pleasant tarmac interlude followed for two miles to the green lushness of Glendale at the head of Loch Pooltiel, a peaceful, pastoral glen with a host of small scattered settlements such as Fasach, Lephin, Holmisdale, Glasphein and Hamaramore. The first of these, Fasach, was to provide our pre-booked bed and breakfast accommodation for that night. En route we passed a small, homely looking restaurant and decided that would be tonight's culinary venue.

In the bright late-afternoon sunshine, Glendale possessed a tranquil, unhurried air and it was difficult to imagine that just over a century ago the Glendale crofters, led by their middle-aged, bearded benefactor, John MacPherson (the Glendale Martyr), rose up in defence of their rights against an authoritarian regime of unscrupulous landowners. In January 1882, the local factor increased his unpopularity by declaring a prohibition on removing driftwood from the shore and owning a dog. These regulations were added to an already long list of others such as prohibiting the cutting of heather and rushes for the purposes of roof thatching. In making these outrageous rules the estate had set in motion a groundswell of unrest resulting in violent clashes between crofting tenants and the 'system'. A month later, under the leadership of John MacPherson, the crofters met at Glendale Church to present a united front against further clearances and for the reinstatement of the dispossessed. Subsequent clashes resulted in the gunboat HMS *Jackal* being dispatched to Glendale to bring the crofters to heel and arrest the ringleaders, including John MacPherson. Their imprisonment in Edinburgh fuelled the resistance machine. The campaign was eventually successful and led to the Crofters Act of 1886 which bestowed security of tenure for all crofters throughout Scotland. In fact, as early as 1904 the Glendale crofters became the only ones in Skye to own the title deeds of their land, an option which did not become generally available until 1976. The rather lamentable sequel to all this is neatly summed up in the statistic which says that of the 212 people now living in Glendale, 150 are English. Scotland's people have for too long had the heart and hope knocked out of them but I sensed renewed optimism that sun-filled July afternoon.

We found our (English-owned) B&B, a modern detached bungalow named Mo Dhachaidh – literally 'my home'. The owners, Mr and Mrs Karlsson, had moved there twelve years earlier after visiting Glendale and falling in love with it. Who could blame them? Mrs Karlsson warmly welcome three foot-weary travellers and assured us that her husband would run us back to Ramasaig in his car to retrieve our heavy baggage. Meanwhile, we organised ourselves and relaxed and readjusted to life under a roof once again. After three nights in a tent it was unashamed luxury to stretch out on the softness of a double bed. The remainder of the evening fell neatly into place. Mr Karlsson kindly transported Mike and me back to Ramasaig, explaining that he often worked in England, returning to Skye most weekends and holidays. We strolled down to the (English-owned) restaurant and indulged in mushroom soup, Ramasaig beef casserole, and a huge wedge of gateau with lashings of cream, all washed down with three cans of Murphy's Irish Stout. Postcards, bought from the (English-owned) shop, were posted and 'phone calls made to loved ones before we limped back to Mo Dhachaidh where our wet clothing was in the process of being washed and dried. The general consensus was for an early night. I retired to my bed, mind focused on and map already folded for tomorrow's jaunt around Dunvegan Head.

* * * * *

I woke refreshed but not relaxed. The room was still an Aladdin's Cave of camping and clothing items. Most of the mess was sorted and packed before I joined Mike and George for a hearty cooked breakfast. Our main packs were deposited at the rear of the house to be retrieved later in the day. At 9.45 we bid farewell to our hosts and set forth under cloudy skies.

A mile-and-a-half of gentle road walking eased us into the day and half-an-hour later we abandoned the Glasphein loop road at a ruin to begin the circuit of Duirinish's northern subsidiary peninsula which ends at Dunvegan Head. Assorted farm tracks and paths soon led to the short grass and heather of the clifftop. From here, almost five miles of continuous near-vertical cliff led north to Dunvegan Head, culminating in Biod an Athair (Sky Cliff), at 1,027 feet the highest coastal cliff on Skye.

A following wind and excellent sheep track made for effortless walking and we were making good time. Wandering closer to the cliff edge, I was startled by the sudden thrash of brown speckled wings as a buzzard peeled away from its precarious perch uttering a loud, gull-like pee-oo cry and soaring gracefully into the void of sea and sky. Three glorious airy miles later we reached the triangulation pillar on Biod an Athair and spent much time to-ing and fro-ing in order to photograph each other standing near cliff edges. Shortly before the summit, the cliff edge dog-legs out, enabling a dramatic photo to be taken of the full 1,000-foot craggy cliff face complete with an ant-like figure at the top. George, who suffers from mild vertigo, stayed well back from the edge while Mike preferred to lie down on his stomach, head peering out over the void. I revelled in the exposure and sauntered along the edge foolishly without batting an eyelid. Yesterday's high point of Waterstein Head was plainly visible from the trig point, rising up beyond the scattered 'sugar-grains' of crofts in Glendale. Looking forward a day-and-a-half, I was sure I could make out the delicate delineation of Stein on the Waternish peninsula.

Beyond Sky Cliff a gradual and increasingly heathery descent was accompanied by the intermittent liquid whistle of a golden plover, its flashing gold and white plumage only fleetingly glimpsed as it flew low over the heather in fits and starts, staying well ahead of us. There was a wonderfully wild spacious feeling of approaching the end of the world, and after about a mile we found a pleasant spot out of the wind for lunch. To my dismay, I discovered that a banana had squashed and split in my rucksack, covering the rest of my lunch in a layer of stickiness. Mike found this a great source of amusement and his laughter, along with increased attention from midges, made this a lunch spot to be remembered. Clearing skies and sunshine soon melted away my annoyance and I basked in the warmth of sun and true companionship.

Dunvegan Head itself was a fairly mediocre affair after the grand clifftop scenery already encountered and we cut across the heathery moor to reach the vicinity of Am Famhair (The Giant), a natural arch on the opposite side of the peninsula. Bog, bracken and blackhouses dominated the walking as we headed south, aiming for the road end at Galtrigill. This section produced a sting-in-the-tail in the form of a deep, thickly-vegetated gorge, with a fast flowing river which, apparently, had to be negotiated before the road could be reached. A bracken-choked, tree-lined descent into the gorge and a tricky river crossing was followed by a steep slippery ascent, tugging on dubious clumps of grass and heather, before normal walking could be resumed. In typical Sod's Law fashion it was only when we had successfully tackled this hazard that we realised it could have been avoided higher up the hillside. Close to this point the map indicated The Manners Stone, a large flat rock which reputedly gives good manners to those who sit on it.

We reached Galtrigill and the road end to begin the trek on the thin thread of tarmac weaving its way along the western fringe of Loch Dunvegan, at the head of which lay the village and campsite which were our point of departure three days ago. The Piping Museum on the map seemed to be further down the road than indicated and was billed as the MacCrimmon Pipe Heritage Centre. History has it that the MacCrimmons held Borreraig (the small township south of Galtrigill) as a free township from the Dunvegan MacLeods and it was home to their famous piping school. Their last pupil was MacArthur, piper to the Highland Society of Edinburgh in the late 1700s. On the coast nearby is a pipers' cave, where pipers used to practise in order to avoid complaints from neighbours! Some distance to the left of the road a beehive cairn-type monument carried the inscription 'The Memorial Cairn of the MacCrimmons of whom ten generations were the hereditary pipers of MacLeod and who were renowned

as Composers, Performers and Instructors of the classical music of
the bagpipe. Near to this post stood the MacCrimmons School of
Music, 1500 – 1800.' Further research showed that the Borreraig
Piping Centre had been opened in 1976 by Canadian descendants,
Hugh and Irene MacCrimmon, and the MacCrimmon legacy was
very much alive in the form of the present hereditary piper to the
MacLeod Chief. The old adage that 'it takes seven years and seven
generations to make a piper' would seem to be an apt slogan for
the MacCrimmon piping legacy.

We were now caught in a game of cat and mouse with rainy
squalls when we endlessly put on and took off waterproofs, a frustrating and rhythm-wrecking necessity. Changing and wide-rang-
ing vistas helped to ease the tarmac miles. We stopped and studied
a ruined chapel whose left gable leaned over at such a precarious
angle that we felt the slightest push would send it tumbling. At
Totaig we bore left at a fork to connect with the B884 just north
of Colbost, home of the renowned Three Chimneys Restaurant.
This pricy, but priceless gem, tucked away in the north-west corner of Skye was originally a tea room selling snacks, afternoon
and high teas. It has now evolved into an evening eating establishment whose colourful cuisine is leagues ahead of its competi-
tors. Three foot-weary chaps stood at the Three Chimneys peering
at the mouth-watering menu like paupers. I was game to go there
that evening but Mike and George's purse-strings couldn't be persuaded – but there would be other occasions ... the teasing slogan
of 'seriously good Scottish food' would tempt me back sooner
than I expected. Behind the restaurant is a blackhouse museum
which also demanded a visit at some future point.

Late afternoon was now upon us, and with still four miles to
the campsite, we strode onwards with renewed intent. A stubby
spout of land nudges out into Loch Dunvegan, producing the long
finger of sheltered sea loch protecting Dunvegan from the full
ferocity of the sea. This little peninsula, culminating in Uiginish
Point, was omitted and it was 6.30 when we finally reached the
campsite. The grand three-day coastal loop round Duirinish was
complete and with it, a major highlight of Skyewalk.

Our first task was to retrieve the car and drive back to Mo Dhachaidh in Glendale to pick up the rucksacks. This done, we returned to pitch tents on a quiet higher area of the site, our previous location now occupied. The view south-west from our secluded but wind-beaten site was dominated by the twin peaks of MacLeod's Tables, the two flat-topped summits about which the rest of Duirinish revolves in a swirl of sea-girt splendour. Curling tongues of cloud licked their level tops and threw them into sombre shadow while closer rolling ridges were dappled in low evening sun, smaller flecks of cloud shadow caressing and outlining their bleached green, sheep-dotted slopes.

The Gaelic/Norse names Healabhal Mhor and Healabhal Bheag for MacLeod's Tables translate as Big Holy Fell and Little Holy Fell, because of their resemblance to two great natural altars. Geologically, the Tables are a result of differential basalt lava flows producing the horizontal stratification also seen in the flat-topped Dun Caan on Raasay. Shifting from fact to what is probably fiction, there is the story of Alasdair Crotach, the seventh Chief of the Clan MacLeod, who visited the King's Palace in Edinburgh and behaved with utmost ease and grace, much to the consternation of the lowland nobility who expected a more unrefined character. Alasdair refused to express admiration and surprise at the rich surroundings despite needling attempts from his hosts, and one earl finally and pointedly asked: 'Have you ever seen in Skye halls so spacious as these, a roof so lofty, a table so ample and richly laden and candelabra so ornate as those around us here tonight?' In response, the MacLeod chief replied that on Skye there was a roof far more impressive, a greater table and vastly superior illumination. The earl, unable to believe what he was hearing, was invited to Dunvegan to see for himself. On arrival, he was accompanied to the flat summit of Healabhal Mor which was covered in a vast array of food and wine and surrounded by scores of clansmen with flaming torches. After the banquet, Alasdair remarked to the earl: 'Truly sir, this is a roof grander than was ever made by human hands; this table, you must confess, is more commodious than any that can be shown even in the royal court; while these faithful vassals of mine are more precious by far than any metallic contrivance, however costly and ornate it may be.' In the face of such indisputable evidence the earl was duly humbled and Alasdair Crotach won the hearts and minds of both Highland and Lowland aristocracy. Thus the name MacLeod's Tables. Fact or fiction, it makes a great story. It is quite possible in a few thousand years that MacLeod's Tables could become the highest tops on an island called Duirinish. The head of Pool Roag to the head of Loch Dunvegan, is connected by a two-mile neck of land rising to only twenty metres above sea level.

As Mike and George were short of cash, we decided to drive twenty miles to Portree to use the cash machine. This manoeuvre ran against the grain of my hang-up with continuity and ethical elegance – it would be ten days before I was really in Portree as part of the walk but I went along for the hurl and the company. Fish suppers were eventually tracked down at the harbour area before we ambled into the Harbour Bar for a pint. A lack of seats and a lack of conversation due to the eclipsing blaring presence of Sky television forced us out and back to the relative tranquillity of Dunvegan. This off-shoot journey to Portree unsettled me and I was glad to return to the place and time I belonged.

Mike deposited George and me at the Dunvegan Hotel before going back to the campsite to leave the car. Half-an-hour later he joined us to indulge in several pints and Bowmore malt whiskies, the latter being a smoky, peaty malt from Islay and my favourite. Today had been a crucial day of the walk. I was now halfway through my intended objective of walking Skye's coastline. However, this halfway point would be properly consummated in tomorrow night's destination, the Stein Inn in Waternish, where I planned to stay three nights. I hoped that the Stein Inn would become a focus for the middle of the Winged Isle walk. I was not to be disappointed.

Route Summary: Carbost to Dunvegan

Note: The following involves the use of Dunvegan as a centre for two nights.

Day 1: Carbost – Ullinish (13 miles – 21 km)

Follow the B8009 south from Carbost to the head of Loch Harport. Once over the bridge, strike off left to a farm and gain the grassy slopes leading to Uchd Mor. Descend to Meadale and follow the shoreline before traversing to a higher vague path ending at Sumardale. Cross the river and swing round to climb the little hillock south of Gesto Bay. At Gesto Bay climb up to the main road and follow it round into Loch Beag and Bracadale. From Bracadale stay with the coast on pathless terrain or continue until the turn-off for the Ullinish Lodge Hotel. If the tide conditions are right an excursion can be made out to the tidal island of Oronsay.

Day 2: Ullinish – Dunvegan (14 miles – 22 km)

From the hotel take the loop road north to Eabost before leaving the road to follow the coast to Colbost Point. Swing round to Eabost West and rejoin the main road at Ose. Follow the road north to Loch Caroy before taking a minor road south to Balmore on the Harlosh peninsula. Reach Harlosh Point by mainly pathless grassy terrain. Rejoin the Harlosh loop road and follow it north to meet the main road again near Roskhill. Follow the main road for two miles to Dunvegan and accommodation.

Day 3: Dunvegan – Ramasaig (18 miles – 29 km)

This is a long day, despite the advantage of a reasonable coastal path, and some parties may opt to split the journey at the MBA bothy in Glen Ollisdal (GR 213344). The route offers what is arguably the finest cliff top coastal walking in Britain, featuring the renowned sea stacks of Macleod's Maidens.

From Dunvegan take the minor road leading to the B884. A left turn and a right turn lead to Orbost, the start of the walk to the Maidens. Note that the stretch of coastline featuring Roag

Island has not been described. (It was the author's original intention to camp on Roag Island.) Follow the track as it swings round
Loch Bharcasaig and enters a forestry plantation. Beyond the forest
the track becomes a path loosely following the coastline for four
miles to Idrigill Point and Macleod's Maidens. The path continues
north-westwards following the cliff top all the way in awesome
surroundings. The MBA bothy in Glen Ollisdal is visible from the
path if overnight shelter is required. Cross the Glen Dibidal river
and gorge and continue to Lorgill Bay. From here to the road-end
at Ramasaig, it is possible to climb high over the Hoe (233m) or
take a low-level route via the Lon Ban track.

Day 4: Ramasaig – Glendale (12 miles – 19 km)

Another superb day's walking, visiting Skye's most westerly point.
Follow the road north from Ramasaig before branching off left
over boggy ground to reach Waterstein Head (296m), a marvellous viewpoint. Descend via the north ridge to the minor road and
path leading out to the lighthouse at Neist Point (Skye's western
extremity). Retrace steps and follow the cliff-top round to Oisgill
Bay. Either stay with the coastline round to Lower Milovaig or
rejoin the road near Loch Mor before following the road to
Glendale at the head of Loch Pooltiel.

Day 5: Glendale – Dunvegan (17 miles – 27 km)

Another very long day, even omitting selected chunks of coastline.
From Glendale follow the cliff-girt coastline north for almost six
miles to Dunvegan Head. This is entirely path-less though good
sheep tracks do exist. The trig-point on Biod an Athair (Sky Cliff)
marks the highest sea cliff on Skye at 313m. From the vicinity of
Dunvegan Head, follow the coastline south to the road-end at
Galtrigill. Continue southwards on the road, which loosely follows the coastline. Join the B884 and continue to Skinidin where
the option exists of heading out to Uignish Point. The above
mileage does not include this option. At the head of Loch
Dunvegan take the minor road leading to Dunvegan.

Accommodation and other information

Ullinish: Ullinish Lodge Hotel (open only in the summer)
Dunvegan: Campsite, hotels and B&Bs
Glen Ollisdal: MBA bothy
Ramasaig: Wild camp only
Glendale: B&Bs

Shops at Struan (near Bracadale), Dunvegan and Glendale

CHAPTER 6

A Waternish Welcome

(Wednesday 22 July – Friday 24 July)

Dunvegan to Stein

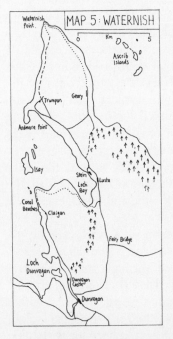

WATERY MORNING SUNLIGHT and a gentle wind whispering on the flysheet nudged me out of my half-awakened state. I rose and dressed quickly, relishing the midge-free conditions induced by the light breeze. Mike and George were slowly shifting about and easing into the familiar pattern of activities involved in striking camp and preparing for the new day. There was no immediate sense of urgency, despite the fact that today's walk involved a fairly extensive trudge round the un-named peninsula between Loch Dunvegan and Loch Bay.

By 10 o'clock we were ready to roll, Mike's car filled, with the heavy gear being left behind at the campsite to be picked up later. Just how we would be transported back here from the Stein Inn later was anyone's guess.

In high spirits we ambled off along our 'pub route' into the village of Dunvegan which looked disturbingly quiet and ghost-like for the height of summer. We bought lunch for two days before enquiring at the castle entrance as to the exact whereabouts of the famous coral beach which we were due to pass that day. Dunvegan Castle is undoubtedly the most visited tourist attraction on Skye and as we passed the entrance visitors were spilling out of coaches and cars. The castle has been home to MacLeod Chiefs for over 700 years and is said to be the oldest inhabited castle in Scotland, although its current mock-Gothic, pepper-box turreted appearance is vastly different from when Dr Johnson visited here in 1773. Then, Boswell said of Dunvegan: 'It looks as if let down from heaven by the four corners to be the residence of a Chief.' I found it hard to agree with this sentiment today. It was only when we had continued along the wooded single-track road for another half-mile that we could stand and look back at the grey, cheerless facade of this pseudo-baronial edifice, its dreariness accentuated by the now light drizzle and vapid sky. Derek Cooper, in his Skye guide, makes the observation that 'Today the outer walls of the castle are covered with a porridge-coloured stucco such as is widely favoured by Inverness County Council for its public housing schemes – a drab and prosaic exterior to the ancient stones within'. Visitors to the castle are not so much interested in the exterior as the lavish interior which contains relics such as the Fairy Flag, the Dunvegan Cup and Ruaraidh Mor's Drinking Horn, the latter holding two and a half bottles of wine and which every new chief is expected to down in one gulp.

We photographed the solemn, Stygian yet sylvan scene of seaweed-blanketed bay backed by the castle and a flourish of trees. A boat of hopeful seal-sighters chugged through the flat waters between us and Gairbh Eilein (Rough Island). The road walking was pleasant in alternate pockets of sunshine and showers with a following wind. Further on, the road crossed the small sea loch of Loch Suardal by means of a causeway. An old harbour with drystone jetty and boathouse pointed to the fact that passengers were ferried across before the advent of the causeway. The next two miles showed a marked improvement in the weather and the landscape and seascape unfolded to reveal rolling, spacious green meadow, backed by a wind-ruffled Loch Dunvegan, its deep blue expanse dotted with white horses. Beyond, and almost on the horizon, the furrowed line of cliffs culminating in Dunvegan Head were thrown into stark relief by the welcome sunshine.

The peppering of steadings and crofts at Claigan marked the end of the public road and a car park marked the start of the half-mile dirt track to the coral beach, a signposted tourist attraction. This grand half-mile was a vibrant changing delight of light and shade. The latter part of the track literally hugged the rocky coast-line on a level section of sun-washed machair. Out to our left, beyond the speckled strip of rocky beach, Loch Dunvegan was a leaden battleship grey and the cliffs were now a dark prosaic wedge clamped to a steel-edged horizon. Directly ahead, a grace-ful curving ivory tusk of sun-bleached whiteness was backed by successive corrugations of seaweed. The immediate foreground was a spread of springy, daisy-sprinkled machair, while a low-lying craggy hill beyond was doused in darkest shadow. Beyond, the vegetated cliffs of the Island of Isay were etched on the hori-zon with startling clarity. For such a small island (only a mile long), Isay has a fascinating but rather gruesome history. In the early 16th century, Roderick MacLeod of Lewis decided to elimi-nate two entire families in order that his grandson might inherit the Island of Raasay and the lands of Gairloch. A banquet was arranged on Isay by him, to which the families were invited and told that they would hear something advantageous. They turned up expectantly and were told during the meal that their personal views were of great importance. Roderick MacLeod then left the hall before each guest in turn was summoned to a room where he had them stabbed to death.

Isay was offered to Dr Johnson by the MacLeods on condition that he built a house on it, but comfort-loving Johnson refused their generous offer. At that time Isay was a well populated and industrious island and by the early 19th century was a big fishing station with its own general store. A final clearance of twelve crofter families took place in 1880 and since then the island has been unproductive. The present owner is the 60s folk-singer, Donovan.

We wandered down on to the curving strand of coral which, from a distance, had had the appearance of white sand. Closer inspection revealed a mass of tiny, brittle, shell-like fragments, which scrunched under our feet. The coral is made by a seaweed called Lithothamnion, lying out from the shore in semi-circular cushions, and when bits break off they are deposited by the tide on the seashore.

Round the Point of Groban na Sgeire (Point of the Rock Skerry) we crossed a carpet of wild-flowered machair to a crumbling stone wall beyond which a jumble of angular rocks provided a fine lunch spot. Our destination of Stein was just visible from this vantage point and as I sat scoffing and staring contentedly out across a cobalt blue sea, I commented to George and Mike that this was leagues better than yesterday's struggle with sticky bananas and midges. In retrospect, that lunch spot was the most idyllic of the entire trek.

All too soon we tore ourselves away and trotted along the grassy promenade on sheep tracks. The peninsula is indented by the V-shaped bite of Lovaig Bay, and the relatively low-lying ground we were on is replaced by a line of high cliffs on the second part of the 'V'. Although these cliffs were only vertical in the upper reaches, with a run-out to the sea, I decided it would be prudent to gradually gain height and stay on the rim of the cliffs. Heather soon replaced sheep-stunted grass and the going became more laborious. Diversion was provided by a couple of stream crossings, ever expanding sea vistas and dozens of spotted orchids and wild thyme.

We turned the northern shoulder of the 'speckled hill', Beinn Bhreac, and continued along a heathery platform, the white walls of Stein and Lusta cottages and crofts now plainly visible across the breeze-ruffled Loch Bay. Beinn Bhreac's seaward slopes are guarded by an almost continuous bastion of crumbling cliffs and it seemed imperative to find a break in these cliffs in order to gain access to the bracken-covered lower slopes. This in turn would lead naturally to the sand and shingle at the head of Loch Bay. Invariably, weaknesses in cliffs are better seen from below than above, but despite this we found what appeared to be a suitable gully. Used to such hurdles in many years as a hillwalker, I lent George my walking pole and we tentatively began our descent. Initially a few massive boulders gave some security in the narrow neck of the gully. The neck gradually fanned out into a slippery, boggy mass of thick vegetation with a covering of oak, hazel and birch trees. Thankfully, my doom-laden scenario of a sudden sheer drop did not materialise and the cliffs spat us out on the bracken-choked lower slopes, only slightly the worse for wear.

We soon found a sheep track through the waist-high bracken taking us to the head of Loch Bay. The last hurdle of the day was the crossing of the Bay River, accomplished on slippery stepping stones and by tossing the walking pole back across for the next person to use. The decision was made to head up to the tiny hamlet of Bay via a grass track and then to the B886 single track road. The straggle of houses comprising Lusta ranged from modern villas with added conservatories, through traditional stone whitewashed crofts to a well-restored thatched blackhouse. The B886 makes a sudden left turn to the sea and the idyllic little backwater of Stein. As we turned down this final stretch with the imposing facade of Bayview House dominating the view, I secretly hoped there would be some form of reception committee awaiting us. In the planning stages I had certainly bestowed the Stein Inn with a kind of kudos. It was a half-way house, a tranquil sanctuary nestling under Waternish's wing, a Rivendell of Skye where various folk, including Heather, had said they might make a rendezvous.

With an expectant spring in our strides, we soon reached the whitewashed front of the Stein Inn, billed as 'the oldest inn on Skye'. We entered an atmosphere of distinctly subdued hush. The barman and two locals were the only reception and they acknowledged our entrance with nods of the head and grunted greetings. This was not the Waternish welcome I had fervently hoped for.

I enquired about the amount of money collected in a charity bottle deposited by me at the Inn some months ago. The bottle was in a fairly prominent position at the end of the bar, but a quick lift indicated little in the way of dosh; unless, of course, it contained a preponderance of notes. A second enquiry regarding transport back to Dunvegan to retrieve Mike's car was equally depressing: 'Naebody going there that I know of but ye could try hitchin' on the road'. We decided to mull over the barman's suggestion with a drink but George and Mike were only in the mood for a coke, whilst I threw caution to the wind and had a pint of Caffreys Irish ale.

For the first time in the whole walk I felt a total anti-climax. During the last few days with Mike and George I had elevated the Stein Inn to some kind of social focus of the entire venture. It would also be their last Skye venue and I desperately wanted their last day and night to go with a bang. Although Mike said little, I could see the disappointment in his face that there was no one here to welcome us and offer us a lift back to his car in Dunvegan. Irrationally, I felt that I had let them both down, though I knew this was stupid.

We sat stiffly round the table, conversation reduced to stilted brief interjections, each of us bound up in his own thoughts. Mike especially realised that there was little point in easing into mellow pub mood until the car had been collected from Dunvegan. As we gazed forlornly out across the water, a Dormobile suddenly drove up and parked outside the Inn. An elderly bearded character emerged clutching a pair of binoculars, the late afternoon sun outlining his craggy features. I immediately recognised the face but couldn't put a name to it. Then I blurted out 'That's Hamish Brown – I don't believe it!' Mike and George looked expectantly at me, only vaguely aware of who Hamish Brown was. I filled them in briefly with regard to his status as Scotland's leading outdoor writer and multi-Munroist, but all the time my mind was chewing over only one thing – would he be willing to give us a lift back to Dunvegan?

Having met Hamish previously in connection with my book *The Munro Phenomenon* for which he wrote the foreword, I felt it only common courtesy to at least pop outside and re-acquaint us. This I did and, to my delight, he recognised me. Immediately I informed him of my coastal ambition, one which he had also nursed for years (see Introduction). He introduced me to his companion Adrian before they both took up my offer of a drink, and yes, they could give us a lift to Dunvegan – things were looking up. In the space of a few minutes the mood had changed from gloomy despondency to heady intoxication – we were back in control once again.

The conversation bounced from Munros to Corbetts to Grahams, the three main hill classifications in Scotland. Hamish had made the first continuous round of the Munros back in the 70s and has since completed at least seven rounds. After only one round, however, we were soon rattling about in Hamish's clapped-out Dormobile en route to Dunvegan. 'Hold on to something', barked Hamish and, lurching from side to side in a camp-chair, I readily followed his advice. The interior of the Dormobile reflected Hamish's off-beat outdoor lifestyle – elasticated, hooked straps could well have been holding the van together but were strategically placed to hold all manner of assorted implements. An 'I love Morocco' sticker betrayed Hamish's long-held fascination for the Atlas Mountains. Every year he made a pilgrimage to Morocco for about three months, living with locals and guiding westerners into the high Atlas. Recently he had completed the first continuous traverse of the whole Atlas range from end to end accompanied by Moroccans and using pack mules to carry gear. He assured me a book would be forthcoming on this fascinating venture. It was far cheaper to live in Morocco than Scotland, he said, and he had even picked up a new wing mirror for the Dormobile there for only £3.

Hamish was a man living in the wrong century. He detested the petty bureaucracy of modern life; the computerised soul-less artificiality of contemporary existence was excess baggage that he could easily do without. I couldn't help but totally agree with him. Part of the reason I enjoyed these walking expeditions was to escape such pressures and to surround myself with the simple uncluttered beauty of the natural world, where the heart could beat to a different rhythm and the mind could fuse in inner harmony with the landscape.

At Dunvegan we said our goodbyes, retrieved the car and drove back to the Stein Inn. Settled comfortably in the car I reflected on the fact that I had now broken the back of the walk. Over 200 miles (320km) completed with only about 150 to go and perhaps the finest walking now over, the light was visible at the end of the tunnel – only this was no tunnel of darkness, more a tunnel of light, landscape and life, a fragile bubble of Highland beauty and calm which would physically burst in two weeks' time but would abide intact within me to old age.

We busied ourselves with the usual chores before congregating in the bar for food. Original stone walls, a large fireplace and tranquil sea views through the sash windows endowed the place with a cosy, quaint atmosphere which was becoming noisier with a steady influx of German, French and English tourists. Where were the locals I wondered? It saddened me that the real heart seemed to have been torn from much of Highland Scotland, especially in the summer months when midges, sheep and tourists are all out in force. Yet, these very tourists are a commodity that the Highlands could not do without. The Highland economy is utterly dependent on tourism and the three of us were contributory factors. The real sadness is, of course, that the majority of Scots do not appreciate the wonders of their own country. I believe Scotland to be the finest country in the world and Skye to be one of the finest parts of Scotland.

A few beers and a few games of pool later we called it a night and retired to our rooms. Tomorrow had originally been planned as a rest day with the walk round Waternish the following day. Circumstances dictated however that the Waternish Walk should happen tomorrow. A relatively early night seemed a good idea before the long 18-mile day. I lay in bed listening to Home County accents drifting up from the still bustling bar below. An American voice exclaimed 'My blow-drier adaptor doesn't work. I'm lost without it.' This comment threw sharply into focus the priorities of someone based in the 'artificiality of contemporary existence'. My immediate priorities were far removed from such materialistic longings. My spirit had broken free from the shackles of greed and gadgetry. That state of complete contentment which psychologists call self-actualisation had been reached. I may have had priorities but I craved nothing. I was happy. Perhaps this happiness was partly due to the knowledge that Heather was coming to Skye on Saturday for two nights. I had 'phoned earlier and on hearing this had immediately booked a room in the Edinbane Hotel. Life was wonderful on that balmy July evening.

* * * * *

At 7.00am I drew back the curtain on the tiny dormer window to reveal an overcast morning with a fine drizzle. The sea loch was a brooding calm and the hills beyond held a single wisp of drifting curling mist. The absolute peace was profoundly uplifting. I quickly captured the scene on film before I began more practical preparations for the day ahead.

It was 10 o'clock before we hit the road, suitably filled with another cracking cooked breakfast, guaranteed to stave off hunger for at least a few hours. In already brightening skies we wandered up the road past Bayview House which I latterly discovered had belonged to Donovan when he introduced a small commune to get away from the 'crap of city life' as one of them had expressed it on BBC Television. As far as I am aware, Donovan now lives in Southern Ireland with his family.

A long pleasant section of road-walking took us leisurely through the scattered hamlets of Hallin and Upper Halistra. Houses and gardens provided interest along the way. In one garden a fishing boat filled with soil made a novel flower bed. Two men and four dogs herding sheep caught our attention and the three miles to the fork beyond Upper Halistra seemed effortless. Here we opted for the left fork, keeping close to the sea, but the side trip out to Ardmore Point was shamefully omitted. Although only a mile out and a mile back, I felt the day was already long enough. Ardmore Bay is a fine natural harbour and it is surprising that no sizeable settlement developed here.

Trumpan Church, near the road end, now a ruin, was the scene of a despicable crime in May 1578 and almost ranks with the MacDonald Massacre at Glencoe. Members of the MacDonald clan arrived by boat from Uist on a Sunday morning under cover of thick mist, with revenge in their hearts for a massacre of a branch of the MacDonalds by the MacLeods on the island of Eigg. The poignant sound of Gaelic psalms was soon replaced by the crackle of burning roof thatch and the barred door ensured that the entire congregation were burned alive except for one girl who rushed to Dunvegan to raise the alarm. The MacLeod Chief immediately unfurled the famous Fairy Flag which was supposed to exert a magic in battle, and his clansmen rallied round to march on Trumpan where the MacDonalds were still pillaging and plundering. The ensuing battle was short but bloody, and the MacDonalds were butchered and buried under a stone dyke. The incident was named Blar Milleadh Garaidh (The Battle of the Spoiling of the Dyke) and is commemorated in a great pibroch.

We spent a quiet few moments looking at gravestones. I was amazed to find flowers placed on the grave of someone who had died in 1906. The names Effie and Flora predominated, but one gravestone and plaque stood out amongst the rest – that of a certain Lady Grange. Her story is a sad one but worth telling. Her husband, a Lord Justice Clerk in Edinburgh, was a staunch Jacobite and one night in 1730 had been hatching plans in the drawing room of their house. Lady Grange, a loyalist, had been listening outside the door and confronted her husband and friends, one of whom was Lord Lovat. Her mistake was to threaten to report them to the Government, which they took seriously, so seriously, in fact, that they arranged another meeting to discuss how to get rid of her. That very night she was kidnapped and taken to the Highlands to spend three years in solitude on a lonely island west of North Uist. Meanwhile, a mock funeral was carried out in Edinburgh with a coffin full of stones. Over the next twelve years Lady Grange was transferred like a piece of baggage to islands as remote as St Kilda, where she gave a letter, hidden in a ball of wool, to a visiting catechist. The letter was to her solicitor in Edinburgh who mounted a rescue plan but, before it could be realised, MacLeod of Dunvegan moved her to Harris and eventually to Skye. Her final years were spent, frail and ill, going from house to house in search of companionship and pity. In 1745 she died in a crofter's house in Waternish, with another mock funeral taking place at Kilmuir Church in Dunvegan, while the real burial was secretly carried out by moonlight in Trumpan Churchyard. May her Ladyship rest in peace.

From the road end near Trumpan a muddy track leads north following the coastline for four miles to Waternish Point, a route I had previously walked. This time, however, two short diversions were made, one to a cairn commemorating Roderick Macleod of Unish, who was killed in 1580 in another skirmish with the MacDonalds. It was interesting to note that the cairn had been restored by the Clan Macleod Society of the USA. The second diversion was to Dun Borrafioch broch, a fairly well-preserved ruin well to the right of the track. As we clambered about on the angular weathered blocks, two ravens croaked overhead, adding to the ancient Celtic atmosphere of the place. The 20th century made its impact once again in the form of a motley collection of old vans, caravans and even an ambulance, which were no doubt the homes of drifters and hippies.

We stopped near a gate and cracked open a packet of wine gums to celebrate Mike and George's completion of a hundred miles, and then plodded on in pleasant sunshine and a refreshing breeze.

Waternish is a relatively low-lying peninsula and possesses none of the high and dramatic cliff scenery of Dunvegan Head or Duirinish. However, it has a peaceful charm which is hard to pin down and is a perfect contrast to its lofty contenders. We passed Dun Gearymore further on but paid it little heed, and reached the end of the track near the ruined two-storey house of Unish. From here to the lighthouse at Waternish Point is less than a mile of tussocky grass and heather, but seemed endless. I needed sustenance, and our lunch stop at the lighthouse, my fourth of the walk, was very necessary.

It was a wild and stormy night on 28 June 1746 when an

unlikely vision of a six-oared boat with Flora MacDonald, her maidservant, Betty Burke, and a trusted follower appeared out of the gloom just off Waternish Point. The maidservant, dressed in flowered calico gown, a quilted petticoat, a hood, apron, mantle and a pair of cotton gloves, was, of course, none other than Bonnie Prince Charlie in disguise. Their trip 'over the sea to Skye' from the Outer Hebrides was rudely extended when their intention to land was thwarted by two sentries of the MacLeod militia who challenged them. They immediately turned and set course for Trotternish across Loch Snizort to land just north of Kilbride Point later that day.

Fully refreshed we resumed our trek, conscious of the fact that the next four or five miles were on completely pathless rough terrain which was, for all of us, virgin territory. Less than a mile further, Creag an Fhithich (Crag of the Raven) uncannily lived up to its name, the hoarse croaking of these largest of British crows sounding from high above. We stopped to watch the black, white and red Caledonian MacBrayne ferry ploughing its way from Uig to the Outer Isles. Less than a mile distant, we could easily make out figures on deck but doubted if they could see us. The long wake stretched out across Loch Snizort, north of the Ascrib Islands and back to Uig Bay, just visible on the lengthy northerly peninsula of Trotternish, still a few days walking away.

Sheep and short grass gave way to tussocky grass, heather and sphagnum moss for two tiring miles on featureless terrain. There were intermittent showers and our rainjackets were on and off

Stein

constantly. The 'pretty river' of Abhainn a'Ghlinne was crossed and we then stumbled across an unmarked muddy track leading to the road end at Geary. Tarmac walking was a relaxing change from four miles of heather bashing but the hard unforgiving surface soon caused aching feet and we still had four miles to go. From Geary to Gillen is an uninterrupted string of crofts and cottages, each with individual character and picturesque appeal, one with a remarkable fuschia hedge.

At Gillen I took the opportunity of checking the route for the day after tomorrow. I was perturbed by a large swathe of conifer plantation to the south which appeared to impinge directly on to the cliff-girt coastline. This would necessitate skirting round the forestry on the western side, avoiding the coastline – or so I thought. As it happened, I needn't have worried. There appeared to be a broad grassy platform between the trees and cliff edge which I assumed would stretch for the four miles in question.

Beyond the road-end at Gillen a muddy farm track led to a new forestry track of rolled black angular stones and rocks, obviously recently upgraded to remove felled timber, but not pleasant for walking. Emerging from the forest we warily passed a group of cows, calves and the odd unfriendly looking bull before rejoining the road just north of Stein. At 5.30pm we had completed the 18-mile Waternish loop – another chunk of Skye's coastline was in the bag and George and Mike's walking was over.

On arrival at the Inn we were informed that a certain Jim and Lucy would be coming over around 7.00pm. Jim (Scanlan) was a teaching colleague of mine and he and his wife had said that they would be on holiday in Skye and would try to rendezvous with me. I was thrilled that at last the clans were beginning to converge on the Stein Inn. Perhaps the Waternish welcome I had envisaged would materialise yet. As I showered and changed I had the feeling George and Mike's last night would be a memorable one.

Well before 7 o'clock the three of us had taken our places in the bar. Jim and Lucy arrived and introductions were made to George and Mike. Lucy is one of those rare individuals who is always at ease and puts other people at ease. An Australian, she possesses that outgoing, flamboyant personality which rarely stands on ceremony and is quick to call a spade a spade. Jim, by contrast, is a quieter more introverted individual who nevertheless has a healthy sense of cynicism and scepticism towards the petty nonsense of contemporary life. Together, they make an ideal couple with a sound, no-nonsense, down-to-earth attitude. I have much time for them both.

Having hoped to join us on the Waternish loop, Jim and Lucy were not too perturbed to discover that we had swapped days and had already completed it that day. We were all in the mood for a chatty, boozy, fun-filled evening and that is exactly what materialised. Personalities gelled perfectly. Lucy's bubbly character contrasted wonderfully with George's quiet, unassuming approach to life and their mutual fascination was interesting to observe.

Several trips were made outside, the first for group photographs, Guinness in hand, in front of the Inn. The remainder were also for photographic opportunities, as bright evening sunshine and showers produced stunning lighting effects in the way of rainbows and isolated sun-soaked 'Godspots'. An iron post displaying a picture of the Inn with an oystercatcher on a rock and surrounded by wrought iron decoration, made a photographic focus, with long evening rays outlining and highlighting its rainwashed features.

George discovered a scallop shell intact on the beach and Lucy, not to be outdone, rushed off to return with a mussel shell. The evening matured as rainbows and reflections were replaced by a smouldering sunset. Inside the cigar-smoke-filled inn Guinness was replaced by the peaty amber glow of Bowmore and five cheery red faces were flushed with fresh air, companionship and life itself. Without a doubt this had been the finest evening yet. My only regret was Heather's absence. In the heat of the moment we decided to book the Three Chimneys Restaurant for Saturday night when Heather would be at Edinbane. Mike and George would miss out but their wallets would be healthier!

Farewells that night were fond and heartfelt. Twilight slipped into darkness and our convivial evening slipped into oblivion, but our memories of it would stay strong.

* * * * *

It was unashamed luxury to crawl out of bed relatively late, casting off the invisible reins for a whole day. This, the eighteenth day of the expedition, was in fact the only day so far in which I would not walk an inch of coastline. The supposed rest day of a week ago at Carbost had entailed the Ardtreck loop with George and Mike – their introduction to a memorable week's walking.

I drifted downstairs to join them for a last breakfast before handing over my main pack which they would deliver at the Edinbane Hotel, my destination for tomorrow night. A final fond farewell and my two trusty companions were off. I was on my own again.

I made the decision to spend the remainder of the morning doing humdrum tasks of washing clothes, writing postcards and diary in order that the rest of the day could be spent in serious relaxation. I scrounged soap powder from the hotel and washed clothes and hung them out in a fresh drying breeze. I wrote postcards and diary in the restaurant over a delicious pot of real coffee. Stamps from a rucksack pocket proved to be non-stick following the deluge of a few days ago and surgical tape found a new use. The bar was my next venue for a long, leisurely lunch and a potter through the papers.

During the afternoon I wandered up to the Captain's House and Dandelion Designs, a craft shop, where I chatted to Pat Myhill, the bearded, softly-spoken English owner. As I entered, the atmospheric strains of gentle Celtic music flowed from a tape-player, while Pat sat at a table hunched intently over a piece of wood, completely engrossed in some sort of engraving. Closer inspection revealed the skilled use of a heated pen to literally burn an image on to a wooden plaque (usually sycamore), using the wood grain to suggest the lines of shore and hills. I was intrigued. Scores of finished plaques were displayed around the shop, and scenes of deserted beaches, crofts and hills, some with poetic inscriptions, made me feel very much at home.

I bought a copy of *Skyeviews*, a quarterly community magazine produced by Skye people for Skye people and interested visitors such as myself. The issue I bought (June 1996) contained a lengthy article by Pat Myhill on the history of Stein, which made fascinating reading.

The village was founded in 1787 by the British Fisheries Society whose main aim was to establish a series of such villages on the west coast of Scotland. From these noble intentions grew Tobermory on Mull, Ullapool, Wick and Lochbay on Skye (as Stein was originally known). Unfortunately, despite the expert services of Thomas Telford, with his grandiose plans for classical curving crescents of houses, wide streets, grand terraces, and a vision which exemplified the formal style of Georgian architecture, the scheme had foundered by 1800. This was also despite the fact that Stein had access to excellent fishing grounds and was the endpoint of what was reputedly Skye's first metalled road which began at Kylerhea (the original crossing point to the mainland). The failure of Stein to reach the heights of the other three model villages was probably due to a large extent to the sizeable land holdings, enabling settlers to live by their crofts alone and have little need of fishing.

However, the Stein which exists today undoubtedly contains the seed of Telford's original proposals and architectural historians have indicated that the smaller, simpler buildings of Stein acted as a catalyst, having a profound effect on Skye architecture as a whole.

As I wandered contentedly out to the pier in the warm afternoon sunshine and gazed back at the whitewashed row of cottages comprising MacLeod Terrace, I was enveloped in the peace and tranquil air of this tucked away gem. I was glad Stein wasn't any bigger. An unknown source had also said that Stein was to be the major port for connection to the Outer Isles (rather than Uig). Presumably if Telford's plans had gone ahead, this plan could have materialised.

The Inn itself has had quite a turbulent history, two of its land-lords having ended up behind bars for fraud! Very recently a plan emerged to demolish most of the original Inn and replace it with a massive out-of-character hotel complete with an 80-space car park cut into the hill behind. Thankfully, a protest campaign resulted in swift relegation of the scheme to the dustbin and the perpetrator to a penal institution – he being one of the fraudulent landlords.

The evening was quiet and relaxing after the jollifications of the previous night. I had plenty of time to muse over the Waternish welcome at Stein and indeed the two-and-a-half weeks walking so far. Less than a fortnight of footslogging remained. I really began to feel that I had broken the back of Skyewalk and conflicting emotions of wanting the trek finished but also my nomadic exis-tence to continue unsettled me. I needed to be walking again.

Route Summary: Dunvegan to Stein (including Waternish Loop)

Day 1: Dunvegan – Stein (15 miles – 24 km)

Follow the A850 north out of Dunvegan and continue on past the entrance to Dunvegan Castle on a minor road, eventually ending at Claigan. From here a track and path lead on to the famous coral beaches. Swing east into Lovaig Bay and gradually ascend the northern slopes of Beinn Bhreac, following the coastline above an obvious tier of cliffs. Descend to shore level in Loch Bay via a suit-able gully and follow the coastline to the mouth of Bay River. Cross the river and either continue round the coast to Stein or ascend to the B886 and reach Stein via the road.

Day 2: Stein – Stein via Waternish Point (18 miles – 29 km)

Follow the minor road north west out of Stein, ending at the vicin-ity of Trumpan Church. If time is available visit Ardmore Point. Follow the good track north past Dun Borrafiach ending at the ruin of Unish. Cross country out to the lighthouse at Waternish

Point. Swing round to follow trackless coastline for four miles to the road end at Geary. From Geary the road continues to Gillen where a forestry track crosses back over to the road leading to Stein.

Accommodation and other information

Stein: The Stein Inn (oldest inn on Skye) is a must (real ale, real food)

Enquire at the Inn about camping

Note: There is no grocery shop at Stein

CHAPTER 7

North to Trotternish

(Saturday 25 July – Tuesday 28 July)

Stein to Rubha Hunish

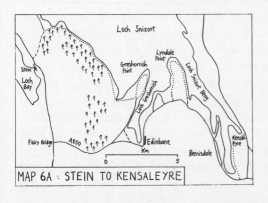

MAP 6A : STEIN TO KENSALEYRE

THE BACON ON MY breakfast plate bore an uncanny resemblance to Skye, the Trotternish peninsula ending in a grisly burnt fragment which I duly cut off. Seeing islands in rashers of bacon – was this the first signs of madness? My lone breakfast gave plenty of time to think of the next phase. The Stein Inn had been a pleasant intermission, and it was now time to move on, to regain the rhythm of walking and restore my restless spirit to the vagaries of Skye's rugged seaboard.

At 9.20 in cloudy close weather, I said my farewells and set off with bulging daypack containing night clothes, trainers, diary, maps, books, food, first aid kit, waterproofs, gaiters, jacket, water bottle and camera! I had borrowed Mike's day rucksack as it was slightly larger than mine.

The first objective was to regain the coast on the east side of the Waternish peninsula at the point where Mike, George and I had crossed back over to Stein two days ago. This prologue was accomplished in increasingly muggy, midgy conditions and I guessed the heavy air would mean rain by lunchtime. Half a mile south of Gillen, I branched off along a muddy track, sweat already pouring from me. Beyond a ruined house I discovered a split new forestry track unmarked on my 1991 map. Unfortunately, it didn't appear to be going my way and I opted for my original plan of following the line of Score Horan, a steep, vegetated inland cliff which rose high above the lost world of a densely forested barb of land enclosing Loch Losait. I felt fully justified in not literally hugging the edge of this thickly forested area and, anyway, in just over a mile Score Horan joined with the coastline once again.

A faint track meandered between forest and cliff edge on a tussocky grass ramp about six metres wide. Beyond the heathery unforested knoll of Cnoc Breac the track disappeared and the true coastal section from Biod nan Laogh (Cliff of the Calf?) was an agonisingly debilitating morass of deep heather, sphagnum moss, bracken, bog and trenches, with some tricky river gorges thrown in for good measure. The walking was nothing if not interesting.

Across the mottled grey expanse of Loch Snizort I could clearly discern the white cottages around Uig Bay, only about eight miles away, yet still a full two-and-a-half days of walking. Directly north, the Ascrib Islands were scattered like steel grey brush strokes, reputedly home to thousands of puffins. I had expected to see these delightful rainbow-beaked sea birds on my Skye odyssey but was disappointed and surprised to learn that they no longer nested on the island. I had only observed puffins once, on the cliffs near Cape Wrath at the end of Scotwalk '89.

The end of the forested section coincided with the weather's turn for the worse and my earlier prediction of rain became a depressing, dreich reality. Ahead, I could only just make out the Greshornish peninsula, a long tongue of smudgy grey undulations poking out to an even greyer washed-out ocean. It held not the slightest temptation, but was one of today's main objectives. The head of Loch Snizort is a five-fingered flourish of little peninsulas, the two main ones separated by the sea finger of Loch Greshornish and the other three poking into the long ribbon of Loch Snizort Beag.

Choking, soaking bracken-covered steep slopes led eventually down to the relative shelter of Loch Diubaig, a tiny cove where a home-made seat in the form of a wooden plank resting on stones made an obvious lunch stop. The rain was now unrelenting and I must have been a miserable sight. I thought of tonight and my first meeting with Heather for two-and-a-half weeks. I thought of our planned jaunt to The Three Chimneys and our rendezvous with Jim and Lucy. I may have been wet and cold, but these thoughts produced a warm fire within me which coaxed me through the next few damp hours.

On the other side of Loch Diubaig a path-cum-track led through a natural gap to Greshornish House beyond which a new natural stone cottage was situated. At this point I struck off for Greshornish Point, about a mile-and-a-half distant across a wet rolling blanket of fairly featureless terrain. Point 97 en route made a mildly interesting detour but was largely included in order to gain higher, drier ground. The theory was sound, the reality as unsound as the clinging morass beneath my squelching boots. Greshornish Point induced little stimulation in the dire conditions and the rain was now sweeping in sheets across the loch, the hills a mass of low cloud.

Various sheep tracks through bracken and tussocks took me back along the east side of the peninsula and to the welcoming feel of tarmac beneath my sodden boots. A mile-and-a-half of automated road walking led to the bleak lonely croft of Lowerglen where a shortcut led over the oddly named Lon Beatha (Marsh of Life) to the main A850 Dunvegan road. A final mile's stint of road tramping followed the loop of the bleak black ribbon to Edinbane, deriving its name – The Fair Face – from its pleasant situation at the head of Loch Greshornish. In today's miserable conditions there was no fair face, just a cheerless scowl.

Having stayed in Upper Edinbane on a previous holiday I was reasonably well acquainted with what I believed to be the only hotel in the village. This hotel was in fact The Lodge where I had imagined my rucksack to have been delivered by George and Mike. However, I discovered that it had been deposited at the Edinbane

Hotel, a different establishment entirely. Conditions as they were, I was glad to get in anywhere. At around 5 o'clock a bedraggled drowned rat of a walker reached the relative luxury of soft dry carpets, a bed and the prospect of a hot shower. Heather had not yet arrived but this meant there was time to remove stinking wet clothing, have a shower and look and smell reasonably human before greeting my wife whom I had not seen for nearly three long weeks.

Dewy-eyed expectancy completely enveloped me in those final few moments before I looked out to see Heather's tiny conspicuous off-green Fiat brighten up the dreary day as she drew up in the hotel driveway. My heart skipped a beat as I rushed downstairs to greet her. Few words were uttered as we hugged each other in an embrace which I wanted to last forever. For the next day or two Skye would take a back seat to the more immediate tender attentions of my one and only. In a flurry of excitement, emotion and tears, we serenaded each other back up to our room. Looking fresh-faced but travel-weary, Heather flopped on to the bed, her bump well pronounced, she being fully six months pregnant.

Our conversation bounced back and forth between both of our experiences during the last twenty days and then turned to the more pressing concern of our proposed rendezvous with Jim and Lucy at The Three Chimneys that evening. My understanding was that they were picking us up at 6.30 but when they had failed to arrive by 6.45 we decided to make our own way in Heather's car. Some thirty minutes later we arrived at the restaurant to find them pleasantly relaxed inside mulling over the mouthwatering menu, seemingly unconcerned about our lateness. Crossed lines somewhere down the line had somehow scrambled my brain into thinking that they were giving us a lift.

We did not fit into the general mould of a traditional evening dinner party, dressed as we were in trainers, jeans and tee-shirts (well, some of us were), and Lucy's prominent Australian drawl with equally prominent character gave us a demeanour somewhat out of place in the cottage-like surroundings. None of these observations struck me much at the time but were related later by Heather who tends to notice such things.

Two hours later and with wallets lighter by £65 per couple, we had enjoyed a three course meal with drinks which was undoubtedly a cut above the rest. The evening had mellowed into dreamy conversation over liqueurs and coffee, different from the Stein Inn of two nights ago, but in its intimate way just as memorable – more so with Heather's company. Outside we parted with hugs, kisses, handshakes and good lucks for the remainder of the walk. We went our separate ways and on the morrow I would once again go mine, but with Heather' presence in the background.

* * * * *

After rain for most of the night, Sunday 26 July emerged sluggishly in a gloomy grey dawn. We were loath to rise, and a brief glance outside revealed heavy uninviting rain-bearing clouds and squalls of rain which turned to myriad silver spears on the black puddles of the car park. The thought of trekking out to the head of a girth of peninsulas in these conditions, when I could be indoors with Heather, did not exactly fire my spirit and I was determined to finish the day's walking as quickly as possible. I knew the temptation to miss out a few smaller peninsulas was doubly strong in the poor weather and the presence of Heather, but the reality as always would be a fine line between two extremes.

My intended finishing point today was the small settlement of Kensaleyre, a mere eleven miles by road. North of the road, one major peninsula and three minor ones poked their fingers out into Loch Snizort and Loch Snizort Beag, making a true coastal circuit a switchback of almost twice this distance. The day would determine which of these polarised options I would drift closer towards. At least I would be carrying a light daypack as we were booked in at the Edinbane Hotel for that evening.

By 10.15am I was off, leaving Heather to go and buy Sunday papers and find a church to attend Catholic Mass. I, being a non-Catholic, and in a sense non-religious, declined such things, gleaning my spiritual highs from intimate bonding with the natural world, though on a day like today I would have preferred intimate bonding with other things. We had arranged to meet in Kensaleyre

151

from 3.30pm onwards, with nearer 5 o'clock being more realistic. This time frame would force me to cut my coastal walking cloth to suit the feel of the day.

Dressed in full wet weather gear, I trudged along the A850 past Borve Campsite where I had originally intended to camp. A police car sped by, the first I had seen on Skye since the walk had begun, an indication of the relatively crime-free state of the island. A tiny corrugated iron Wee Free church contrasted remarkably with the grand white crow-stepped gabled one at the mouth of the river Tora. The Kildonan loop road was omitted, despite its wandering nearer to the coastline, in the pretence that it was more meaningful (at least if all else failed) to make an attempt on Lyndale Point, the tip of the first and major peninsula of the day.

At a forested section I finally forsook the easy security of the road and followed a track out to Lyndale Farm. From here it was a literal bog-slogging tussocky trek northwards to the trig-pointed high spot of Torr a'Chruidh (Hillock of the Horseshoe). A further half-mile across a wide valley saw me standing forlornly on a secondary high point, once more saturated from boots upward and hood downward, in a steady depressing drizzle. Through the gloom I could see Lyndale Point and that was enough. I returned along the eastern edge of the peninsula through pockets of bedraggled bog-cotton, their normally sprightly white heads now bent and bowed, heavy with moisture. When I finally reached the road I had completed the hour-and-a-half detour – I felt reasonably pleased that this hurdle was over.

Now conscious of time, I stormed the next few road miles, deciding to omit a visit to the promontory of Rubha nan Cudaigean and the little settlement of Knott, though in different circumstances I mused that this would be an interesting side excursion. The next mini-peninsula of The Aird was also by-passed despite the presence of a mile-long minor road going almost to the tip. As I strode through Bernisdale along the old road which runs parallel to the main road, pangs of guilt seized me and I was determined to make a mark on the more pronounced final peninsula of Skerinish which lay between here and Kensaleyre.

I discovered that sizeable sections of the A850 could be by-passed using the old road, but beyond the Skeabost House Hotel this became very overgrown with bushes touching each other from both sides. I was amazed at how quickly and effectively nature's hand took over from that of man's.

Skeabost means 'the sheltered house' and it is dominated by the hotel, a late Victorian house with a splendid interior of pine panelling, huge stone fireplaces, old baths, oil portraits, a library and a richness redolent of a bygone era. The hotel even has its own small golf course which was visible from the old road. In 1539 a gory battle between the MacLeods and MacDonalds took place in Skeabost and a number of dismembered heads were later seen floating down the river Snizort. Skeabost was the birthplace of Mary MacPherson, a Skye poet, who was sentenced to a term of imprisonment for an alleged petty crime, much to the outrage of herself and local people. During her eleven-year spell in confine-ment, her frustration and rage culminated in a series of poems expressing disgust with the Clearances. She died in Portree in 1898 and a plaque to her memory was erected in 1966 at Skeabost.

Beyond the vicinity of the hotel I crossed the river Snizort (thankfully bereft of floating heads) by an old stone bridge and turned off left following a minor road towards two houses. A vague path gradually ascended bracken-covered slopes and disap-peared in a large copse of trees where I was rewarded by the sight of a short-eared owl fluttering between the branches. There was a grand view across Loch Snizort Beag of the Skeabost House Hotel sitting in isolated grandeur under a canopy of trees. As I left the shadow of the forest, the weather finally began to lift out of the doldrums and patches of blue sky appeared with a watery sun turning millions of water beads on the grass into sparkling dia-monds. Waterproofs were shed and sweat poured off me as I climbed higher to Tote House. I crossed the boggy shoulder of Ben Tote and reached the narrow road which led to Skerinish House.

It was now twenty to four and I was fully aware that Heather would now be waiting in Kensaleyre, only a direct mile away. Beyond Skerinish House the map indicated a fort and chambered cairn on a small knoll which would probably have been worth a visit. With time pressing, however, I reluctantly followed the road to the house before heading downhill on a path which gradually faded into boggy ground lower down. Whilst descending, I spied a tiny green dot by the church in Kensaleyre which I recognised immediately as Heather's car. By ten past four I was there to greet my wife, who was happily ensconced knitting a tiny suit for our forthcoming arrival in October. I had imagined she would have seen me descending the hill but she had been too wrapped up in her knitting.

I was surprised to learn that she still hadn't been to Mass. The three o'clock one at Broadford would have suited but she didn't want to be late to meet me. She planned to run me back to Edinbane where I would shower and change while she headed to Portree for the five o'clock service. Back at the hotel, in Heather's absence, I made myself presentable, wrote my diary and settled down with a copy of *The Sunday Post*, a paper which doesn't place heavy demands on the brain. An article on tics, those horrible little insects which burrow themselves into the skin, made interesting but rather disturbing reading, especially since I had been the object of their unwelcome attention during the walk. Various horrific phrases such as facial paralysis, meningitis, heart trouble, arthritis, Lyme's disease, shot out of the page and into my consciousness with alarming force. Surely one miserable little beasty couldn't be responsible for all these ailments? I took comfort in the fact that I had no red rashes (yet) which are an early symptom of Lyme's disease, an ailment producing semi-paralysis.

Following Heather's return from Mass at Portree, we decided to opt for a cheaper alternative to last night's extravaganza and drove to Dunvegan for fish and chips in the hotel bar. The return to Edinbane was a delight in the soft evening light and gentle conversation helped me unwind from the rigours of the day. Two pints were downed in the lounge bar at Edinbane before we retired to our room. It was wonderful to have an early night.

* * * * *

The second morning in Edinbane dawned cloudy and drizzly and

Heather's deliberations about heading back south today or tomor-row were over – she would go today. Bag packing was unusually complicated. There was a small pack for carrying today, a main pack to be dumped at the Duntulm Hotel for tomorrow night, a small bag of night clothes to be left at tonight's destination of Uig and another bag for Heather to take home!

During the drive back to Kensaleyre with Heather, the rain fell in sheets and the rhythmic beat of the wipers together with the heat of the car had a soporific effect on my already dulled senses. There was a flat end-of-holiday feel to the morning and, for a moment, I felt like just giving up and driving back south with my wife. I seemed to be cornered, checkmated by the pawns of fate which dictated Skye weather. Ironically, it was the drive north to Trotternish's tip which enlivened and revitalised my flagging spir-its. By Uig, blue skies had broken free from the strangle-hold of low cloud and by Duntulm it was another world of warm sun-shine and renewed optimism.

The Duntulm Hotel is the most northerly hotel on Skye and although it wasn't on my pre-booked accommodation itinerary, it certainly featured highly as a wet weather alternative. I only hoped that whoever was in charge would allow me to leave a pack there for a couple of days. A good dose of 'I'm doing this for charity' and 'the hotel would be rated highly in the subsequent book', etc, seemed to work wonders and my pack had a safe home until tomorrow night. We returned south to Uig to drop off evening clothes at the Ferry Inn before finally rejoining the cloud and over-cast skies at Kensaleyre Church where I had met Heather the day before.

Fond and fervent goodbyes were made and we hugged as we had hugged on Heather's arrival at Edinbane less than two days ago. Our brief encounter on our island had been all too brief and at twelve noon I took to the road with a spring in my step but a tear in my eye. It would be ten days before we would meet again.

By road from Kensaleyre to Uig was only nine miles, but it lay at an infuriating just-too-far-from-the-coast distance to be realisti-cally construed as a coastal walk, and I knew a good proportion of today's trek would need to be off-road in order to satisfy my coastal ambitions. The first few miles were fine, the road less than half-a-mile from Loch Snizort Beag, and a steady plod in steady drizzle took me to the turn off left to the township of Kingsburgh, a corruption of Cisborg or tax-town, built at the entrance to Loch Snizort in order to levy taxes on passing ships. On the night of 29 June 1746, Bonnie Prince Charlie slept at Kingsburgh House after a dreary midnight walk from Monkstadt (north of Uig). Boswell and Johnson were entertained in this very same house in 1772 and Dr Johnson, hearing the story of the Prince's wanderings, actually slept in the same bed as had Charlie. The Laird of Kingsburgh at this time was none other than the husband of the legendary Flora Macdonald who had been Charlie's guiding Skye-light. Boswell narrates:

'There was a comfortable parlour with a good fire, and a dram went round. By and by supper was served, at which there appeared the lady of the house, the celebrated Miss Flora Macdonald. She is a little woman, of a genteel appearance, and uncommonly mild and well bred. To see Dr Samuel Johnson, the great champion of the English Tories, salute Miss Flora Macdonald in the Isle of Skye, was a striking sight; for though somewhat congenial in their notions, it was very improbable they should meet here.'

The Kingsburgh House in question is sadly no longer, but the present house sits pleasantly within trees not far from the site of the old one. All this was second-hand information as the miserable weather did not readily inspire a visit. I had already discovered substantial stretches of old road which I eagerly adopted, thus relieving the drudgery of a hard road and heavy traffic – if only for a short while. It wasn't until about a kilometre past Hinnisdale Bridge that I finally found a half-decent track going left in the direction of the coast. Beyond a farmhouse, a mud-bath track led to a ruined castle which I had spotted on the map – Caisteal Uisdein, or Hugh's Castle. As castles go, this one was a small affair, a plain rectangular stone construction perched on a small hillock with cliffs dropping thirty feet or so to the sea. A barbed wire fence surrounded it with various intrusive signs claiming 'Danger – steep cliffs' and 'Do not enter – falling masonry'. The second demand seemed somewhat self-regulating as I could find no sign of a door. Had it been blocked up, I wondered? I thought it strange that this castle, being fairly out of the way and un-sign-posted, had such a profusion of danger signs whereas Dunsgaith, way back in Sleat, had none and was in a more dangerous state with easier access. Subsequent research showed that the castle had been built in the 16th century as a monument to Uisdean MacGhilleasbuig Chleirich, one of Skye's more murky characters, who had hatched a plan to murder his chief. His evil intentions were discovered when the letter outlining his plan was sent by mistake to the chief himself rather than to a close friend. The unfortunate Hugh was duly captured and taken to the dungeon at Duntulm Castle where he was fed on salt beef and salt fish without water until he died of thirst. More of this later...

I lunched peacefully in the lee of the castle, a friendly meadow pipit swooping and diving around the walls to land on the fence in the hope of a titbit. At the same time a welcome ray of sunshine appeared – a column of light breaking through the curtains of cloud signalling a vast improvement in the weather. Within minutes I was bathed in warm sunshine and blessed with renewed vigour. I continued north on freshly cut meadow grass. A tractor passed by and the driver gave a friendly wave, seemingly unconcerned to see a walker where none would usually be. The beautifully secluded and sheltered bay of Poll na h-Ealaidh (Pond of the Song) was soon reached with its sprinkling of white crofts and cottages – a veritable revelation of timeless serenity. A group of children played and splashed about in the blue sea, their far off laughter ringing and underscoring high summer, creating flashes of my own distant childhood. I crossed a tinkling, trickling burn and nodded to a woman cutting grass at the side of her well-groomed cottage.

Cuidrach (the name of the settlement) is connected to the main Uig road by a winding single-track road which I shunned in favour of a path north past a larger house and through the gap between

Cnoc Fadail and Cnoc Steud. This was a heat-trap, a verdant oasis of sweet smelling gorse bushes and a maze of sheep tracks. I scuttled along feeling on top of the world. Uig was hardly three miles distant and it was only three o'clock. I had every reason to be satisfied and content. Once again life was wonderful.

A mile on I crossed fields and passed through a wooden gate, dropping steeply down an overgrown path to the deserted pebble beach at Camas Beag (Little Bay), a smaller nibble out of the bigger bite of Uig Bay itself. I lingered, before climbing up beyond the burn to follow the edge of the cliffs forming the eastern boundary of Camas Beag. Rhythm was frustratingly hampered by a profusion of barbed wire fences, but in the vicinity of Rubha Riadhain the clifftop heath was a riot of wild flowers. Tiny white eye-bright, purple orchids, trailing St John's wort, thyme and delicate yellow tormentil made a lush and colourful carpeted foreground to the rippled blue-grey surface of Uig Bay and Ru Idrigill.

Beyond the point of Rubha Riadhain a fast flowing stream cut a steep furrow in the hillside and I reluctantly made a beeline for the main road via a newish house and driveway north of Earlish. Sauntering along the road I enjoyed fine views of Uig, the name literally translating as bay, some say one of the most beautiful on Skye, though I could not agree. The more gentle intimate charms of Poll na h-Ealaidh an hour or so ago were more worthy of comment. The final mile downhill was a pleasant and fitting end to a textbook day. A tourist was crouched in a field, camera in hand, taking photographs of white ponies against a background of Uig's round tower, a folly built by a certain Captain Fraser, who owned much of the surrounding land in the 19th century. A grand villa, which he also built for himself overlooking the bay, was swept away in a massive storm in 1877 when the River Conon broke its banks.

At 4.30 I reached the rustic charms of the Ferry Inn. At four-and-a-half hours this was the shortest day's walking so far. A long, lazy, boozy evening lay ahead – if this was roughing it I wanted more. Two hours later I was sitting at the window of my bedroom watching a Cal-Mac Ferry ploughing a grand fan-like furrow through the waters of the bay heading for the Outer Isles. The introduction of the car-ferry to the Outer Hebrides in 1964 has put Uig on the map and drawn it from its pastoral backwater status.

Next door I could hear a couple arguing, so I put on the television to drown their din. The weather forecast was awful for the next few days but I had at last learned to ignore these – Skye has its own set of weather rules. I switched off the television and immersed myself in a copy of the *Daily Mail* which seemed more like a life-style magazine than a messenger of current events. An article on an amazing character who was attempting to 'run the world' caught my eye. Apparently he was only days away from breaking the 10,603 miles distance running record, yet his incredible journey was only half completed with Australia, the Americas and Africa still to go. He was running the full length of every continent. After dodging bullets, escaping bandits and negotiating police roadblocks in Tibet he commented 'I hope my effort shows that people can use their legs more for getting about'. A comparison of his monumental task with my paltry 360-mile walk round Skye made my efforts seem like a stroll in the park. We all do things for different reasons. I am sure the return on my investment was just as great – if not greater – than Mr Marathon Man.

It wasn't long before I gravitated towards the bar and homed in on the Ferry Inn fraternity. I sat on a stool at the bar tucking into an excellent meal while listening to Van Morrison and Tom Petty and the Heartbreakers. The barman was a Geordie, a jovial character and a great talker. The owner of the Ferry Inn was a lightly-built, grey-bearded Irishman who had visited Uig years before and vowed that he would eventually return to live here. He must have loved Skye to forsake the Emerald Isle for the Winged Isle. Both being keen photographers, we had a stimulating discussion on the merits of Skye as a photographer's paradise.

The evening developed into a full-blown drinking binge and locals and visitors blended and bevvied together in that unique, cordial atmosphere that is only found in a few pubs on a few nights. I felt lucky I was in such a pub on such a night but then, maybe I had something to do with it, being in a blethery mood. Sitting at the bar was a smartly dressed young man with dark-rimmed glasses who had never left Skye in his life. He watched every single TV soap religiously and had them taped if he was unable to see them live. I thought back to the Old Inn at Carbost and a girl who had also never been off the island – maybe I could introduce them ...

Well into the evening, when I was fairly 'well-oiled', the owner came over and thrust a mobile phone into my hand. Heather's voice came over loud and clear intimating her safe arrival back in Perthshire. She seemed glad that I was obviously enjoying myself in a semi-intoxicated state, but not surprised! Minutes after the phone-call I was offered a delicious curry-based dish consisting of chillies, garlic, herbs and other unidentified ingredients, made by the owner himself – an on-the-house surprise which went down a treat after countless pints of ale. More pints and a few drams later I was handed my one and only walking breathable T-shirt which had been washed and put out on the line to dry. Unfortunately, some bright spark had decided to finish it off in the tumble dryer. Being a type of nylon man-made fibre, it ended up with several small holes produced by the intense heat. A not dissimilar thing happened on Scotwalk '89, when a Helly Hanson top was ironed – the heat caused the material to melt and stick to the iron. Thankfully, I was too far gone to really notice or really care and stole off to my room having enjoyed thoroughly the craic of the evening. I was aware of nothing until the following morning.

* * * * *

I sat at the breakfast table with a thick head, staring out at a wind-less humid morning and gulping down orange juice in a vain attempt to rehydrate my listless body. After breakfast, as I packed in my room I glanced outside to see heavy rain, and consoled myself with the possibility that it might clear the humidity. An incoming ferry loomed out of the grey and approached the pier, its tannoy system fully audible. Despite the rain, I wasted no time in setting off, making a quick visit to the shop for fruit, chocolate and drinks.

I was well aware that today would be highly significant. It was the day I hoped to reach the northernmost point of Skye. From there all roads led south and back to my starting point at Kylerhea. A relatively short day, an estimated thirteen miles, the route was largely on fairly unspectacular coast until the vicinity of Rubha Hunish at Trotternish's northern tip.

Initially I followed the main road looping in a wide arc round the bay until it hair-pinned back to head north over the moor. At the hairpin I forsook the road for a rough path clinging to the steep southern slope of Creag Liath, and a short while later I was standing by the cairn above Ru Idrigill, the northern promontory of Uig Bay. The rain was now off, but ominous low cloud was spilling tendrils over the low-lying muted green hills across the bay. I set off north on a path leading steeply down to green swathes of sheep-shorn raised beach. Ahead, a prominent rocky knoll, labelled Dun Skudiburgh on the OS map, is actually Skudaborg (Norse origin). To its left, a large basaltic sea stack known as the Stack of Skudiburgh, was dwarfed by the knoll. I suddenly heard barking ahead and two collie dogs appeared from nowhere seemingly resenting the presence of an intruder. I decided to ascend the knoll and was quite surprised to discover the dun in a reasonable state of preservation (relative to some other Skye duns).

The dun was an excellent vantage point for the next stage of my route north, a broad mottled green expanse of low-lying moor, its left edge a wriggling line of unbroken coastline as far as the eye could see. From here it looked easy enough but the reality was to prove different. I made my way down and attempted to follow the shoreline. I was soon forced up on to long, wet, tussocky grass, alternating with endless stretches of bog and a string of awkward fences. Sheep and cows looked on curiously.

Bonnie Prince Charlie's intended landing place on Skye (after his stormy sail from South Uist) had been Waternish Point, but he was thwarted by militia who were stationed there. His actual landing place was the wide bay between Kilbride Point and Prince Charles's Point, where I stopped for a breather and bite to eat.

From here, the Prince's Skye guardian, Flora Macdonald, had gone up to Monkstadt House, about half-a-mile distant, to seek help from her kinswoman, Lady Macdonald, only to discover that soldiers searching for the Prince were camping nearby, while their captain was actually in the house. Cool as a cucumber she chatted to him and diverted his suspicions when he questioned her about the Prince. Later that afternoon the party set off south for Kingsburgh.

Monkstadt (Monk's Town) derives its name from the monastery which once stood on the island in Loch Chaluim Chille (Saint Columba's Loch). A glance at the OS map shows Eilean Chaluim Chille (Island Chaluim Chille) on flat contourless ground north of Monkstadt, riven with drainage ditches. The loch has long since been drained but its location is obvious from the map. Monkstadt, now a ruin, was built in 1732 and is reckoned to be the first house on Skye to have had a slated roof.

Somewhere on the long dreary stretch of coastline north of Prince Charles's Point I made the decision to cut directly across the moor to reach Camas Mor, thus omitting Rubh a' Chairn Leith, a rounded headland which didn't appear to hold much interest. In retrospect it may well have given me less toil to have stuck rigidly to the shoreline. A wet and boggy mile-and-a-half later I arrived at the road end by the Sgeir Lang slipway. My boots were so sodden that I fished some old Sunday newspapers out of a nearby waste-bin to stuff them with later. I lunched at two well-placed picnic tables just as a watery sun brightened up the rather sombre gloom of the day.

I wandered up the narrow road and passed several pleasant cottages before coming across an old farm building with a green corrugated iron roof and brightly coloured door and windows. On the wall was a sign 'Macurdie's Exhibition' and on the door a second sign proclaiming 'Open – just come in'. I was surprised to say the least – what on earth was an exhibition doing in some far-flung corner of Skye? An exhibition of what? My inquisitiveness drew me to a small poster on the window with the question 'What is Macurdie's Exhibition?' Underneath were a variety of visitors' comments such as 'unique', 'Pure dead brill', 'hilarious', 'bizarre', 'unbelievable', 'Nothing like this in Texas', and other superlatives which obviously smacked of a totally off-the-wall experience. Underneath these comments was written 'Now in its 6th year and slightly world famous. What have you got to lose but your marbles? Come and have a look.' How could I refuse such a zany invitation? Anyone with any sense of imagination, curiosity and fun could not fail to accept the offer. I removed my pack, propped it up on the wall outside and entered the creaky door, expecting the unexpected.

Inside what appeared to be an old animal byre was at first glance a random collection of assorted items and pieces of script written on wooden boards. Closer inspection revealed humour of Monty Python brand and proportions. An old set of weighing scales contained a wooden white painted fish with the word 'Glasgow' written on it. On the wall above was the remark 'A Big Plaice'. Hanging on the wall was a puppet figure mouthing the words 'Excuse me. Have you ever seen Macurdie's wife?' Next to this was an old electricity meter mouthing the reply: 'No, but I'd love to meter'. A section on 'common seabirds' showed a shaving razor sitting on an old gas-bill (razorbill), a rubber gloved 'hand' grabbing an oyster-shell (oystercatcher) and a miniature highlander with bagpipes standing on sand (sandpiper). These were just a tiny number of a huge selection of deliciously outrageous, offbeat, madcap items which kept me occupied for a full half-hour. The exhibition was obviously the brainchild of someone with a creative imagination and a sense of humour to match. I would have loved to meet the creator – he had surely cheered up the hearts of many a visitor on a dreich Skye day, including myself. I gladly paid a fifty pence donation (as requested) and returned outside with a wry smile on my face.

The surreal nature of the day, spawned by Macurdie's Exhibition, further manifested itself just a few moments later further up the road in the shape of a weird bunch of hippily dressed mums and kids. One of the women was clothed in black skintight trousers with white polka dots. Coloured beads were draped round her neck and her matted hair was a profusion of coloured rags. The others' dress was a variation on this New Age theme.

The map indicated I was in the hamlet of Kilmuir, a typical Skye straggle of crofts strung across several hundred acres. The Gaelic name of Am Fearann Stapagach translates as 'the land of cream' but it is also fairly fertile, being also known as the Granary of Skye. Kilmuir Churchyard contains a granite memorial to Flora Macdonald and Johnson's tribute: 'A name that will be mentioned in history and, if courage and fidelity be virtues, mentioned with honour'.

I made a slight detour across a field blazing with buttercups to photograph the stark remains of a large church with just a gable end and two walls left standing. In the background an ominously black sky hung heavy over the shadowed scarp slopes of Suidh 'a 'Mhinn – the weather was worsening again.

I briskly continued on up to the main road and turned north, anxious to put in some easy road miles to Duntulm, now only about three miles distant. Less than a mile up the road the tourist honeypot of the Blackhouse Museum and the monument to Flora Macdonald was buzzing with swarms of noisy trippers pouring out of vast air-conditioned coaches. This was not the Skye I was looking for and I gave it the thumbs down. I passed the mile-long Score Bay and out to the left on a raised beach I spotted several tell-tale ruins amongst the tangle of bracken; residual relics of the Clearances yet again. And so on to Duntulm, an area steeped in history and legend and boasting a fine hotel where I retrieved my main pack and negotiated the filling of water bottles. True to Skye form, the sun made an appearance once again and a night at the hotel was not an option.

A short distance from the hotel stands the remains of the ancient Duntulm Castle perched precariously on a rocky headland rising sheer from the waters of the Minch. Originally a Pictish fortress forming one of a chain of duns or forts across the north coast of Skye, it was seized by the Vikings and held by them until they lost control of the island after The Battle of Largs in 1263. Almost 300 years later, King James V commented on its commanding position, strength and charm, and it was around this time that the castle began to look as it does today, albeit a lot less ruinous. Traditionally, Duntulm is a MacDonald stronghold, the first mention of a MacDonald chief occupying the castle being in 1616, when Donald Gorm set about improving the existing building. It is said that he moved here from Dunsgaith Castle in the Sleat peninsula, the castle I had visited en route to Ord from Point of Sleat nearly three weeks ago. The castle was abandoned around 1730 in favour of Monkstadt, the house mentioned previously and supposedly built by stones from Duntulm. Behind Duntulm Hotel is the little hill of Cnoc Roll (Hill of Rolling) which takes it name from a rather gruesome ancient test. A wrongdoer was rolled down the hill in a sealed barrel. If he survived without injury he was set free, otherwise he was taken to another hillock where he was judged by the Chief. If able to make a good case of his innocence he might be released. Failing that he was taken to a third hill, called Cnoc na Croiche or Hanging Knoll, where he met his end.

The sheer magic and romanticism of this northern tip of Skye's great Trotternish wing is gracefully captured by Alexander Smith in *A Summer in Skye* as he is gazing out from a window in the Duntulm Hotel:

'Through the window I beheld the spectral castle, the sea on which the light was dying, the purple fringe of Harris on the horizon. And seated there, in the remotest corner of Skye, amongst people whom I had never before seen, girt by walls of cliffs and the sounding sea, in a region, too, in which there was no proper night, I confess to have been conscious of a pleasant feeling of strangeness, of removal from all customary conditions of thought and locality, which I like at times to recall and enjoy over again.'

Having spent a night with Heather in the Duntulm Hotel after a glorious fiery sunset, I knew exactly what he meant.

Duntulm Castle

For most folk with little time and lots of money, Duntulm is the north of Skye. A glance at the map, however, reveals a wild cliff-girt peninsula poking another mile-and-a-half north to the true northerly point of Rubha Hunish. I had half a notion of camping there, but had got wind of a useful little hut from Hamish Brown which could offer some overnight refuge. I had visited Rubha Hunish on a previous occasion and could vouch for the existence of this hut but was still tempted to wild camp at the Point itself. The next hour or so would tell ...

In strengthening sun and clearing skies I set off along the rocky beach below the castle, finding the weight of a full pack a shock to the system. I could scarcely believe that the last occasion I had carried a full load was on day seven while en route from Camasunary to Glenbrittle – this was now day twenty-two. I had enjoyed a fortnight of light loads but I knew my last week could be very similar to the first.

North of the castle is the big bite of Tulm Bay, with rocky teeth, and the long sliver of Tulm Island, a prominent wedge backed by scattered skerries far beyond. I slithered and stumbled along seaweed-covered rocks, taking delight in the wonderful light and the rock pipits flitting and dipping in darting displays. A flock of herring-gulls made a raucous din almost as if welcoming the return of the sunny weather.

Towards the end of the bay I turned to photograph the sun-dappled scene. In the foreground, a lichen-encrusted rock pavement was riven with deep channels. In the middle distance, the low-lying moor and hills caught the sun in a display of translucent luminosity, their flanks dotted with brilliant white cottages, the more substantial form of the Duntulm Hotel stealing the show. The whole of this water-colour scene was backed by the brooding, dark, crouching line of hills marking the start of the great Trotternish spine marching southward to Portree in a twisting twenty-mile switchback.

Beyond the bay I began the 100-metre climb up the southerly top of Meall Tuath (North Hill) and flopped down in the heather for a breather, the heavy pack of prime concern. In the space of only fifteen minutes since my last photo stop the lighting had changed remarkably. The grand sweep of sheep-studded green before me was awash with sun and the Trotternish spine beyond had relinquished its scowl for a fresh, friendly profile. The short climb had brought me into a gentle cooling breeze carrying the briny scent of the seashore. There was a halcyon, heavenly feel to those few precious moments which was a tonic to the soul. At the top of this hill the view is a revelation to those who are paying a first visit to this secluded spot. Beyond and below, the final tongue of green sward pushes out for half a mile to the last of Skye at Rubha Hunish. There is a truly Lost World sensation to this remarkable little peninsula, for its access is barred by a curving bastion of sheer cliffs seemingly offering no chink in their armour. However, between here and Meall Tuath is a deep, natural furrow which gives access to the only break in the cliffs.

I crossed this furrow and made the short climb to Meall Tuath where stood the small building which could be my home for the night – a tiny, flat-roofed, long since deserted coastguard's hut, perched almost on the edge of sheer cliff, dropping 300 feet to the Hunish peninsula below. I entered the musty interior, removed my pack and looked around. Unlike the gloomy innards of a stone bothy, there was a bright, almost spacious feel to the place, created entirely by the presence of the extensive look-out window on three sides of the front of the building. A wooden high chair was positioned at the window in front of a broad shelf table and to its right along the wall below the window was a full length bunk-type sofa with a foam pile base covered with old curtain material. An ancient stone fireplace was set into the back corner by the door with a makeshift pipe and teapot serving as a chimney flue. On the white wooden panelled wall was a slightly mildewed, badly faded map of north Skye. To the left of the entrance door was a bunkroom with the latest in air-conditioning – a nine-inch diameter hole in the wall open to the elements.

Within seconds I made the decision to stay and began spreading wet gear, food items, stove, plastic bags and assorted paraphernalia on every level surface. I secretly hoped I would get the place to myself. I decided also to postpone the trip out to Rubha Hunish until tomorrow morning, thus giving me a long, lazy evening to relax in this unique refuge.

Sitting on the high chair and gazing out to sea was a bit like being at the helm of a ship, I surmised. There was a wonderful edge-of-the-world feel, with an expansive panoramic vista of a silky, sparkling ocean, intermittently encrusted with fleeting filaments of diamond-like brilliance as shifting shafts of sunlight caught the surface. A tiny black fishing boat silhouetted in the low sun drifted lazily across the scene, producing a fine filigree of lacy phosphorescence in its wake. The jet-black, back-lit skerries of Fladda-chuain and Sgeir nam Maol were rocky anchors on this shifting stage, while way beyond, the nebulous brush-strokes of the Shiants and Outer Hebrides hung amorphously on the razor-sharp horizon.

I cast my mind back three weeks to the lonely lighthouse at the Point of Sleat, the churning grey ocean and the dismal weather. That was the southernmost tip of Skye when the walk was barely a pup. Since then I had traversed the whole western seaboard of the Winged Isle; 250 miles of contorted coastline to the northernmost tip. In the same way that the Point of Sleat had been a pivotal point of the journey, so was Rubha Hunish: a point from which to view past and future in clearer perspective – except that now there was much less future.

After my meal I amused myself by reading through the various comments in the bothy-book – an old notebook in which people could record their feelings. Some of the entries made compulsive and fascinating reading ... 'I can't believe I found a book here. I can't believe this pen works and, of course, I can't believe this place is real. Who is setting me a trap?' Someone with a more poetic turn of phrase was obviously as impressed with the place as I:

'Not just a view but a feeling
The colours, the sound
The waves and the wind
With us but far away.

Not just a place, it's a space
to belong or be gone
In yourself or in others
Each to his own
will take away
an unforgettable memory'   (Sarka-Jo, 29 June 1996)

For me, these few lines seemed to say it all.

A couple of other users expressed their admiration in a more practical way by apparently hiding three bottles of 10-year-old Talisker whisky and ten pounds in a tin box within a 100-yard radius of the hut. This alleged action was validated a few pages on when someone reported finding the first two bottles. Further proof was evident with the existence of two empty Talisker bottles used as candle-holders on the window ledge. And the third bottle? I spent a half-hearted ten-minute spell outside searching but expected nothing and found nothing. With a 300 foot drop less than ten yards from the building and in fading light, I didn't feel even a bottle of malt was worth the risk.

In those last hours of gloaming on that magical evening, a malt would have gone down well, but I was already experiencing utter, inner calm and a profound sense of spirituality. The absolute silence and peace of this place was uplifting and inspiring. I saw the mainland Applecross hills bathed in late evening sunshine away across to the eastern horizon. The grass was waving in the wind just outside but I couldn't hear a thing. I felt as if I was almost floating, caught in a timeless snapshot. I imagined this place would be the spiritual highlight of the walk, in utter contrast to the social highlight of the Stein Inn.

I looked up to see a strong pinprick of light winking on and off far across the Minch, somewhere on the Outer Hebrides, and immediately thought of the weak struggling light of Sleat lighthouse. I had journeyed a metaphorical lifetime since that gloomy day. The kaleidoscope of events and experiences which had unfolded between these two geographical extremities were now only memories – but what wonderful memories.

Route Summary: Stein to Rubha Hunish

Day 1: Stein – Edinbane (14 miles – 22 km)

Retrace the last two miles of the Waternish loop route, following the forest track. At GR269591 turn off right along a muddy path to a ruin and a new forest track. Follow the forest edge along a grassy promenade above the cliffs of Score Horan to the vicinity of Biod nan Laogh. Continue to keep to the coastline on awkward pathless terrain above the cliffs. Several river gorge crossings are unavoidable. At the end of the forest, traverse hummocky, heathery hillside until the little bay of Loch Diubaig is reached. Follow a path round the head of the bay and either leave it before it heads towards Greshornish House to follow the western boundary of the Greshornish peninsula, or continue to the House and reach Greshornish point from there. Return along vague sheep tracks on the eastern side and reach the road at Greshornish House. At Lowerglen take a track across the Lon Beatha to reach the A850 road leading to Edinbane in less than a mile.

Day 2: Edinbane – Kensaleyre (15 miles – 24 km)

Depending on how religiously the coastline is adhered to, this route can be in excess of 20 miles. From Edinbane follow the A850 north past Borve campsite. The first major peninsula ends at Lyndale Point and this can be reached via the track to Lyndale House. The Kildonan loop road is optional. Return from Lyndale Point along the eastern boundary on tussocky terrain to rejoin the A850. The next two small peninsulas separated by Loch Treaslane are optional and are not included in the above mileage. At Bernisdale, the main road can be avoided by using the minor road running parallel. In the vicinity of the Skeabost Hotel the old road can be followed over the old Skeabost Bridge. Turn immediate left along a minor road leading to two houses. Beyond, a vague path traverses upwards through a wood to Tote House. From there swing round the northern flank of Ben Tote to reach the minor road to Skerinish. From here a path leads to Dun Cruinn. Return to Skerinish and follow a path east to the A856 near Kensaleyre.

Day 3: Kensaleyre – Uig (11 miles – 18 km)

Much variation possible on road and coastline. From Kensaleyre follow the A856 north, with a possible side visit to Kingsburgh. Note that if the true coastline is followed before Hinnisdal Bridge, then the river will have to be crossed. A small track leads down, past a farm to Uisdein Castle from where good level farmland leads to the road-end at Cuidrach. Continue directly north on a path leading to Camas Beag. The Point of Ru Chorachan may be worth visiting but is not included in the above mileage. Continue to follow the coastline along the tops of the cliffs until forced up onto the A856 just south of Uig.

Day 4: Uig – Rubha Hunish (14 miles – 22 km)

Take the A855 road out of Uig. At the hairpin bend above the pier follow a path leading out to Idrigill Point. Drop down to Dun Skudiburgh on another steep path, and continue northwards on pathless grassy ground to Prince Charles' Point where he landed on Skye. Follow the coast north for another mile-and-a-half before heading directly across boggy ground to Camas Mor. Alternatively, stay with the coastline to reach here. Take the Kilmuir road and rejoin the A855, following it north-east past Flora Macdonald's Monument and eventually to Duntulm Castle and Hotel. From here, leave the road and head north along the beach at Tulm Bay before climbing to Meall Tuath. An obvious cleft in the hillside leads to an initially precarious path winding down the cliffs guarding the entrance to Hunish, Skye's northern-most tongue of land. Rubha Hunish is the northern tip of Skye.

Accommodation and other information

Edinbane:	Two hotels (Edinbane, The Lodge) plus various B&Bs. Campsite at Borve. Grocery shop in Edinbane
Skeabost Hotel:	Expensive!
Kensaleyre:	B&Bs

Wild camping may be possible near Skerinish but enquire first.

Uig:	the Ferry Inn, Hotel, B&Bs, shops
Duntulm:	Hotel
Rubha Hunish:	Wild camping or Coastguard hut on clifftop

CHAPTER 8

South to Portree

(Wednesday 28 July – Saturday 1 August)

Rubha Hunish to Portree

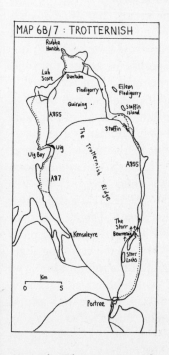

MAP 6B/7 : TROTTERNISH

I WOKE EARLY TO the sound of torrential rain battering on the roof of the hut and turned over to grab more sleep. However, I was up sooner than expected to answer a call of nature, entailing a trip outside. The heavy rain had subsided to a light drizzle, but the humidity and windless conditions instantly produced clouds of midges forcing me back inside quicker than I would have liked. The passionless light of morning was a world away from last night's dream state. I was at least thankful that I hadn't decided to camp.

Following a welcome pick-me-up of tea and porridge I packed a small daysack and set off on the brief trek to Skye's northerly point of Rubha Hunish. The 80-metre descent through the break in the cliffs was much steeper and rockier than I remembered and was made doubly difficult due to the rain and midges. The rain caused the rock to be extremely slippery, being highly polished anyway through the action of countless feet. The slowness and extra concentration thus required gave the midges more time to bite, reducing me to futile, foul-mouthed cursing and swearing. To top it all, I had full waterproofs on, which caused me to sweat profusely. If I had only done this last night in favourable weather – hindsight is a wonderful thing.

Slowly but surely I slithered my way down the twisting, greasy trail which literally clung to the cliff-face in several places, as did I. Eventually the gradient relented and the path fanned out in a chaotic jumble of scree and fallen rocks. A further short but easy grassy descent took me finally on to the broad sweep of lush grassy hummocks leading out to land's end. For bird lovers, Rubha Hunish has little equal on Skye and on my previous visit we had spent a good hour or so perched on the edge of cliffs photographing a variety of ornithological specimens. Today, time and weather dictated a briefer circuit of the peninsula. I headed briskly for the Point itself, often, like the summit of a misty mountain, a distinct anti-climax. Sea and sky were reduced to an amorphous grey mass with the stubby outlines of the Shiant Islands giving aerial perspective to the washed-out scene. In the immediate foreground a small skerry hosted a cluster of shags and guillemots, giving a living presence to this far-flung corner.

I turned and began to follow the north-eastern edge of Hunish and the most spectacular part of the excursion. Facing me, over half-a-mile distant, were the vast crumbling mural precipices forming the girdle barrier to this Lost World. Perched on the edge, I could just make out the tiny squat square of the lookout hut. The remainder of the return route passed by stupendous cliff scenery, much of it eroded and split, creating massive fissures and several worthy sea stacks. One such fissure, barely 20 feet wide, overhung at the top and plunged 100 feet to murky depths. Its dank, greasy, moss-laden walls were festooned with birds occupying every conceivable ledge, nook and cranny, their raucous cacophony reverberating around the confined space. Guillemots, kittiwakes, herring gulls and the odd great skua joined in the general racket. Further on, I positioned myself on the cliff edge to photograph the tapering wedge of Bodha Hunish, a fine sea stack. A glorious display of bushy pink sea thrift and yellow lichen-covered rock made a fine foreground.

A short while later I reluctantly began the long, gradual ascent away from this wild, exposed, clandestine domain, a truly mystical spot belonging only to the birds. I felt an intruder and, in a sense, that is all that Man could ever be in the presence of such awesome surroundings.

By 10.15 I was back at the hut and involved in the mundane ritual of packing my rucksack in preparation for departure. Psychologically, I felt as if I had broken the back of the walk. All roads now led south. South to Staffin, Portree, Sligachan and, finally, Kylerhea a week from now. This was the first day of the walk that I knew there was less than 100 miles to go, a crucial turning point of the venture. There were no more wild circuitous peninsulas – the eastern seaboard of Skye is a bit like that of mainland Scotland, long straight runs of cliff and shoreline indented by minor sea lochs, such as Loch Sligachan and Loch Ainort. Yet I felt no sense of anti-climax at this prospect, no sense of wishing that it was over. I knew that profound sadness would be felt at Kylerhea when it was all over. Like life itself, once the end is in sight there is a yearning, itching desire to make every day count, to live life to the full, to savour every experience as if it was the last. This was exactly what I intended to do for the final week of Skyewalk.

Just as I was leaving the lookout hut, two people suddenly appeared as if from nowhere. I nodded and said 'Good morning' before striding off to follow the cliff-edge, a weak, watery sun trying to punch a hole in the cloud layer. I turned constantly to enjoy views of Rubha Hunish – this was grand clifftop walking. My original intention to climb Ben Volovaig, a 111 metre hill on the stubby Aird peninsula, was abandoned and I cut directly through a natural trough in the heathery moor to reach Port Gobhlaig, oddly translated as Dung Fork Port, a beautifully secluded natural harbour. I followed the minor road round the bay and attempted to find the coastal path shown on the map which, in actuality, was a figment of the map-maker's imagination. At the tiny hamlet of Balmacqueen my sights were set on reaching the famed Flodigarry Hotel in time for a bar lunch and I bee-lined up to the main A855 Portree road. In the original scheme of things today had been planned as a half-day with the night spent at or in the environs of the Flodigarry Hotel. This plan had been made partly because Heather might have met me – now no longer the case.

The road on the eastern side of Trotternish rarely strays more than half a kilometre from the coast, but the lie of the land is such that, in many instances, the coastline is frustratingly not visible. A viewpoint shown on the map tempted me away from tarmac after less than a kilometre of road walking and I was rewarded with a fine view of the twin stacks of Stacan Gobhlach and Eilean Trodday beyond. The whole of this section of coastline from Port Gobhlaig southwards for two to three miles is prolific with sea stacks but this was unknown to me at the time. Prior research was obviously not complete. Here was yet another excuse to return to Skye in the future, if any was really needed.

I returned to the road, the view south now dominated by the true northern termination of the so-called Trotternish Ridge, a serpentine spine stretching for over 20 miles from the north of Trotternish almost to Portree in the south. This ridge is very different in character from the Cuillin though no less distinctive. The basalt plateau from which Trotternish has been carved has tilted up eastwards to form a continuous steep escarpment, a spine of high ground rarely rising above 2,000 feet and with the underlying sedimentary rocks exposed to the east. Subsequent Ice Age action has resulted in older strata shearing away in great slivers producing, along with other erosion, spectacular rock formations such as The Storr and The Quiraing with their tottering spires and crazy pinnacles.

I had visited both these popular tourist venues on many previous occasions but there was one major undertaking which I have still to accomplish – the complete traverse of the Trotternish ridge. In the early 1980s I had traversed the Cuillin ridge in a day, a rocky 12 km switchback with eleven Munro summits requiring good scrambling skill, a head for heights (and exposure), long arms and a good insurance policy. The Trotternish ridge requires none of these, but a high level of stamina and fitness is essential especially if the traverse is fitted into a single day. I had toyed with the idea of just abandoning the coast and following this ridge instead, but however appealing this seemed, I knew that it would be stretching things to then call the expedition a coastal walk round Skye. Sadly, it would have to be left for another occasion – yet another reason to come back!

The Flodigarry Hotel would be an ideal starting point for a north-south traverse as it stands in a perfect position beneath the north end of the ridge. I arrived there at one o'clock more concerned with ordering a pint and a meal at the bar. Minutes later I was in relaxation mode inside the hotel with a pint of beer shandy half drunk and soup, steak pie and chips ordered.

The bar I was seated in was once the billiard room of a plush private house built by wealthy Skyeman, Major R.L. Macdonald, a descendant of Flora's. The interior contains much Moorish decoration and bears testimony to the time he spent in the Middle East. Flodigarry was the home of Flora Macdonald herself following her short spell in prison – she did some time in the Tower of London for the part she played in helping Bonnie Prince Charlie to escape. Much of her married life was spent at Flodigarry and five of her seven children were born here.

Standing as it does in splendid isolation below the Trotternish ridge and with grand seaward views from its imposing battlements, not to mention its Flora Macdonald connections, Flodigarry has a long-standing tradition of mystery and romance, some of which had flowed into my own life. Heather and I spent the first night of our honeymoon at Flodigarry before shifting to slightly less luxurious surroundings in a cottage in Portnalong. The fact that one night's lodgings for two at Flodigarry cost nearly the same as the remaining week at Portnalong gives an indication of the wallet-denting properties of this hotel.

I rejoined the road south and within minutes stopped to photograph a sheep sitting under a sign for the Flodigarry Hotel. I was now actually ahead of schedule and for the first time during the walk did not have a pre-planned venue for the night's accommodation. The sky was brighter, my pack seemed lighter and I was pleasantly refreshed and recharged following the Flodigarry fester. I passed the next few road miles by counting foreign cars and British. In half-an-hour the tally was 11 British and 9 foreign, which confirmed my hunch that Skye was hoaching with Europeans. I chatted to an English couple at the side of the road who were watching a buzzard through binoculars. Their knowledge of ornithology was far superior to their geographical expertise – they thought Skye was only 25 miles from end to end. (It is at least twice that.)

South of the little township of Digg the road dropped and swung in a wide arc round Staffin Bay, one of the finest, sandiest bays in Skye. Today it looked benign and beautiful. In the depths of winter it can be storm-lashed and wild and the pounding of surf on sand is heard for miles around. Staffin is more a collection of small villages than a village itself. The name derives from the Norse word Staffr, meaning pillar, a reference to the basaltic pillared rocks in the area. The island of Staffa, near Iona, with its world-famous basaltic columns, has the same Norse derivation.

I strolled on past the neat, well-kept crofts and cottages of Brogaig and Stenscholl. Near the turn-off to Marishader I stopped at The Oystercatcher, a village hall, general store and restaurant rolled into one modern building. Planning to camp somewhere that evening, I went into the store to stock up on a few basic provisions. My ears caught a conversation spoken in Gaelic between two women; it was the first time during the walk that I had heard the Highland native tongue. Staffin is one of the few places on Skye which has managed to retain its younger generation and its native Gaelic. The fact that it is one of the best and most productive farming areas on the island has played a large part.

I enquired (in English) as to the whereabouts of a campsite and was delighted to be informed that one lay only a mile further on. It was marked on the map but I hadn't noticed. The site was off the road to the left in a fairly secluded spot and seemed small enough to be free of that rowdy atmosphere which was the hall-mark of other sites. The owner was a real Skyeman with a real West Highland accent, rolling off the tongue like wavelets on a Hebridean shore: 'Och, ye've come a long way right enough ... That's a fine stick ye've got (a reference to my walking pole) ...Chust camp anywhere ... a wee bit higher to be away from the midges'.

I followed his advice and camped higher. The midges still bit. A shower, a rest and a mug of tea later, I was revived enough to want to explore the hill and coastline beyond the campsite. In favourable weather I followed a vague path upwards through cropped heather and grass. Ten minutes later I was rewarded with a corker of a view north over Staffin slipway to Staffin Island, Eilean Flodigarry and, still visible in the far north, Eilean Trodday. From where I was standing, a well-engineered crazy-paving-type track zig-zagged steeply down below fluted basalt cliffs to the grassy run-out before the jetty. I swiftly descended the track to emerge on a minor road near a semi-ruined building and small car park for the jetty.

The gentle stroll along the road was a tonic in the soft evening light. Low-lying Staffin Island, just a few hundred yards away, is used for grazing and has a small fisherman's bothy with a newer building alongside. I rounded the sharp bend of An Corran and discovered an idyllic little beach of dark sand. Several children were running and playing, their laughter mingling with the sound of kleeping oystercatchers. Further on, several folk had found the perfect pitch by the Stenscholl Rover and for a moment I wished I had also camped there. The low sun transformed the water of Staffin Bay into a shimmering display of silver sequined move-ment. The low-lying farmland beyond was thrown into a wave-like relief of bleached greens. Beyond and above, the more omi-nous, brooding Trotternish ridge was grey and cloud-capped.

I soon reached the main road about half-a-mile north of the Oystercatcher complex and was tempted inside to sample the cui-sine. Pie, beans and chips wasn't exactly five-star food but this, together with soup, made me a satisfied customer – until I noticed sausage roll, beans and chips written on the 'specials' blackboard for £2 less! Piped background music was pleasant and in keeping with the mood of the walk – an album called 'Celtic Heart', featuring Runrig and Capercaillie.

I strolled back to the campsite lamenting the absence of a pub and thinking that if there was one planned, a good name would be The Staff Inn. Many Skye parishes are still too parochial and puritanical to view pubs as anything other than dens of sin. I passed a Wee Free church and heard psalm singing – perhaps the Kirk was an evening substitute for the pub. Just beyond, in a field, three tractors were involved in haymaking in the late evening sun. Rather than drinking and playing, Staffin folk seemed to be working and praying. I began to understand more fully the reasons behind Staffin's air of productivity and prosperity.

At the site I was rudely brought back to reality by a bunch of noisy German and Italians; so much for this being a quiet place. As I was snuggling into my sleeping bag it suddenly struck me that I hadn't phoned Heather. It would have to wait until tomorrow. I fell asleep and dreamed of a wild campsite tomorrow night.

* * * * *

I woke very early itching and scratching, wondering if midges had found their way into the tent. There seemed to be no wind and I dreaded getting up. Sleep engulfed me once more and I was woken by the wonderful sound of tent fabric flapping in the wind – an answered prayer. I wasted no time washing, dressing and breakfasting. Porridge with real milk (bought yesterday) was a rare treat, as was tea.

At ten past nine I lifted my pack on to my shoulders and set off, making a beeline for the coastal cliffs via a succession of bogs and fences. The weather had a menacing feel – raw and grey with cloud cover well down on the lower slopes of the gloomy hills. The threat of rain was more of a promise.

My pre-planned itinerary for today was Flodigarry to Rigg. Since I was at least four miles ahead of schedule already, I figured on reaching the wild ground east of the Storr Lochs where there were sure to be suitable wild camping sites. I knew that this would be the last chance of such a camp for the remainder of the walk.

A more immediate concern was to reach the vicinity of Kilt Rock, vertical columnar basalt cliffs which resemble the pleated folds of a kilt. I soon reached the crumbling cliff edge and a fence which followed the line of cliffs southward to Loch Mealt and the tourist viewpoint. This point provided the best view of Kilt Rock with a waterfall plunging over the edge, a foreground to the cliffs beyond. Lower down the cliff the horizontal strata even gave the impression of tartan. These 400 hundred foot high cliffs were the scene of a particularly heart-rending tragedy in the 1960s when a young Indian couple were honeymooning on Skye. They had decided to view Kilt Rock on a wild and windy day. Whilst standing at the edge, one unusually violent gust caught the young bride's billowing sari and propelled her to her death on the storm-lashed rocks far below. Today there is a safety rail and plenty of warning notices.

Kilt Rock

South of the viewpoint the twisting line of cliffs continued, dropping vertically for a few hundred feet before a grassy run-out gave way to the rocky shoreline and the white frayed edge of the grey ocean. I continued my cliff top romp, revelling in the grand surroundings but ever conscious of my boots becoming saturated once again. Clean, dry socks this morning were already damp. After about half-a-mile I dropped down to the road, disturbing a couple of sparrowhawks, their 'flap and glide' flight very distinctive.

I was on the lookout for a telephone box and found one at the tiny straggling hamlet of Herishader. My attempts to 'phone Heather resulted in the frustrating knock-down of 'The number you have dialled has not been recognised – please try again'. I did, another two times, with exactly the same result. I 'phoned the operator and finally got through.

Within seconds of Heather speaking I knew all was not well. I sensed that something was gravely wrong. She informed me that the doctor had seen her on Tuesday (two days ago) and had diagnosed pre-eclampsia, a condition in pregnancy which can mean that the placenta is breaking up. My heart and jaw dropped like a stone. She sensed my anxiety and tried to reassure me, telling me that her mum and dad were there doing everything and that she was resting and taking it easy. The doctor would give her another check-up in a week's time. I knew she suffered from high blood pressure but took consolation from the fact that she was now six-and-a-half months pregnant and past the real danger period. We discussed the possibility of my abandoning the walk but Heather would hear none of it. She wanted me to finish it and she knew I wanted to finish it, but guilt niggled at me that I was putting my walk before my wife and unborn child. If her mum and dad hadn't been there, I would like to think that I would have made the decision to return home.

Not surprisingly, my thoughts ran deep as I continued the walk. The now steady rain and surrounding gloom gave a dark, sombre mood to the day. I was in desperate need of company, a long chat to unravel the knot of worry, emotion and depression that was tightening within my head. I thought how so much can change on a long walk – mood, weather, scenery, being alone, not being alone, feelings – every day had been a unique blend of these basic ingredients (and other flavourings). Not one day had even been remotely like another yet the walk was becoming a composite whole. How different, how refreshingly contrasting the last three weeks had been, compared to the daily routine of a work environment.

At Culnaknock I made the surprising discovery of the Glenview Inn and Restaurant. A film was ready to be posted and there was a post box nearby. I decided to go in, partly to escape the dreich weather, partly to address the film envelope, partly because I craved a coffee but mainly because I needed cheering up.

No-one seemed to hear me enter, mainly because no-one was about other than an elegantly dressed girl hoovering the hallway with apparent indifference to my damp presence at the doorway. Eventually she directed me to sit on a chair near reception and informed me that I would be attended to in due course. I took the opportunity to address the film envelope before I was finally shown into the lounge. Despite the rather austere, frosty reception and lack of company, the pot of coffee was delicious. The Glenview Inn had a distinctive country house atmosphere rather than a country pub. I asked whether Rubha nam Brathairean (Brothers' Point) was worth making a detour for. This is a small peninsula east of the Inn. 'On a good day, yes' was the brief reply. As the rain was unrelenting and mist had crept down even further, even the reviving effects of the coffee couldn't coax me out on the 3 km return trip. I subsequently learned from Ralph Storer's *50 Best Routes on Skye and Raasay* that he rated it as 'one of the most exciting spots on the Trotternish coastline', offering an exposed scramble on a narrow ridge to reach the point itself. If I had known that then, I might have responded to the tempting challenge. I might also have had a tragic slip whilst attempting the scramble on wet, slippery rock. Who knows? Perhaps fate intervened on that dank and dour day. It was yet another addition to my ever-lengthening list of Things Still To Do On Skye.

Dreary but dreamy roadwalking followed, my interest maintained by discovering sections of old road in places. Another viewpoint at Inver Tote was crawling with tourists clicking away. I hurried and scurried on along the raw ribbon of tarmac, its grey, glistening surface the only permanence against a background of confused thoughts and emotions. I lunched in an old slate quarry, hunched, weatherbeaten and travel-weary. Again I craved company. Rain dripped off my hood and a cold dampness chilled me to the very bone. I was at the lowest ebb of the walk since that second day way back in Sleat – the Garden of Skye – to which I would soon return.

I vowed that if I came across a Bed and Breakfast before the Power Station track at the Storr Lochs then I would gladly accept it. I plodded on for several miles in constant drizzle and with a total absence of guest houses. The bleakness of the rain-sodden landscape and my damp, forlorn state made the thought of wild camping a nightmare – yet I knew I could have little choice. The relatively early hour of 3.15 implied the possibility of road-bashing on to Portree, another eight miles. However, this would have meant omitting the huge chunk of coastline from Bearreraig Bay to Portree, as the road pushed inland between these points.

Just as I had resigned myself to a miserable night in the tent, a white bungalow appeared on the right just before the road to the Power Station with an encouraging B&B sign. Too good to be true, I thought, as I knocked on the door, fully expecting a 'fully booked' response. A pleasant, homely woman opened the door and considered my request with some hesitation. She only had a twin and double room and did not normally let these to single people, but after some deliberation she agreed. My offer to pay more was rejected outright and she welcomed me in with open arms to the warmth of her cosy croft house.

Minutes later I was lying in a hot bath, not quite able to grasp the stroke of good fortune that had hit me. Later, a huge plate of fresh mackerel, potatoes, carrots, onions and mushrooms, followed by lashings of ice cream and peaches, found their way to my stomach and heart. My hostess, Christine MacKinnon, had done me proud. Her brother, Angus, had caught the mackerel the day before.

Christine, a nurse, was a local, born and raised in Staffin, whilst her husband, Roddy, was a painter and decorator hailing from Stornoway. Our conversation turned to crime on Skye (or lack of it) and I was surprised and shocked to learn that drugs are a big problem with young people. Car break-ins were becoming more common but these were usually blamed on groups from the mainland focusing on car parks used by hillwalkers and fishermen. Had the Skye Bridge made any difference to crime levels I asked? They reckoned not – the tolls put them off! I was envious when I heard that Roddy had spent six months on remote St Kilda, doing general manual work and painting and decorating army billets. This was one port of call high on my list of 'must visits' and had been for as long as I could remember.

While Christine disappeared to prepare some supper I watched the news on TV. A heatwave in Texas had lasted for 26 days with hundreds of people dying from heat exhaustion. Free fans had been supplied to houses and the harvest was useless. Scotland's harvest would probably be useless for the opposite reason of too much rain – it's a topsy turvy world I thought. The forecast was for it to clear up slightly tomorrow, followed by fine on Saturday, then unsettled after that. I took it all with a pinch of salt and tore into a 'bedtime snack' of lobster meat on toast, the lobsters, like the mackerel, caught by Angus. I was stuffed. The knot of worry and depression had finally unravelled all due to my homely highland hosts, the MacKinnons. I went to bed a contented and satisfied man.

* * * * *

I wouldn't have expected anything other than a huge cooked breakfast and I wasn't disappointed. Grapefruit, followed by two eggs, three sausages, bacon, mushrooms and tomato was a firm foundation for a full day's walking. Whilst eating, I turned over some logistical possibilities in my head. From here to Portree via the coast was essentially wild pathless walking which I preferred to tackle without the burden of a full pack. I hit on the idea of leaving the pack at the B&B, doing the walk with a daypack and returning by taxi to retrieve the full pack later. Christine wouldn't hear of the idea. Roddy was going to Portree anyway, so he would transport my pack and leave it with a friend who worked in the Tourist Information Centre. Good fortune again seemed to be on my side.

I was staggered when I was told that the B&B charge was only £15, particularly with the five-star dinner and supper plus double bed. I insisted that I wanted to pay more but Christine's stance was firm, saying that if I wrote a cheque for more she wouldn't cash it. Her Scottish thrawnness was as marked as her highland hospitality. On the door of my bedroom was a sign with the words 'Come as a guest, leave as a friend'. In many guest houses this would express a hollow sentiment; at Bearreraig Cottage it made perfect sense.

We exchanged fond farewells before I took to the road, fully charged by the heart and hearth of my generous hosts. The weather wasn't wonderful but still a vast improvement on yesterday's wash-out. Grey moisture-laden skies allowed only a half-hearted trickle of sunlight to momentarily flicker on Loch Leathan's ruffled surface. I turned to look back at Bearreraig Cottage and was blessed by the sight of a diaphanous rainbow arching delicately over the tiny white building, itself dwarfed by the gaunt, grey cliffs of the Trotternish Ridge high above and beyond. Curtains of curling mist played around the higher summit of The Storr and as I left the vicinity of the loch, the rocky finger of the Old Man of Storr poked defiantly through the shroud of cloud.

At Storr Lochs Cottage there is a visitor area with three information plaques, one describing the power station which opened here in 1952. Hydro-electric pipes drop 450 feet to the generating station in Bearreraig Bay, accompanied by 674 concrete steps and a pulley-operated railway. Skye finally got its electricity in 1953 with the opening of this power station but most of the power now comes from the mainland via the pylons crossing the Kylerhea narrows.

The other two plaques concerned fossils and dinosaurs and made fascinating reading. Scotland's first dinosaur finds were made a few miles from this spot including, amazingly, dinosaur footprints preserved in mud. According to the plaque, 170 million years ago, during the Jurassic period, the Isle of Skye did not exist and the area in which I was now standing was the bottom of a shallow tropical sea. I gazed across to the cliffs guarding the bay and learned that they had taken 13 million years to form from sand and mud laid down in that sea. The rock and fossils contained within are of international importance. As I started up the grassy slopes to follow the clifftop southwards, I was in awe of the time scales involved and attempted to grasp the sheer enormity of 170 million years. If one year of this time represented just one minute, then the Jurassic period would still be over 320 years ago, well before the Jacobite Rebellion. My own utter insignificance in time as well as space was made mind-blowingly apparent.

The cliffs opposite tiny Holm Island turned out in reality to be less well defined than they appeared on the map and, rather than plunge to the sea in a single drop, they possessed many wide grassy promenades. I gradually traversed southwards and upwards to a level but tussocky and boggy area above the point marked with Prince Charles' Cave. The Bonnie Prince landed on this section of coastline on returning from a night on the Isle of Raasay but it is doubtful if this cave was actually used by him. On a clear day the long Island of Raasay would stand out proud but if anything the weather had worsened, with a grey featureless gloom out to sea.

I climbed up on to the crest of the highest tier of cliffs where the going was good on dry, short grass and sheep tracks. Rabbits appeared from holes like bullets from a rifle and disappeared again as quickly. At the secondary high point of Craig Ulatota (roughly translating as 'the crag of the mound of the grave by the wall of the house'!) I was enveloped in clammy, cold, wind-driven mist and didn't hang about. On the descent, a window on the world framed two croaking ravens flying out from the cliff face, only to vanish in the mist churning up from the gloomy depths below. I soon reached the bealach before the 392 metre high point of the day, the swirling mists adding drama and mystery to the view southward past the awesome cliffs to the washed-out but unmistakable profile of Ben Tianavaig beyond Portree Bay. Sithean Bhealaich Chumhaing (roughly 'narrow fairy col') at 392 metres was a wild and windy spot. The triangulation pillar provided a modicum of shelter from the raw wind and the views were poor in the flat monochrome conditions. Even the sea, far below, was only vaguely visible. I was reminded sharply of Dunvegan Head with Mike and George and found it difficult to believe that this was only ten days ago. Apart from Ben Tianavaig these would be the last high coastal cliffs of the walk.

I abandoned my wind-scoured perch on the edge of the world

and began the long slow descent. As I lost height, the right-hand side became clear, but vaporous tongues of mist continued to boil up and over the cliff edge on my left, as if to pull me over into the inky void from which they had risen. Great buttresses and pinnacled prows suddenly loomed out of the shifting sheets of cloud, as did tantalising snippets of coastline far below. Within half-an-hour I had emerged into a different world free from the clutches of wind-tossed cloud and one of green, sheep-studded pastures and views of the welcome familiarity of Portree houses. The return to civilisation was personified by the meeting of two hikers on their way up.

Near Torvaig I finally stumbled on an old farm track and followed it to some farm buildings before crossing two stiles and making my way out on to the fine viewpoint of Ben Chracaig, a prominent knoll commanding a superb view of Portree harbour. I sat and stared for a while, allowing the peaceful surroundings to make an impression. My eye was drawn to the colourful, pastel-hued terrace of two-storey, dormer-windowed houses comprising Portree's harbour facade. Various yachts and other vessels were moored on the placid, slate-grey water. From my eagle's eyrie I could see and hear the splashes of fish jumping in circular fish farm cages below. A large sailing craft ploughed into the sheltered harbour, wheeling gulls screaming in its snowy wake.

The name Portree is an Anglicisation of Port an Righ, literally translating as the Port of the King, referring to King James V who anchored here in 1540 on his expedition to assert sovereignty over the rebellious Highland clan chiefs. The event made such an impression on them that they changed the name of the place from Kiltaraglen (chapel at the foot of the glen). According to Martin Martin it was 'the Convenience of the Harbour which is in the middle of the Isle, made 'em chuse this for the fittest Place'. In due course the lochside fishing village became Skye's only true town and its capital, today boasting a population of some 1,600 souls.

Reluctantly, I left my perch and drifted down a zig-zag path through bracken and shrubs to a picnic area with tables and viewpoint. A happy horde of adults, kids and puppies were romping around in high spirits. 'How old are they?' I asked one of the women (referring to the puppies, not the kids). 'Eight weeks', she replied. 'How far have you come?' she asked. '300 miles', I answered – 'just round the coastline!' I continued on my way leaving one silent, astonished woman amongst her riotous crew.

My original intention had been to spend two nights in Portree with a rest day in between. In the event, I only managed to secure accommodation for the second night (tomorrow night) and had planned to camp somewhere tonight. Despite my failure to find a roof for my head, having contacted the tourist office from home a few months back, I secretly hoped that I could find somewhere 'on spec' this evening, and not have to resort to camping. My luck was in. After a few attempts, a B&B called Ben Lee, high above the harbour on the Staffin road, offered me a single room. The owner was a soft-spoken elderly gentleman who had spent most of his life as a shepherd on the hills I had just walked over.

As arranged, I collected my main pack from the Tourist Information Centre before returning to Ben Lee to unpack, wash a few items of clothing and shower. I went out again to buy a newspaper, camera film and draw cash from the 'hole-in-the-wall'. Later still, I opted for a Chinese take-away meal and stole off to find a quiet spot to eat it on the little circular path round the hillock above the harbour. This hillock is the Meall, or less elegantly, the Lump, which was planted with trees and shrubs by Dr Ban, an idealist who imagined Portree could one day be like Oban, and who built the round lookout tower on its summit. The last hanging in Skye took place on The Lump in 1742.

I sat on some steps leading up to the tower to start my meal. Lack of salt in the chicken and sweetcorn soup, together with a cloud of midges, forced a retreat to the B&B. My cramped single room was a jumble of clothes and other paraphernalia strewn everywhere – Chinese food cartons added to the general mayhem.

Refreshed, I wandered back outside with the intention of 'phoning home and finding some night-life. Public telephones are situated in Somerled Square, the hub of the town, where a short shopping street leads to the whitewashed cottages above the harbour, of which Ben Lee was one. Somerled is said to have been the 12th-century founder of the Clan MacDonald, and how Portree looks today owes much to Sir James MacDonald whose ambition was to create a village which would encourage education, trade and local industries. Many of the street names, such as Bosville Terrace, Wentworth Street, Beaumont Crescent and, of course, Somerled Square, reflect the part played by Sir James.

Portree's sheltered setting behind a natural harbour and beneath towering hills, with its liberal scattering of broad-leaved trees, gives it an attractive, upright and prosperous air, but its continued survival is utterly dependent on its one major industry – tourism. Most people either love or loathe Portree. Personally, I can take it or leave it. It is a harsh truism that many places which are tourist dependent develop a tacky, touristy flavour, often resulting in a bad taste in the mouth. Portree has not quite succumbed to the tourist onslaught to the extent of, say, Pitlochry, Callander or Oban, but it still has its share of tartan stuffed toys, Isle of Skye car stickers and mugs, and assorted cheap and tawdry gimmicky items bearing the hallmark of crass vacuity.

My 'phone call to Heather was more upbeat and optimistic than that of yesterday morning and our conversation was animated and enthusiastic. I was surprised and delighted to be told that Mike was so uplifted by his walking on Skye when he had joined me with George a few weeks back, that he would be returning to meet me again with his wife, Eva, at Sligachan, in two nights' time. He would not be walking this time but introducing Eva to the magic of Skye – she had not set foot on the island before. I had hoped for the company of friends at the Sligachan bar and Mike and Eva filled the niche perfectly. Once again I fell into a jovial, buoyant mood – 'Time for a few pints', I mused.

I mooched down to the Harbour Bar, the only true pub in Portree, in the sense of not being connected to a hotel. I drank a pint of Caffrey's Irish Ale outside to escape the din of Sky television blaring from a corner. The deplorable aspect of this was that tourists, looking perhaps for a quiet drink or some live Scottish music, were turning away in droves. I drifted up to the Tongadale, a hotel bar where I ordered a pint of Caledonian 80/-. Lack of atmosphere and music sent me searching once again, this time to the Portree Hotel whose main bar was absurdly lacking in customers for a Friday night. My eye was drawn to a notice advertising the Skye Folk Festival from 10 o'clock to 1 o'clock in the village hall. A payment of £5 at the door followed by further inflated prices for canned fizzy beer did little to encourage me.

Just as I was resigning myself to an early night, the faint but unmistakable strains of live fiddle music hit my ears. I traced the source to the Royal Hotel lounge bar, overlooking the quay. To say the bar was crowded would be an understatement. Hordes of customers clutching glasses were hovering around outside like midges around a camper. Inside was a seething mass of sweaty bodies – a shoehorn would have been useful for getting more in. Undaunted, I struggled through the human zoo to the relative safety of the bar and eventually ordered a pint of MacNab's Real Ale, a local beer which I had never heard of before. I subsequently discovered that MacNab's Inn once occupied the present site of the Royal Hotel. It was in this thatched building that Bonnie Princes Charlie bid his final farewell to Flora, passing to her a lock of his hair; and here, 27 years after that event, Boswell and Johnson had 'a very good dinner, porter, port and punch'.

I supped my pint and glanced around. Everyone had lost all traces of self-consciousness and were tapping and moving rhythmically to a fiddler and two guitarists sitting centre-stage belting out an endless, seamless, frenzied string of Irish/Scottish jigs and reels. The whole place was pulsating, the effects of alcohol and live music creating an hypnotic atmosphere.

At the heart of the maelstrom my eyes fell upon an old man sitting next to the musicians. His grey, crinkled hair was combed back and his ruddy, gnarled, shrunken features exuded more character than the whole crowd put together. He was utterly lost in the music, imitating the actions of the fiddler, and obviously enjoying himself to the full. He was undoubtedly one of a few locals in a bar filled with tourists. I thought it lamentable that he looked so out of place – until it occurred to me that it was the crowd who were out of place. He attempted, several times, to converse with others around him but was sadly and unkindly ignored. I felt an overwhelming urge to go over and talk to him but the heaving swell of bodies wouldn't allow it. His eyes sparkled and betrayed a love of life and a lifetime of experiences. Sometime later, as the music began to wind down, a tray-bashing young local blade led the old man out. They were obviously good friends, even perhaps grandfather and grandson. I felt relieved.

With no real urge to linger, I metaphorically stubbed out the fag-end of evening, drank up, struggled out and strolled up to a soft bed and dreams at Ben Lee.

* * * * *

I woke to the sound of screeching gulls in the harbour and drew back the curtain to greet a new day, and a new month for this was the first of August. The pretty facade of the harbour houses was reflected in the water, gently wrinkled by a soft wind. The sky was overcast and dark but shafts of sunlight skipped over the distant hills, promising better things to come. I photographed the peaceful morning scene and thought of the day ahead. Rather than stagnate in Portree, I had decided to climb Ben Tianavaig, the small but distinctive hill sitting south-east of Portree. Being a grand coastal hill, it was on my itinerary and was suitable for a circular trip, ending at the guest house on Viewfield road which was pre-booked for this evening. Yet again, I would have the luxury of carrying only a light daypack.

I shared breakfast with an Oban girl whose other half wasn't yet out of bed and who, apparently, wouldn't be for some time. She would be returning to bed following breakfast. A late night at the village hall ceilidh seemed reason enough for spending most of the day in bed. By 9.30 I had left Ben Lee, slightly annoyed at having to relocate to a new guesthouse. Pre-booking does have some disadvantages. Cathy McLeod's B&B was a huge change from last night's quaint, terraced town house. Hers was a modern, spacious, detached out-of-town bungalow. I found the front door open and a jumble of used sheets and towels cluttering the hallway. Cathy appeared and assured me that my main pack could be left there until the evening.

I set off southward down the main A850 road at a sprightly pace. The day had lost its early bright sheen and low cloud was disappointingly obscuring the summit of my objective, Ben Tianavaig. A slight smirr of rain seemed to confirm that the weather was on a downer and I resigned myself to another soaking. I was glad to abandon the traffic tourist trail of the A850 and saunter along the quiet single-track road leading eventually to The Braes. An even tinier road led to Penifiler, a straggle of farm buildings and crofts, with a B&B establishment at the end of the road where Heather and I had stayed on a previous occasion.

Here I romped off across heathery moor, heading in the direction of Camas Ban (White Bay), lying directly opposite my eagle's perch of yesterday. A succession of craggy bluffs and heathery dips led to the high ground above the sheltered bay where I stopped for a short breather. A fragmented line of vegetated cliffs extended eastwards for a mile to the foot of the north ridge of Ben Tianavaig. I followed the tops of these cliffs but was forced downwards by a frustrating series of deep trenches, destroying any sense of rhythm. In one, an antiquated ruined stone house, nestling again a rock wall with its own rowan tree, betrayed man's long gone presence. In another, I came across a sheep standing shakily in a burn, its head rocking back and forth and foaming at the mouth. I coaxed it out of the water but it seemed hardly aware of my presence. It was obviously very ill (possibly pneumonia) and I vowed to tell a shepherd of the poor beast's predicament.

As I climbed up to the rocky promontory marking the foot of the ridge I was aware of sun on my back and light and warmth flooding the previously gloomy scene. A massive, flat, sun-warmed rock on the lip of the crag was a marvellous invitation to sit and stare. Directly northwards, yesterday's high cliffs were tearing asunder their cloudy mantle to reveal a sky of exquisite ultramarine blue. To the west, the sprinkling of houses forming Portree was still in deepest shadow, while eastwards the island of Raasay was thrown into pin-sharp relief, its sun-carved features a feast for the eye. From the dark, drizzly ashes of an hour ago, a fiery phoenix of sun-bleached splendour was in the process of being reborn. The old Skye magic was doing its stuff.

The mile from where I sat, to the summit of Ben Tianavaig, involved only 200 metres of gradual ascent following the edge of an almost continuous cliff. Despite the improvement in the weather, the mist doggedly clung on to Tianavaig's summit and the climb seemed a long slog with crags and buttresses looming in and out of the ever thickening mantle. As I reached the triangulation pillar perched on a craggy hillock, rivulets of cloud chased past in a bullying wind, gradually thinning out to leave acres of blue sky. Then, in an instant, another wave of cloud washed over me, leaving only grey clamminess, the wind and a few sheep for company. I was as dogged as the mist, however, and sat it out on the summit waiting for the full-blown clearance which had to come.

Like the sheep, I nibbled, and waited. Minutes later the mists parted, like dark curtains drawing open on a bright sunny morning. My window to the world was a revelation. Directly across the deep blue Sound of Raasay the distinctive flat-topped summit of Dun Caan stood out proudly, where Dr Johnson danced a reel in sheer exuberance at the majestic surroundings. A final flurry of mist produced an arc of light, like a colourless rainbow. I almost expected to see a broken spectre, a shadow of myself cast on the mist by the sun, but it never appeared.

I climbed over to a subsidiary grassy summit and gazed across the expanse of wind-ruffled blue ocean to white foam-flecked beaches and rocky headlands. The tiny white crofts of Camustianavaig, Lower Ollach and Upper Ollach were scattered sugar grains on emerald green. In the distance, the peaks of the Red Cuillin were still cloud-capped and the Black Cuillin totally obliterated in a shrouded cloak of menacing grey.

My gaze again turned east to the long island of Raasay, Skye's largest offshore island. Raasay has a fascinating and at times tragic history. Like many other Scottish islands, it has had its fair share of unscrupulous landlords. Raasay and Rona to its north both paid dearly for their support of Bonnie Prince Charlie, and the reprisals following the Jacobite rising resulted in the burning of Raasay House and all the cottages on the island. Raasay was an inspiration to Boswell and Johnson who spent four days in the rebuilt Raasay House as guests of the then laird, John MacLeod. Throughout their Highland journey, but especially in Raasay, they were struck by the contrast between the wildness of the landscape and the warmth and elegance of their reception. It has been said that the short time he spent on Raasay was possibly the happiest in Boswell's life. Judging by Johnson's reel-dancing on Dun Caan, the same might no doubt be said for him.

The late, great Gaelic poet, Sorley Maclean, was a native of Raasay. Two of his most famous poems, 'Coilltean Ratharsair' (The Woods of Raasay) and 'Hallaig' (a ruined township on the east side of the island) exude such a sense of place and people that Raasay seems elevated to a symbolic landscape in which the black, etched, unattainable, 'antlered' Cuillin become the only permanence in a 'sea of sorrow' and 'morass of agony'. In the years before his death Sorley Maclean lived in the little township of Braes, in a house which enjoyed panoramic views across to the sylvan slopes of his beloved island.

Sorley Maclean will forever be a spiritual inspiration to the local people but practical inspiration must surely be in the form of one man named Calum MacLeod. In 1966 Calum single-handedly started to construct a two-and-a-half mile road to his home at Arnish in the north of Raasay, using only a pick, shovel and wheelbarrow, taking over ten years to do it. He undertook the task because the local authority would not extend the existing road to his township. When he started his monumental labour there were seven families in Arnish, but on completion ten years later only he and his wife remained.

Today, Raasay has a population of around 150 and is partly owned by Highlands and Islands Enterprise and partly by the Government. There is a hotel on the island and Raasay House is now an Outdoor Centre. Perhaps the most unusual but environmentally friendly way to see the island is by Heavy Horse-drawn Carriage, a relatively recent innovation run by qualified Scottish tour guide, Annie. I have been to Raasay on two occasions and look forward to future visits to do the famous East Coast walk and other delights.

I had spent almost an hour on the summit of Ben Tianavaig, snacking, photographing and dreaming. It had been a high point of the trip. In terms of altitude it was also the highest point yet. The summit may have been only a meagre 413 metres (not even 1,400 feet) but the views were out of all proportion to the hill's elevation. This was one of the few hills that Heather had climbed before me. Having lived at Camustianavaig directly beneath the hill for a spell, she had good enough reason.

As I was about to move off, I noticed a figure ascending the south ridge and decided to hang about until he arrived at the summit. Moments later, an exuberant Dutchman, besotted with Skye landscape, greeted me with 'Wonderful, wonderful' and asked me to use his camcorder to take footage of him walking to the other subsidiary summit. I gladly obliged before asking him to return the favour by taking a photo of me on the same spot, with my camera. Unfortunately, a delicate wreath of cloud floated by as he pressed the shutter, throwing the background into a washed-out flatness. However, the resulting transparency captured the atmosphere of that magical hour.

I said goodbye to my Dutch friend and sauntered off down the springy, well-defined escarpment forming Ben Tianavaig's south ridge. This was a grand, effortless descent of almost constant gradient affording further opportunities to soak up the magnificent surroundings. Unfortunately, I stuck with the ridge too long and became ensnared in a sun-blasted hollow of ankle-biting bracken with an awkward barbed wire fence. This frustrating end to a classic climb raised my temperature and I was glad to find a picnic table in Tianavaig Bay where I removed my fleece jacket and sat down for a drink. This delightfully peaceful corner of Skye was Heather's home for six months while she had taught in Portree High School.

The 7 km roadwalk back to my guesthouse was punctuated by a surprise meeting with a pupil in the school where I worked. Iona

MacDonald and her father stopped their car and we chatted briefly before they resumed their journey to their home at Penifiler. I mentioned the distressed sheep and they assured me that the shepherd would be notified.

That evening I dined at the Aros Centre, an all-encompassing tourist experience comprising restaurant, craft shop, exhibition and audio-visual display, an innovative attempt to reclaim some of Skye's cultural heritage and give tourists a painless introduction to the history of the island – a great venue for a rainy day. Soup, haddock and a couple of pints were soon given short shrift and I mentally readjusted myself for the final phase of the venture. The original game plan had been to take four days from Portree back to Kylerhea but I subsequently decided to cancel a night's accommodation at Kyleakin (the bridge entry point to Skye) and cover the ground from Broadford to Kylerhea in one long day. In short, three days of the walk remained, none of which would require a camping stove and associated food. I planned on leaving these (and other) items at Cathy MacLeod's guesthouse. The main pack plus tent, mat and sleeping bag, could hopefully be left at the Sligachan Hotel following tomorrow night's camp there, resulting in my carrying a light pack for the final couple of days.

I strolled back to the guesthouse. The serrated spire of Sgurr nan Gillean soared high above a sliver of cloud, and a late evening sun was picking out the craggy features of Ben Tianavaig. The chug-chugging of a fishing boat broke the silence of evening, the silvery fan of its wake spreading across the flat-calm surface of Loch Portree. What had started as a rather nondescript day had turned out to be one of the finest of the trip.

* * * * *

Route Summary: Rubha Hunish to Portree

Day 1: Rubha Hunish – Staffin (11 miles – 18 km)
Follow the cliff top at Meall Tuath and cut through a natural cleft

to Port Gobhlaig. An excursion out to Rubha na h-Aiseig is optional but not included in the above mileage. Swing round the bay on a minor road and reach Balmacqueen by a path and track. Either follow the coast to the Flodigarry Hotel from here, or rejoin the A855 via a minor road. The pure coastal option is recommended owing to a profusion of sea-stacks and cliff scenery. South of Flodigarry, follow the main road to Staffin Bay. At Stenscholl take the minor road marked Staffin Slipway via An Corran. Note that this point can be easily reached from the campsite at Clachan and is recommended as a circular route from there.

Day 2: Staffin – Storr Lochs (12 miles – 19 km)

From the campsite, head east to the coast across open heath and follow the cliff top past Kilt Rock to the viewpoint. Continue along the top of the cliffs or, alternatively, walk on the main road. The side trip out to Rubha nam Brathairean is recommended. South of there the road continues to follow the coastline but more coastal scenery is visible by keeping to the cliff top. At Rigg, the road turns inland and, about a mile south of here, conifer plantation makes it difficult to stay with the coast. South of the plantation are Storr Lochs.

Day 3: Storr Lochs – Portree (8 miles – 13 km)

From the power station at Bearreraig Bay climb easy slopes to follow the high clifftop above Holm Island. Continue south, gradually climbing higher, eventually reaching the triangulation pillar on Sithean Bhealaich Chumhaing, a fine viewpoint. Descend easy slopes to a track at Torvaig. At a farm, head south to Ben Chracaig, directly above Portree Bay. From here a good well-used path leads to Portree.

Accommodation and other information

Flodigarry Hotel:	Food and/or accommodation
Staffin:	B&Bs. Campsite at Clachan
Storr Lochs:	Excellent B&B (Bearreraig) at start of Power Station road – wild camping possible
Portree:	Hotels, B&Bs, shops, bank, campsite 1 mile north of Portree (on A855)

CHAPTER 9

Back to the Garden

(Sunday 2 August – Tuesday 4 August)

Portree to Kylerhea and Glenelg

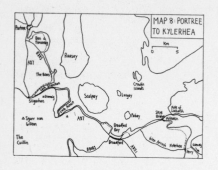

AT BREAKFAST I ENQUIRED about leaving a carrier bag with stove and food items to be picked up after the walk. I was met initially with a negative response. Continued persistence on my part moderated the initial reply of 'We don't really have enough room' to 'Well, I suppose we could put it in the shed outside'. This was indeed a marked contrast to the amiability of Christine MacKinnon two nights ago. Some equanimity was restored by the huge, hearty breakfast, which I couldn't finish.

Ten past nine saw me off, retracing the road miles of yesterday until I passed the turn-off to Camastianavaig. The lower tops were clear of cloud but, true to form, Sgurr nan Gillean was buried in a billowing mass of grey. I was now in the long straggling district known as Braes, comprising the several scattered townships of Conordan, Lower Ollach, Upper Ollach, Gedintailor, Balmeanach and Peinchorran, although the last three of these deserve the title of The Braes. A generally prosperous and prim air about the neat, well-kept cottages and gardens indicated an abundance of money and senior citizens. Several old folk were either tending grand colourful gardens or resting in equally grand conservatories. A cottage, delightfully named Fairburn Stepalong, was surrounded by an incredibly extensive, well-manicured garden, the result of many years of careful thought and loving attention.

The peaceful, rural air which characterised Braes on that soft August morning was far removed from the stormy events of 1882. It was then that the head of steam raised by long-standing crofters' grievances finally exploded in a series of cataclysmic and revolutionary events. The Battle of the Braes, as it has come to be known, is in most people's minds the event which symbolised the crofters' struggle against the all-powerful landed gentry and their subsequent emergence into calmer waters. I make no apologies for telling the story in full here.

In 1882, Braes was anything but prosperous and peaceful. Poverty and hunger, born of greed and selfishness on the part of Lord MacDonald, had a stranglehold on the Braes crofters. One Peinchorran crofter of the time remarked, 'The principal thing we have to complain of is our poverty. The smallness of our holdings and the inferior quality of the land is what has caused our poverty; and the way in which the poor crofters are huddled together and the best part of the land devoted to deer forests and big farms.'

Conditions for the crofters deteriorated even further when cotters evicted from land on the south side of Loch Sligachan (to enlarge deer forests) were moved to already overcrowded Braes, thus subdividing the available land into even smaller holdings. The decision in 1865 by MacDonald Estates to deny the Braes crofters their long-established right to graze their stock on Ben Lee, a grassy hill lying north of Loch Sligachan and west of Braes, sowed the seed of reaction and revenge.

For seventeen long years the Braes people harboured and nurtured a growing grudge against the establishment, until the lease on the use of Ben Lee was due to expire in 1882. During this period the Braes men attended the Kinsale fishings in south-west Ireland, an annual excursion necessary to augment their feeble income. There they learned of similar problems to their own and that a group called the Irish Land League had been formed to fight for a radical overhaul of the conditions of agricultural workers and smallholders. Security of tenure was a demand at the heart of their agenda. By organising meetings, refusing to pay rents, intimidating landowners and ostracising those who rejected the Land League, they were eventually successful in their demands.

Taking a salutary leaf out of the Irish book, the Braes crofters got together and signed a polite letter to Lord MacDonald, asking him to restore their previously held pastures on Ben Lee for an agreed rent. His Lordship not only refused but insultingly rebuked his tenants for having the insolence to ask. Now thoroughly provoked, they decided to let their sheep graze on the hill and marched to Portree to inform MacDonald's factor that 'their rents would not be paid that day, or any other day, until Ben Lee was returned to them'.

The response of Lord MacDonald was swift and savage. He ordered the eviction of twelve Braes crofters as an example and as an encouragement to the rest to abandon their rebellious stance. On 7 April 1882 a Sheriff Officer approached Braes with eviction papers but was confronted by a crowd of almost 200 crofters who grappled with the official, seized the documents and, to the accompaniment of jibes and cheers, burned the writs before his very eyes.

The situation was now deadly serious. By 'interfering with an officer of the law in the execution of his duty', the Braes rebels had moved from committing a civil offence to a criminal offence. For Sheriff William Ivory of Inverness-shire, this was the signal to muster all the force that he could against what he saw as an undisciplined band of upstarts who should be treated with no more respect than the Boreraig and Suisnish crofters 30 years before. (In my case, 300 miles before.) There being insufficient policemen in Inverness-shire, the Chief Constable of Glasgow sent up a posse of 50 officers to support the Skye police in the arrest of the five men supposedly mainly responsible for the attack on the Sheriff Officer.

Twelve days after the attack, on a day of cold wind and rain, the massive contingent of chilled, soaking police constables tramped miserably along the Braes road from Portree. Behind, Sheriff Ivory sat stately in a luxurious and weathertight carriage. He and the police were in for a nasty shock. Although the Sheriff had planned a dawn assault and managed to capture the five men, the Braes folk arranged an ambush at the northern end of Gedintailor, a narrow pass with a sheer drop to the sea below and a steep scree slope above. About 100 men, women and children pelted the astounded posse with a hail of sharp rocks in an effort to make them give up their five prisoners. A pitched battle resulted, the air thick with sleety rain, stones, sticks and Gaelic curses. Blood, sweat and tears mingled freely with the dreich April rain. For a while it appeared that the crofters would free the prisoners, but a final, frantic charge took the police through the frenzied crowd to the eventual safety of Portree.

The five men were fined in court the following day but the money was promptly paid by the Braes folk and the prisoners released. However, the Liberal Government of the time saw the Braes rebellion as an extremely serious situation and dispatched warships and marines to land at Uig to quell any subsequent riots and deal with any insubordination. The overkill reaction of the Government and the harassment of what most people saw as quiet, law-abiding country folk, led to huge protests throughout Britain. The Battle of the Braes and its sequel was now national news. In the wake of such widespread outcry, the troops were withdrawn and Gladstone set up a Royal Commission to investigate the crofters' grievances. After a lengthy hearing in Skye, the Crofters' Holdings Act was passed in 1886, guaranteeing fair rents and security of tenure.

Just before the narrow road swept down to the shore at Gedintailor, I stopped at a stone monument, a modest, unpretentious affair with a Gaelic sentence and its English translation inscribed on a simple white background:

'Near this cairn, on the 19th of April, 1882, ended the Battle fought by the people of Braes on behalf of the crofters of Gaeldom.'

As I stood and read these brief words, a film crew, festooned in gadgetry, was hovering about in the background. An interview with a local appeared to be being conducted and I guessed it was for a radio programme. It was a suitable testimony to the people of Braes that their battle of over a hundred years ago was still national news.

The road at Gedintailor split into two, running parallel with each other, to join together once again over a mile further on. I took the easterly one and was greeted by an American couple sitting in a garden and favourably commenting on the weather. Were they the owners, or holidaymakers? Opposite this section of road is an odd sickle-shaped peninsula which I had remembered seeing from the summit of Ben Tianavaig. I decided to head out to its inviting arm of sandy beach and find a pleasant spot for lunch. A car park charging a pound to park a car left me astounded. An overgrown path meandered down to beautiful Camas a' Mhorbheoil with its rock pools and scores of jellyfish. As I set foot on the sand, the middle distance exploded in a flurry of wings as a crowd of sandpipers and oystercatchers took to the air in a barrage of shrill, staccato shrieks. Ben Tianavaig presented a marvellous profile across the silvery grey water: a sweeping sward of green and scarp slopes. I found a comfortable rock and spent an indulgent half-hour eating, drinking and dreaming.

I dumped the pack and wandered out to the point (Dunan an Aislidh) where a jumble of rocks marked the remains of the dun. If there was ever to be a bridge from Skye to Raasay (God forbid) then it would be built here – Raasay is only just over half-a-mile from this wild spot. Caves marked on the map are only accessible at low tide but I had a potter around, searching for them, before collecting my pack to complete the final road mile to Peinchorran, the end of the road.

From here a footpath hugs the shoreline beneath Ben Lee's steep southern flank, leading in three-and-a-half miles to the Sligachan Hotel and campsite, my destination for this evening. Time was very much on my side and I felt no pressing need to break any records. The unsightly scar of the Sconser Quarry and the noise of traffic on the A850 across Loch Sligachan detracted somewhat from what was otherwise a delightful coastal ramble. I passed an idyllic camp spot on a springy area of short grass by a stream outflow, but the carrot of food, drink and Mike and Eva's company at the Sligachan Bar proved too strong.

The steep, scree-ridden slopes of Glamaig and its off-the-shoulder number of An Coileach dominated the view across the loch. It was this mountain in 1899 that Gurkha soldier, Harkabir Thapa, ascended and descended in an astounding 55 minutes (37 minutes up and 18 minutes down) – an amazing record by any standards but more so as he completed the task in bare feet. Such was the interest in and admiration for this feat that an annual Glamaig hill race continues to this day. The current record, set in 1994, stands at 46 minutes (with running shoes). Glamaig is one of the Red Cuillin range of rounded, rolling summits, in stark contrast to their craggy, castellated cousins, the Black Cuillin, sitting just across Glen Sligachan. The Black Cuillin form a crenellated half crown of spiky summits, around the jewel in the crown of Loch Coruisk, that dark ribbon of water I had visited three weeks previously. The serrated spire of Sgurr nan Gillean (peak of the young men) is the worthy end peak of the ridge and on a clear day should have presented a fine profile from the path I was now walking, but was obliterated by cloud.

Towards the campsite, the path petered out on an area of tidal mud flats and tussocky grass, the flood plain of the river Sligachan and its associated tributaries. Sligachan (the emphasis is on the 'Slig') translates as the shelly place and occupies a wild windswept position at the head of Glen Sligachan. There is little here but a hotel and campsite and even the latter is a relatively recent addition. The sweep of green grass of the campsite was, long ago, the site of a horse and cattle market, one of the main trysts on the route south to Crieff in the Southern Highlands. The first one took place in October 1794 and was attended by 4,000 people with another 1,600 cattle, horses and ponies. A huge tinker camp accompanied the fair where whisky flowed freely and music, song and dance lasted long into the night.

The modern equivalent is the nightly gathering at the

Sligachan Hotel annexe bar and restaurant. This relatively recent extension to the hotel was built to cope with the swelling numbers of climbers, walkers and outdoor enthusiasts who use Sligachan as a base camp for their pursuits. When I frequented Sligachan in the early 1980s there was no campsite and no extension bar. The days of camping near the old stone bridge over the river and cramming into the poky climbers' bar for a few pints are well and truly over – an old man of the hills wistfully reminisces!

The campsite was busy but not crowded and I found a passable place to erect my shelter for the evening. Just as I was about to set off to the washhouse I noticed a figure purposefully striding across to the campsite from the direction of the hotel. I recognised the figure immediately as Mike Wilson, but he obviously hadn't seen me in the colourful chaos of other tents. I walked across to meet him. When he saw me, his eyes lit up and his face broke into a welcoming, cheeky, cheerful grin. We shook hands and greeted each other in a series of one-liners. It was marvellous to be back in the bosom of an old friend. Ten days had passed since Mike and George had left the Stein Inn in Waternish – it seemed like months ago.

Mike drove his car down to the site with his wife, Eva. He would sleep in his tent while Eva, who was not keen on camping, would sleep in the car. The way things turned out that night, Eva was definitely the winner.

By the outrageously early hour of half-past four in the afternoon, the three of us were wiring into our first drinks in the spacious surroundings of the Sligachan bar/restaurant. We agreed that it could be a very long evening and that we would need to pace ourselves. In the bar was another of my charity donation bottles. This particular one was gratifyingly heavy. We ordered a meal and another drink and gently eased ourselves into the convivial ambience of an evening's craic.

The Sligachan bar of today is the very antithesis of the cramped climbers' bar of yesteryear. The natural wood decor, sheer spaciousness and various ante-rooms of a snooker/pool hall and children's play area, give the feeling of being in a more urban environment rather than in a tract of wild moor surrounded by mountains. On a dreich day it is not surprising that the place is hoaching with both climbers and tourists. Sligachan's climbing history betrays its presence by a selection of sepia, monochrome photographs on the wall, a brief slice of mountaineering memoirs.

It was in the Sligachan Hotel that the great Norman Collie spent his final years. In 1886, Collie, a Professor of Chemistry, came to Sligachan to fish. The weather was fine and the fishing poor so he walked the hills instead. One day he stood marvelling at two climbers high on the pinnacle ridge of Sgurr nan Gillean. He thought it 'perfectly marvellous that human beings should be able to do such things'. After discussion with the two climbers that very evening, Collie immediately telegraphed London for a climbing rope. The minute it arrived, Collie and his brother were off to the heights of the Cuillin – the rest is history, as they say. For the next 56 years much of Collie's life centred around Sligachan and the Black Cuillin and, although he climbed in other great ranges of the world, Skye was his second home. For many, Collie and the Cuillin were synonymous. He soon became a legendary figure with routes and peaks, such as Collie's Ledge, Collie's Route (The Cioch) and Sgurr Thormaid (Norman's Peak), littering the main ridge. Collie did much climbing with General Bruce and the aforementioned Harkobir Thapa (of barefoot Glamaig fame), but it was a local rock-climbing guide, John Mackenzie, who became his trusted climbing companion – almost his alter-ego. John climbed Sgurr nan Gillean in 1866 when he was just ten years old, an incredible feat for the time. He grew up to become Skye's original climbing guide, leading thousands of clients, both novices and experts, in their personal quest, with an unblemished safety record. After John Mackenzie died in 1934 Collie was never quite the same, for they had been inseparable companions for half a century. At the outbreak of war in 1939, Collie remained at Sligachan, totally alone apart from the hotel staff. Too frail to climb, he reverted to his early passion of fishing. The last glimpse we have of Collie is from pilot and author, Richard Hillary, who penned 'The Last Enemy' and ultimately gave his life in the Battle of Britain. Whilst convalescing in the hotel with a friend he wrote:

'We were alone in the Inn save for one old man who had returned there to die. His hair was white but his face and bearing were still those of a mountaineer, though he must have been a great age. He never spoke, but appeared regularly at meals to take his place at a table tight-pressed against the window, alone with his wine and memories. We thought him rather fine.' On his death bed, several friends attempted to get there to be with him. Only one, a Mr Lee, was successful and was with him when he died on 1 November 1942, aged 83. With him, the great golden age of Cuillin climbing sank into oblivion with the setting sun. The stage was set for the post-war crowds.

As a member of those crowds, I was sitting in the hotel dining room on the evening of 31 May 1982, celebrating a very special event. I had just spent fifteen glorious hours traversing the complete Cuillin ridge, once a feat thought to be possible 'only for the gods', now a fairly common occurrence (the record is now a staggering three-and-a-half hours end to end!). Sitting alone with his wine and memories wasn't Norman Collie, but a more up-to-date Cuillin devotee and photographer, William Arthur Poucher, author of the classic *The Magic of Skye* and *The Scottish Peaks*. I rose from my seat to introduce myself and steal an autograph. He too has now passed away, leaving a legacy of fine photographic volumes.

The Sligachan bar gradually filled out, and the three of us slowly chilled out, as the alcohol took effect. Our conversation ranged from wild camps to wildcats and wilderness to silliness, all to a background of awful out-of-key Scottish music. The bar used to have a good repertoire of Runrig, but their music was notable by its absence.

At some point during the evening we noted the weather worsening. A constant stream of 'drowned rats' squelched in from a wild and wet outside. As the door opened to let in another straggling line of sodden refugees, I could feel the draught and see rain bouncing off the puddles. The canvas awning above the door was heaving to and fro in the strengthening wind. We looked at each other with amused but worried grins. Two of us would be camping in this. Our minds were temporarily diverted from the weather by a lass from New Zealand who had spotted my Skyewalk T-shirt and came up to ask me how I was doing. I felt genuinely honoured by this appreciative gesture.

At 11 o'clock we took the bull by the horns and made our way outside into the maelstrom. Trousers and light trainers were literally soaked within seconds by the raging wind-driven rain. After what seemed like ages stumbling and squelching and being battered and buffeted by gusting wind, we reached our tents. The campsite was a chaotic quagmire of flapping fabric. Waves of rain swept over in unbridled intensity. My tent was almost unrecognisable – the rear guy line had been forced out and the flysheet front zip was open. The wind's ferocity almost flattened the tent. I attempted to put things right before diving inside, my 'goodnights' to Mike and Eva dying immediately in the howling gale.

Remarkably, my sleeping bag seemed dry and I removed every item of sodden clothing before snuggling into the relative warmth of chilled goosedown. I thought back to Duirinish exactly a fortnight ago and our wet and windy camp at Ramasaig. Tonight was far worse; in fact, these were the worst conditions in which I had ever camped. My chilled body slowly thawed out and turned to toast as I lay back and felt the wind's power ram the inner tent into the sleeping bag. Sleep was snatched in short bursts, the wild, dark night punctuated by numerous fumbling attempts to re-zip the outer flysheet. The last camp of Skyewalk was a night to remember.

* * * * *

A sluggish dawn and drumming rain provided little impetus to move. Some time later I emerged from my battered tent to a scene of devastation. Like the morning after a wild party, the campsite was a battlefield of bulldozed tents, littered items, and shell-shocked campers. In a steady rain I dodged puddles to reach the washroom. I was greeted by a line of weathered, weary faces, some poking out of sleeping bags. Many had preferred the safety of a building to sleeping in a tent and had spent the night there. I really couldn't blame them. Joseph Mitchell recorded this scene at the Sligachan cattle market in 1837:

'It had been raining all night and as most of the people had either been up drinking or sleeping on the bare ground during the night, they had a dirty and dishevelled appearance. The gentlemen had a bleary and unshaven aspect, the horses ungroomed, and there being no stables, little gillies with kilts, bare heads and bare legs were mounted and with much glee were riding backwards and forwards along the road...'

Very little had changed 150 years later.

I wasted no time in packing up and joining Mike and Eva for breakfast in the Sligachan bar. Lashings of hot tea and a big fry-up were especially welcome on that grey, gloomy morning. My rendezvous with Mike and Eva had been short and sweet, but their warmth and friendship had been an invaluable boost in the dire conditions. Like Mike, Eva has a kind-hearted, homely spirit and together they make a wonderful couple. They helped to give me the spiritual sustenance needed for the last two days of Skyewalk.

It was almost 10 o'clock when I deposited my main pack in the hotel and bade farewell to Mike and Eva. They drove off up the glistening thread of road, heading for Portree and touristy things. I turned to face the wind and weather and the long twenty-mile march to Broadford. For the first time on the walk I almost wanted it to be over. My chosen trail was wearing thin – the end was, if not in sight, within my grasp. Yet I felt no need to hurry. If you need to hurry then you shouldn't be walking, I maintained. For me, the journey is all, the destination nothing – more so when the journey is on foot and the destination is the starting point.

I crossed the old stone bridge over the Sligachan river, now a raging torrent of peaty brown water with cotton wool 'stoppers' of foaming white frenzy. The three dreary road miles up the south side of Loch Sligachan passed uneventfully and I made good time – not that it mattered. I reached Sconser just as the little car ferry was leaving for Raasay. The miserable conditions had reduced Raasay to a gloomy film smeared on a formless void. What a difference from Ben Tianavaig two days ago. Before 1976 there was no Caledonian MacBrayne ferry service to Raasay. Only a lengthy campaign by the islanders resulted in the present ferry and helped stem the island's declining fortunes.

As well as a ferry terminal, Sconser boasts a hotel and Skye's only municipal golf course. The Sconser Lodge Hotel was built on the site of the Old Inn visited by Johnson and Boswell in 1773. It has always appeared to me to be a slightly down-at-heel establishment, its grey colour on a grey day like today further fuelling my feelings.

Between Loch Sligachan and Loch Ainort the main A850 road climbs to the 140 metre bealach separating the Red Cuillin from a group of small hills on a stubby two-pronged peninsula. The 'old road' leaves the A850 at Sconser to follow the coastline of this peninsula, a route I had never taken. I was glad my first trial would be as a pedestrian and not as a motorist.

The start of this scenic route was marred by the extensive slate quarry, a permanent blot on the landscape. The whole site was like a set from *Doctor Who*; vast excavations and assorted Heath-Robinson-type machinery were strewn everywhere. However, it was a source of employment and probably would be for some time yet. Beyond the ugly scar of the quarry the outlook softened and I appreciated the absence of the charging brigade of tourist traffic on the A850. Since the opening of the new road some years ago this coastal loop had become a quiet backwater but I was still astounded by the almost total absence of vehicular traffic.

As I rounded the first point, another of Skye's offshore islands, Scalpay, became visible, drifting tendrils of cloud brushing its rolling features. Scalpay is a rough, heathery, hilly island with a highest point of almost 400 metres. I have often studied the island on OS Map 32 and planned possible walking routes for the time when I might pay it a visit.

Scalpay certainly didn't escape Johnson and Boswell's notice. (Was there anywhere in the Highlands they didn't go?) Dr Johnson wanted to buy the island and 'found a good school and an Episcopal church, and have a printing press' but his enthusiasm diminished on discovering that ownership required spending at least three months a year on the island. From having a population of 90 in 1841, Scalpay today has only seven, but this is at least an improvement on the early 1960s when only two souls lived there. There is no regular public access but private charter can be arranged from Broadford or Portree. Provided permission is obtained from Scalpay House, it is possible to camp on the island and there is also a holiday cottage to rent opposite Ard Dorch on Skye.

The sheltered bay containing the tiny settlement of Moll is home to the man-made austerity of fish farms. Men working in oilskins were tiny stabs of bright orange, providing the only real colour in a background of bleached grey-greens. Even the roadside heather struggled to be noticed. It had rained on and off since Sligachan but turning the headland at Maol Ban signalled a major improvement. The two straight road miles along the northern shore of Loch Ainort's sea finger were accompanied by a constant kaleidoscopic change in climatic conditions, creating a marvellous show of light and shade. For a short while the sun punched through the gloom and threw the immediate foreground into blazing, blinding brilliance. Beyond, the hulking forms of the Red Cuillin were black as night, ominous cloud shuffling uneasily around their partially obscured summits. Directly across the loch, Glas Bheinn Mhor's steep, dark, northern scree slopes were a deluge of ribboned white torrents.

Taking advantage of the break in the weather, I had a break myself and sat down for a bite. Marauding midges took advantage of me sitting down and began biting too. I swiftly moved on – crisps in left pocket and can of juice in right hand. Towards the head of Loch Ainort more fish farms appeared. A curlew gave a plaintive wail somewhere across the loch. A bobbing dipper played cat and mouse with me at the side of the road. A salvo of oystercatchers exploded at the edge of the loch in a volley of black, white and orange. This was road-walking at its best.

At the head of the loch the sun had retreated and a raw bleakness again enveloped the day. The old single-track road looped round the flat flood plain of the Allt Coire nam Bruadaran, crossing it by a fine stone bridge before finally rejoining the busy A850. The road-stroll up the other side of Loch Ainort was enlivened by another change in the weather. Cloud had lifted off Scalpay to reveal a mottled green and brown sun-speckled landscape. I took the small loop road at Luib partly to escape the traffic and partly out of interest. Had I not been tethered to the coastline, it would have been logical to follow a hill track from here to Strollamus, passing the southern flank of Am Meall, and cutting out three-and-a-half bustling road miles. A coffee shop looked inviting, but I resisted.

I rounded the point to Ard Dorch (Dark Head) and noticed the holiday house on Scalpay. By now the weather had vastly improved and life and colour were flooding back into everything. Despite the change for the better, I felt at a low ebb and opted for a Mars Bar stop at the bridge crossing the An Slugan. I had already walked over fourteen miles today and an energy boost was long overdue.

The next two miles were hot, hard road-bashing in the now warm afternoon sunshine. Scalpay's hills smouldered and I sweltered. The day had matured beyond recognition. Skye walking never palls. At a little forested, squat peninsula the road heads inland to reach Broadford in only one-and-a-half miles. Here I had a choice. I could adopt the quick and easy option of staying with tarmac or I could follow the coastline round the peninsula into Broadford Bay. As time was on my side and the weather fine, I decided to take the second option. Energy had also returned and the encouraging 'Forest Walk' label on the map tickled my exploratory instincts.

A forestry track led quickly to a small bay and jetty and I met a crowd of casual afternoon walkers coming the other way. Beyond here the path quickly deteriorated into a boggy trough ending at a shingly beach. The next mile was the sting in the tail of the day. A meandering line of low vegetated cliffs forced me up and down like a yo-yo. Thankfully the tide was partly out and a dry rock pavement beneath the crags was a great bonus. Beyond the forestry plantation the coastline opened out to a broad shingle beach. It was here that I noticed the unmistakable low curve of the Skye Bridge, arching in a single sweep to the mainland. Suddenly the end of the walk seemed close. This time tomorrow I could actually be back in Kylerhea, the beginning and end of my great dream.

I turned slowly southwards across sunlit machair and gazed across Broadford Bay. A threadlike sliver of light delicately illuminated a brilliant green strip on the opposite side. White sun-washed crofts were a perfect contrast to the murky, misty hills beyond. I crossed a stile and trod uneasily through a herd of high-land cattle. These beasts always look fearsome but are usually quite docile and unconcerned with humans. A track led me to the pier and the dubious delights of Broadford.

Skye's second largest town, Broadford has changed out of all recognition since 1843 when, according to Anderson's Guide, it consisted only of three houses and an inn. Now it is a long, strag-gling, centre-less thoroughfare of stark houses, hotels, guest houses, shops and garages. It is not one of my favourite places on Skye. Behind it towers Beinn na Caillich, a massive scree dome and another member of the rounded Red Cuillin family. The 'Hill of the Old Woman' is topped by a huge cairn, supposedly covering the remains of a Norwegian princess.

I soon tracked down my night's accommodation. The Sheiling, 2 Lower Harrapool, was an old stone dwelling belonging to Catherine Shearer, who had moved to Skye from Falkirk and opened a reptile centre, of all things. Catherine seemed a kindly, slightly eccentric soul. She showed me to my cosy room. She did-n't do dinner but recommended The Claymore restaurant and bar just a few hundred yards up the road. Although my socks and boots were wet there was no possibility of changing – all extra clothing had been left at Sligachan. Dry socks, shoes, jeans and shirt would have to wait until tomorrow evening when I would be back at my car. Two pints, soup, spaghetti bolognaise and apple crumble with ice-cream were a real treat, as was a long soak in the bath later. Tonight was my last evening on Skye soil.

* * * * *

I was wakened by the sound of geese cackling in a nearby field. Huge flocks of wild geese regularly fly across my home in Perthshire, their remarkable formation, flight and call at the very heart of wild beauty. In evening flight, they are inspirational. Grounded, they become menacing, noisy things to be avoided at all costs.

I had slept well. Outside, it seemed fairly bright but the old adage of 'bright too soon, rain by noon' was to be well and truly justified. Following a hearty breakfast, I packed my gear, said goodbye and set off. Within minutes I was donning waterproofs and the scene was set for the day.

The low-lying Ardnish peninsula on the east side of Broadford Bay was my first objective. To reach it I took the little B road to Waterloo, so named because of the large number of veterans of Wellington's army who once lived there. An incredible 1,600 Skyemen fought at the Battle of Waterloo. An old stone house called Honeymoon Cottage set me thinking. Heather and I were obviously not the only ones to honeymoon in Skye.

I soon reached the end of the road at a couple of modern bungalows and a gate. An overgrown path quickly became a choking morass of bog and bushes and any thoughts of reaching the scattered skerries at the head of Ardnish were laid to rest. I was fully aware of the distance involved today and the nature of the trackless terrain between Kyleakin and Kylerhea. The weather had by now also deteriorated to a dreich drizzle.

After a frustrating deviation, I finally reached a footbridge at Lower Breakish shown on the map. This turned out to be three slippery wooden spars with protruding nails. Brawn and balance saw me across to a stile and a field of long, wet grass leading up to a large house. Lower Breakish consists of two parallel straight roads, both north of the A850, and lying between it and the coast. It is not a part of Skye I would choose to live in, being too flat and too close to Broadford. I walked on the southerly Breakish road, rejoining the main road at Ashaig.

From here to Kyleakin was only five miles of road-walking, following the coastline all the way. To its left, the old road could be adopted in small chunks and these were taken to avoid traffic. I passed the signpost indicating the turn-off to Kylerhea – just eight road miles. Temptation resisted, I ploughed on with hood up and head down, the rain now coming down in torrents. Further sections of old road had signs saying 'Dangerous – peat bog' and 'Danger – slurry lagoon'. The narrow strip of land between the road and coast had apparently been the scene of a few accidents in the past.

The final few miles to Kyleakin were done on automatic pilot. Dreams of a bar lunch and a pint were forgotten when I passed a shop and decided to go in and stock up instead. I muttered something to the shopkeeper about the dreadful weather before leaving some money and a watery trail through the shop. Further along, a roundabout displayed a huge sign; 'S.K.A.T. NEWS – BEWARE – BOGUS TOLL COLLECTORS AHEAD'. S.K.A.T. stands for 'Skye and Kyle Against the Tolls', an organisation formed in the wake of the Skye Bridge to protest over the level of the toll charges.

Had I been literally on the coastline at this point, I would have had to go right under the bridge. Nevertheless, I still intended to do this but from the other direction. At the roundabout I turned right and followed the road downhill to Kyleakin, the old ferry terminal now dominated by the colossal, concrete geometry of the Skye Bridge. I headed directly across the grass frontage to reach the shingle beach, now alarmingly slippery in the heavy rain. A few hundred yards stumbling to the left and I was directly underneath this gargantuan man-made creation. High above my head the concrete span stretched to the first immense pillar before leaping across in one seamless, striking arc to Eilean Ban, almost a quarter-of-a-mile distant. There is no doubt in my mind that Skye's physical link with the mainland possesses an austere, simple elegance contrasting so profoundly with its rugged, natural background, that it paradoxically harmonises with it in an unobtrusive and unpretentious manner. The simplicity and purity of its design reflect the simplicity and purity of the natural landscape of which it is now a permanent part.

This is all in direct contrast to the ugly obscenity of the highest bridge tolls anywhere in Europe. Some wit has remarked that the Skye Bridge toll booth is the only place where you get mugged and are then given a receipt. The real tragedy was (and still is) the Tory Government's dogmatic and narrow-minded policy of pursuing a privately financed scheme in order to pay for the bridge. The so-called Private Finance Initiative is, at best, unjustified; at worst, a bungled botch-up job which is a blatant and insulting injustice both to the Skye people and to everyone using the bridge.

There are those who argue that the cost of the old ferry was the same as the bridge tolls, so what is all the commotion about? Consider this: the level of ferry fares was well above the operating costs but the surplus was used to cross-subsidise other ferry services within the Caledonian MacBrayne network, i.e. the money was being sensibly used to further boost the Highland economy. More than half the cost of the bridge toll goes into the cost of actually collecting it in the first place. The rest is lining the pockets of 'fat cat' Bank of America shareholders and subsidising the most expensive, unjust government stitch-up of the millennium.

So determined was the Scottish Office to thrust the project through on a privately tolled basis, that they failed to provide any consultation with local people and bridge users. Neither did they carry out any formal risk analysis. Blinkered and blinded, they blundered into a major contract totally oblivious to the potential costs to the public purse. A public enquiry into the project was not held until after the contract had been signed and the toll level set – a bit like closing the stable door after the horse has bolted. Rather than admit to their errors, the Scottish Office continued to churn out propaganda and lies to cover up their wrongdoings. This included a statement to the effect that public funding was not costed as it would be 'misleading'. If their intention was not to mislead the public, then they have failed miserably.

One of the most blatant lies peddled to the public was that a publicly funded bridge could not have been constructed for at least twenty years. According to the National Audit Office, construction costs at the time were given as £20 million, with public funds amounting to nearly £15 million put into the P.F.I. The balance of £5 million could easily have been generated from another five years of ferry profits. With Objective One funding (secured after the contract was awarded) the final result could have been a completely toll-free bridge for nearly £5 million less than the current financial fiasco.

The Scottish Executive continues to cloak its subversive, prejudiced dealings under the misleading title of a Private Finance Initiative. In fact, the amount of private money in the Skye Bridge amounts to less than 2% of the total bridge cost!

To add even more insult to an already fatal injury, Skye Bridge Ltd saw fit to raise the toll charges from what was already nearly £5 to almost £6 in the summer (these charges are one way only!). The Cal-Mac Ferries adopted this tactic in order to pay additional staff involved with marshalling the unavoidable queues of traffic. No such marshalling is required at the bridge, so why the inflated charge?

The tragic aftermath of this catastrophic 'cock-up' is that the already delicate economy of Skye has taken such a blow that it may require years to recover fully. A survey at the toll booth indicated that during the summer as many as 50 vehicles each day were turning back due to the level of toll. The removal of tolls would add £2.5 million to the Skye economy and increase tourist visits by 10%.

In the wake of all this, is it any wonder that an organisation such as SKAT was formed to fight the injustice of the whole debacle? The reader may not be surprised that I am a member of SKAT and proudly display a sticker on the back of my car. Displaying SKAT stickers is one thing, but a few hundred others have gone further and refused to pay the tolls, resulting in an eventual trial at Dingwall Sheriff Court. The lengthy business of being charged, put on trial and possibly arrested has itself been a major bureaucratic nightmare and the details will be spared here. Suffice to say that the first arrests of non-payment protesters took place on 4 June 1997, when over 100 people, led by pipers, marched around the square in Portree, in defiance of the verdict.

One wonders whether Skye has made much progress since 19 April 1882 and the Battle of the Braes. Renewed optimism following the voting in to power of the Labour Government in 1997 and the establishment of the Scottish Parliament in 1999 was to crack under the political hammer of misplaced trust and broken promises. Labour's vow to seriously tackle the toll problem was lamentably shunted to the sidelines on the pretence that most Scots couldn't care less about the tolls. Presumably 'most Scots' refer to those living in the Central Belt and if this group doesn't allegedly care less, then there is no political mileage in pursuing the campaign. Such is the stunted, selfish thinking of modern government. The wheel of injustice and persecution has turned full circle from the Braes to the Bridge. Once again, like the Clearances, the people of Skye are being held to ransom by an unbending and unscrupulous wall of authority.

Perhaps it was appropriate that the day was clamped in a chilling dampness and torrential rain. I took one last look out to Eilean Ban, where Gavin Maxwell had spent some time studying otters in splendid isolation. His island was now debased to a mere stepping stone for the great concrete cord tethering An t-Eilean Sgitheanach to the mainland.

I wandered back up to the road and into the small community of Kyleakin, once a thriving village and tourist haunt, now a virtual ghost town in the wake of the bridge. Kyleakin takes its name from Haakon, the Norse King whose fleet anchored here en route to Largs in 1263. There was a detached, discarded feel about the place, accentuated further by the drab weather. I found myself scurrying through the wet streets, skipping puddles, anxious to reach the familiarity of the ruined Castle Maoil, standing on a wind-blasted rocky promontory east of the pier where, for scores of years, in all weathers, the ferry had ploughed its way across Kyle Akin delivering its human cargo. During all my years of using this ferry to land on Skye, rushing to pay homage at the hallowed altar of the Cuillin, I am ashamed to admit that the side chapel of Castle Maoil had been denied my attention – until now.

I searched, and found the path leading to the conspicuous,

eroded, twin towers of this romantic ruin, a maritime marker for the ferry-goer, a symbolic sentinel standing guard over the Kyleakin narrows. I trudged around a small cove containing a boat shed and railed slipway. A sign warned of tides but it didn't concern me, as I wasn't returning that way. A steep mud-caked trail led upwards through the heathery hillside to the castle. The scant ruins of Dun Akyn (Norse for Haakon's Fort) were once a proud fortress against Norse raids and later became a home of the MacKinnons of Strath. In bygone days it was said that tolls were lifted from boats passing the Kyles. Legend also has it that Saucy Mary, a Norwegian Princess, stretched a chain from the Castle to the mainland, ensuring that no boat sailed through without paying up. The modern counterpart to Saucy Mary's Chain is the Skye Bridge toll booth. Is the bridge perhaps the twisted truth of an ancient prophecy? I took a gloomy photograph of the old and the new together; the rustic simplicity of the ruins and the geometric simplicity of the bridge collided and juxtaposed – oddly harmonious bedfellows. In the murky vapidity, the bridge's bold profile had already faded to a tenuous stretched thread.

South of Kyleakin, Loch na Beiste (Loch of the Otter) produced an unavoidable dogleg around its head which, on the map, appeared a fairly harmless route. The reality was very different. The terrain south of the castle was a morass of heather-clad hillocks and sphagnum moss bogs. Stumbling and sweating in rain gear I forged a tortuous trail on to Cnoc na Loch, a small knoll supporting the remains of old Second World War concrete pillboxes. The outlook from this vantage point was utterly depressing. My proposed coastal route visible across Loch na Beiste was devoid of any obvious walkable line. The steep hillside was clothed in deciduous forest to sea level and the shoreline itself was a thin line of crags and boulders. If I was to reach Kylerhea at all that day, I was going to have to climb high – very high. My eyes drifted upwards into mist shrouded hills and waves of rain sweeping across the bleak scene – Skyewalk wasn't in the bag yet.

A more immediate concern, however, was to reach the head of the sea-loch. Ahead, a trough-like depression was a jungle of thick

bushes and low trees. I made the decision to try and reach the
shoreline and spent the next fifteen minutes bush-whacking my
promising. A thin ribbon of slippery rocks and seaweed led in a
few hundred metres to a section of cliffs
plunging almost vertically into the
water. If I failed to discover a route
along their base I would be
forced back up through thickly
vegetated slopes with at least
50 metres of ascent.

With heavy heart I began edg-

Castle Maoil   ing my way along a ledge and flake system at the
foot of the cliff. The rock was greasy but a slip would result in a
'dooking' rather than serious injury – or so I told myself.
Eventually I found myself at the crux of the section. A final projecting rib of cliff with a partially overhanging nose of rock lay
between me and the bouldered shoreline beyond. I crept along a
narrow shelf until the angle of the cliff forced me outward. I knew
I was fast approaching the knife-edge boundary between advance
and retreat. Retreat was unthinkable and yet to continue seemed
utterly foolhardy. For a moment I was paralysed on the horns of
a decision-less dilemma. I glanced at my right hand clinging to a
crack in the rock. My fingers were white with the pressure. In my
other hand the trekking pole was as useless as an ashtray on a
motorbike. Almost without thinking, I swung my left hand and
threw the pole the few metres to safety beyond the overhanging
nose. In doing this I had freed my left hand and effectively tilted
the balance in favour of going on. I carefully lowered my body and
grabbed a hold of the ledge on which I was standing. In one adren-
alin-powered pendulum movement, I swung my whole body forward until my feet made contact with the rock on which lay the
pole.

Ten minutes late I reached the relative safety of the head of
Loch na Beiste and waded uncaringly through the river's outflow.
High on adrenalin and soaked in sweat and rain, I flopped down
on a wet rock to quench a raging thirst. It had taken an incredible

one-and-a-half hours to cover the mile from the castle to here. Yet what lay ahead looked far worse and would take far longer. The hideously rocky, vegetated nature of the coastline was undeniably the least walker-friendly of the entire trip. It was as though I was being thrown one last great gauntlet in order to prove my worth to tread the full length of Skye's coastline. As on the second day of the walk, almost four weeks ago, I had imagined the Winged Isle itself to be testing my worthiness for such prolonged intimacy. Its final, ferocious examination was to provide a true test of my grit and determination.

I brooded and pondered over my next moves. Thick bracken and trees pushing down to water level dictated a long climb up to bare heathery hillside some 150 metres higher. This, however, proved a nightmare. A forest of bracken gave me twenty minutes of frustrated fern-bashing, in some instances the bracken stretching above head height. Underfoot was a quagmire of bog and rotten moss-laden wood. Higher still I grappled with two deer fences, eventually reaching firmer heathery hillside. Having gained what I reckoned to be enough height to escape the clutches of bracken and trees, I began a gradual rising traverse eastwards, aiming roughly for a gap between Carn an t-Seachrain and the higher Graham of Beinn na Caillich (another Hill of the Old Woman). The next major hurdle was the crossing of a series of river gorges, these slowing the rhythm – what there was of it.

Some two miles and much climbing later, I reached the boggy bealach. I was now engulfed in thick water-laden mist and struggling into the teeth of wind-driven rain. Hunched, harassed and weather-beaten, I wandered on, all sense of direction now gone. A compass was an item which I thought would not be needed on a coastal walk – or was it in my main pack? A series of enormous poles loomed out of the grey clag, but turned out to be mere fence posts. A small lochan shown on the map failed to materialise and I began to seriously doubt my position. The mist seemed to be distorting space, time and even my own sanity.

After what seemed like hours, a faint, feeble wriggling line emerged from a grey sludge, and then a muted white shape far in the distance. A few steps later and I realised I was looking at the mainland coastline across the Kylerhea narrows. The white shape was the ferry house. The end was in sight. A faint whisper of movement through the gloom could have been the ferry, or my mind playing tricks.

I crossed a deer fence and gradually descended through a new forest plantation, intent on finding the forestry track I had spotted a month ago. The descent proved to be almost as horrendous as the ascent from the Kyleakin side. Trenches, deep bracken, choking heather – all conspired to stretch me to breaking point. Lower down, I found myself on a heathery spur between two deep gorges. A steep descent was made into the left one, followed by a heather-tugging tussle to extricate myself up the other side. A final exhausting descent took me to the track where I had to negotiate a near vertical craggy drop just to reach it.

It was a drenched and weary figure who trudged the last mile to the ferry at Kylerhea. I passed several folk who had walked along to Otter-haven, a shoreline nature centre where it was possible to view otters in their natural habitat. At that moment otters were the last thing on my mind.

The final half-mile of track frustratingly passed the ferry point and I was forced to dogleg back along the road. As I reached the end and beginning of my journey at Kylerhea I was surprised at my lack of emotion – that would come later. All I wanted now was a dry change of clothes and a hot cup of tea. Roddy and his son were there working the ferry as they had been doing day in, day out, for the last month while I had flirted on my grand flight of fancy round the furthest reaches of the Winged Isle. They remembered me – just; but little was said as I dragged my dripping body aboard along with three cars.

Cold, wet exhaustion enveloped me. I felt numbed both physically and spiritually. The end was an anticlimax in every sense, but I knew that, psychologically, I was yet to come to terms with Skyewalk.

On the road walk to Dalmor, the Chisholm's B&B, the weather perked up briefly and a watery sun threw a layer of glitter on the sea. Beyond, the hills of Skye were still shrouded in mist. As I walked, I warmed up and my spirits rose. Mentally and emotionally I was still Skye-walking. It would be a while before my tangled emotions would unwind and allow me to view the walk as a holistic entity.

A hearty welcome awaited at the Chisholm's. Within seconds of arrival I was sitting in the warmth of the kitchen with a mug of tea in my hand. Chaotic conversation could only be the result of trying to compress four weeks of colourful experiences into half-an-hour.

Unfortunately, they were unable to put me up that night but a B&B beyond the Glenelg Inn, belong to a Margaret Cameron, had a spare room. Reluctantly, I pulled the plug on our cosy kitchen chat and bid a poignant farewell and thank you. My old but trusty VW Polo came to a spluttering, rude awakening from its month of hibernation. It felt strange to be driving after such a prolonged absence from being behind the wheel. My new venue was a big modern bungalow where I revelled in a hot bath and a change of clothes.

The end of the day, and the symbolic end of the walk, was the Glenelg Inn where, a month ago, I had spent the last evening on the mainland, poised on the brink of my Skye sojourn. Now I was there again, sitting at the bar, cigar in hand, fondly reminiscing and rekindling the fiery dream which was no longer. The wet beginnings in Sleat, homely Fiordhem, the wild camp at Borreraig, Camasunary and the Cuillin, lazy days and crazy nights at Carbost Inn, the wonderful week with Mike and George and the Stein gathering, my meeting with Heather, ethereal Rubha Hunish, the glorious day on Ben Tianavaig, the storm at Sligachan, the final rain-lashed day – these were just a sprinkling of the myriad gems in the memory's treasure chest. Like the grounded geese I had heard first thing this morning, there were days, like today, which were a vexation to the flow of the walk. Others, many others, like scores of gleeful geese in full formation flight, were truly inspirational.

Yet the walk was more than just a collection of days. It had been an exploration, a probing through not just a contorted geographical space but also a contorted historical time. The bare bones of geology and the bald carcass of history were glaringly and often distressingly evident in the form of bleak, blackhouse remains sucked dry of human motion and emotion, of hearth and heart. The endless ebb and flow of geography and geology, of history and mystery, of time and tide, of wavering weather and wonderful company – all had woven into a tangled path round Skye's coastline. In their wake trailed a single shimmering thread of experiences, now matted to a colourful tapestry of cherished memories.

As I wallowed in these memories and ordered my third pint of Gillespie's, I was conscious of background music. Nothing unusual in that, except that I was listening to what seemed at the time the most haunting and most appropriate piece of music that I had ever come across. The track was a simple Celtic melody played on Uilleann pipes, but for me it was the musical manifestation of the walk in every sense. Its slightly mournful, pensive air struck a chord and tugged at my heart. I was completely captivated. Enquiries resulted in the empty cassette box being set in front of me. The album was 'Pipedreams' by Davy Spillane, an Irish musician of whom I had never heard. The track which had impressed me was 'Midnight Walker'. More to the point, however, were the titles of some of the other tracks: 'Shifting Sands', 'Stepping in Silence', 'Shorelines' – these had obvious associations with my activities of the previous month. I vowed one of the first things I would do on my return home would be to buy the album on CD.

I downed my pint and called it a day. The music was finished, the walk was finished, the final note had been struck. The midnight walker strolled out from the smoky, hustling atmosphere of the pub to the soft summer highland air. The heaviness of the gloomy sky was punctuated by a thin ribbon of flushed yellow and pink above the low hills of Skye – a western whisper of sun-tinged cirrus. Before the walk had begun I had had an unsettling feeling that Skyewalk might leave me jaded and weary with the magic and mystery of the Winged Isle. I needn't have worried.

Route Summary: Portree to Kylerhea and Glenelg

Day 1: Portree – Portree via Ben Tianavaig (11 miles – 18 km)

This is described as a circular route though could, of course, be tackled as part of a linear route to Sligachan. Leave Portree heading south on the A850 and turn off left at the Braes road. Take the minor road to Penifiler before heading cross country to the clifftop above Camas Ban. Follow the top of these cliffs eastward for just over a mile to the foot of the north ridge of Ben Tianavaig. Ascend pleasant grassy slopes to the summit – a marvellous viewpoint. Descend the prominent south ridge and gradually swing round west to descend to Camastianavaig. Follow the road back to Portree.

Day 2: Portree – Sligachan (14 miles – 22 km)

Retrace the first part of the Ben Tianavaig route but continue along the B883 to the Braes. A side excursion to the beak-shaped peninsula containing Dun an Aislidh is well worth the effort. Reach the road end at Peinchorran and from there follow the coastal path, hugging the north shore of Loch Sligachan. This reaches Sligachan in three-and-a-half miles.

Day 3: Sligachan – Broadford (20 miles – 32 km)

This is a long day and almost entirely road walking. Follow the A850 from Sligachan along the south shore of Loch Sligachan. At Sconsor take the old road following the coast round to Moll and into Loch Ainort. Rejoin the A850 at the head of the loch and follow the road all the way along the coast to Camas na Sgianadin. Leave the road along a forestry track as far as possible before continuing along the coastline on tricky craggy terrain at the edge of a forest. At the end of the trees the going becomes easier. Reach the pier at Corry and the road into Broadford.

Day 4: Broadford – Kylerhea and Glenelg (15 miles – 24 km)

This is not a particularly long day but the section from Kyleakin to Kylerhea is possibly the most walker-unfriendly of the entire trek. Follow the A850 east from Broadford with the option of an excursion out to Rubha Ardnish via Waterloo (not included in the above mileage). Continue along the main road before visiting Lower Breakish on minor roads. Rejoin the main road and follow it all the way to Kyleakin. Cross the river in Kyleakin and turn left along the road leading to Castle Maoil via a path round a small cove. From the castle to the head of Loch na Beiste involves extremely awkward going in deep heathery hillocks and small trees. From the head of the loch, climb upwards through deep bracken and trees, gradually traversing eastwards. Cross a couple of deer fences to keep above the main mass of trees. It is probably best to head for the gap containing Loch an t-Seachrain before gradually descending south east to pick up the forestry track leading to Kylerhea. Alternatively stay with the pylons round the point but expect very heavy going.

Accommodation and other information

Sligachan: Hotel and campsite
Broadford: Hotels, hostel, B&Bs, shops, campsite south of Lower Breakish
Kyleakin: Hotels, B&Bs, bridge to mainland
Kyerhea: Be sure to catch the ferry – there is no accommodation in Kylerhea

Postscript

THE FOLLOWING DAY I returned to Skye by car on a mad-dash tour to collect deposits of gear and donation bottles in such diverse venues as Fiordhem, Stein, Uig, Portree, Sligachan and Strathaird. This was more tiring than a day's walking. On the long drive south to Perthshire I was flushed with the anticipation of being reunited with my wife and family.

Two-and-a-half months later, Heather gave birth to Ruaraidh, a healthy, bouncy boy and my only son. Sometime around then, I began the long process of writing this book, a task which was monumentally more difficult than the walk itself. Writing a book of this nature is a bit like trying to release a butterfly from a locked box. Sometimes the key is found and the butterfly is set free. On other occasions the butterfly is dead or the key cannot even be found.

At the end of the day, the reader will decide if I have been at least partially successful in conveying some of the magic and mystery of the Winged Isle through the act of walking its coastline.

Some other books published by **LUATH** PRESS

WALK WITH LUATH

Scotland's Mountains before the Mountaineers

Ian Mitchell

ISBN 0 946487 39 1 PBK £9.99

In this ground-breaking book, Ian Mitchell tells the story of explorations and ascents in the Scottish Highlands in the days before mountaineering became a popular sport – when bandits, Jacobites, poachers and illicit distillers traditionally used the mountains as sanctuary. The book also gives a detailed account of the map makers, road builders, geologists, astronomers and naturalists, many of whom ascended hitherto untrodden summits while working in the Scottish Highlands.

Scotland's Mountains before the Mountaineers is divided into four Highland regions, with a map of each region showing key summits. While not designed primarily as a guide, it will be a useful handbook for walkers and climbers. Based on a wealth of new research, this book offers a fresh perspective that will fascinate climbers and mountaineers and everyone interested in the history of mountaineering, cartography, the evolution of landscape and the social history of the Scottish Highlands.

'*... will give you much to think about next time you're up that mountain.*' THE GUARDIAN

'*To have produced a work of such significance that is also fun to read is an achievement.*' HIGH

Mountain Days & Bothy Nights

Dave Brown and Ian Mitchell

ISBN 0 946487 15 4 PBK £7.50

Acknowledged as a classic of mountain writing still in demand ten years after its first publication, this book takes you into the bothies, howffs and dosses on the Scottish hills. Fishgut Mac, Desperate Dan and Stumpy the Big Yin stalk hill and public house, evading gamekeepers and Royalty with a camaraderie which was the trademark of Scots hillwalking in the early days.

'*The fun element comes through... how innocent the social polemic seems in our nastier world of today... the book for the rucksack this year.*' Hamish Brown, SCOTTISH MOUNTAINEERING CLUB JOURNAL

The Joy of Hillwalking

Ralph Storer

ISBN 0 946487 28 6 PBK £7.50

Apart, perhaps, from the joy of sex, the joy of hillwalking brings more pleasure to more people than any other form of human activity.

'*Alps, America, Scandinavia, you name it – Storer's been there, so why the hell shouldn't he bring all these various*

and varied places into his observations... [He] even admits to losing his virginity after a day on the Aggy Ridge... Well worth its place alongside Storer's earlier works.' TAC

LUATH WALKING GUIDES

The highly respected and continually updated guides to the Cairngorms.

'*Particularly good on local wildlife and how to see it*' THE COUNTRYMAN

Walks in the Cairngorms

Ernest Cross

ISBN 0 946487 09 X PBK £4.95

This selection of walks celebrates the rare birds, animals, plants and geological wonders of a region often believed difficult to penetrate on foot. Nothing is difficult with this guide in your pocket, as Cross gives a choice for every walker, and includes valuable tips on mountain safety and weather advice.

Ideal for walkers of all ages and skiers waiting for snowier skies.

Short Walks in the Cairngorms

Ernest Cross

ISBN 0 946487 23 5 PBK £4.95

Cross wrote this volume after overhearing a walker remark that there were no short walks for lazy ramblers in the Cairngorm region. Here is the answer: rambles through scenic woods with a welcoming pub at the end, birdwatching hints, glacier holes, or for the fit and ambitious, scrambles up hills to admire vistas of glorious scenery. Wildlife in the Cairngorms is unequalled elsewhere in Britain, and here it is brought to the binoculars of any walker who treads quietly and with respect.

LUATH GUIDES TO SCOTLAND

These guides are not your traditional where-to-stay and what-to-eat books. They are companions in the rucksack or car seat, providing the discerning traveller with a blend of fiery opinion and moving description. Here you will find '*that curious pastiche of myths and legend and history that the Scots use to describe their heritage... what battle happened in which glen between which clans; where the Picts sacrificed bulls as recently as the 17th century... A lively counterpoint to the more standard, detached guidebook... Intriguing.'*

THE WASHINGTON POST

These are perfect guides for the discerning visitor or resident to keep close by for reading again and again, written by authors who invite you to share their intimate knowledge and love of the areas covered.

Mull and Iona: Highways and Byways

Peter Macnab

ISBN 0 946487 58 8   PBK   £4.95

'The Isle of Mull is of Isles the fairest,
Of ocean's gems 'tis the first and rarest.'

So a local poet described it a hundred years ago, and this recently revised guide to Mull and sacred Iona, the most accessible islands of the Inner Hebrides, takes the reader on a delightful tour of these rare ocean gems, travelling with a native whose unparalleled knowledge and deep feeling for the area unlock the byways of the islands in all their natural beauty.

South West Scotland

Tom Atkinson

ISBN 0 946487 04 9   PBK   £4.95

This descriptive guide to the magical country of Robert

Burns covers Kyle, Carrick, Galloway, Dumfriesshire, Kirkcudbrightshire and Wigtownshire. Hills, unknown moors and unspoiled beaches grace a land steeped in history and legend and portrayed with affection and deep delight.

An essential book for the visitor who yearns to feel at home in this land of peace and grandeur.

The West Highlands: The Lonely Lands

Tom Atkinson

ISBN 0 946487 56 1   PBK   £4.95

A guide to Inveraray, Glencoe, Loch Awe, Loch

Lomond, Cowal, the Kyles of Bute and all of central Argyll written with insight, sympathy and loving detail. Once Atkinson has taken you there, these lands can never feel lonely. 'I have sought to make the complex simple, the beautiful accessible and the strange familiar,' he writes, and indeed he brings to the land a knowledge and

affection only accessible to someone with intimate knowledge of the area.

A must for travellers and natives who want to delve beneath the surface.

'Highly personal and somewhat quirky... steeped in the lore of Scotland.'
THE WASHINGTON POST

The Northern Highlands: The Empty Lands

Tom Atkinson

ISBN 0 946487 55 3   PBK   £4.95

The Highlands of Scotland from Ullapool to Bettyhill and Bonar Bridge to John O' Groats are landscapes of myth and legend, 'empty of people, but of nothing else that brings delight to any tired soul,' writes Atkinson. This highly personal guide describes Highland history and landscape with love, compassion and above all sheer magic.

Essential reading for anyone who has dreamed of the Highlands.

The North West Highlands: Roads to the Isles

Tom Atkinson

ISBN 0 946487 54 5   PBK   £4.95

Ardnamurchan, Morvern, Morar, Moidart and the west coast to Ullapool are included in this guide to the Far West and Far North of Scotland. An unspoiled land of mountains, lochs and silver sands is brought to the walker's toe-tips (and to the reader's fingertips) in this stark, serene and evocative account of town, country and legend.

For any visitor to this Highland wonderland, Queen Victoria's favourite place on earth.

NATURAL SCOTLAND

Wild Scotland: The essential guide to finding the best of natural Scotland

James McCarthy

Photography by Laurie Campbell

ISBN 0 946487 37 5   PBK   £7.50

With a foreword by Magnus Magnusson and striking colour photographs by Laurie Campbell, this is the essential up-to-date guide to viewing wildlife in Scotland for the visitor and resident alike. It provides a fascinating overview of the country's plants, animals, bird and marine life against the background of their typical natural settings, as an introduction to the vivid descriptions of the most accessible localities, linked to clear regional maps. A unique feature is the focus on 'green tourism' and sustainable visitor use of the countryside, contributed by Duncan Bryden, manager of the Scottish Tourist Board's Tourism and the Environment Task Force. Important practical information on access and the best times of year for viewing sites makes this an indispensable and user-friendly travelling companion to anyone interested in exploring Scotland's remarkable natural heritage.

James McCarthy is former Deputy Director for Scotland of the Nature Conservancy Council, and now a Board Member of Scottish Natural Heritage and

Chairman of the Environmental Youth Work National Development Project Scotland.

'Nothing but Heather!'
Gerry Cambridge

ISBN 0 946487 49 9 PBK £15.00

Enter the world of Scottish nature – bizarre, brutal, often beautiful, always fascinating – as seen through the lens and poems of Gerry Cambridge, one of Scotland's most distinctive contemporary poets.

On film and in words, Cambridge brings unusual focus to bear on lives as diverse as those of dragonflies, hermit crabs, short-eared owls, and wood anemones. The result is both an instructive look by a naturalist at some of the flora and fauna of Scotland and a poet's aesthetic journey.

This exceptional collection comprises 48 poems matched with 48 captioned photographs. In his introduction Cambridge explores the origins of the project and the approaches to nature taken by other poets, and incorporates a wry account of an unwillingly-sectarian, farm-labouring, bird-obsessed adolescence in rural Ayrshire in the 1970s.

'Keats felt that the beauty of a rainbow was somehow tarnished by knowledge of its properties. Yet the natural world is surely made more, not less, marvellous by awareness of its workings. In the poems that accompany these pictures, I have tried to give an inkling of that. May the marriage of verse and image enlarge the reader's appreciation and, perhaps, insight into the chomping, scurrying, quivering, procreating and dying kingdom, however many miles it be beyond the door.'
GERRY CAMBRIDGE

'a real poet, with a sense of the music of language and the poetry of life...' KATHLEEN RAINE
'one of the most promising and original of modern Scottish poets... a master of form and subtlety.'
GEORGE MACKAY BROWN

Scotland Land and People
An Inhabited Solitude
James McCarthy

ISBN 0 946487 57 X PBK £7.99

'Scotland is the country above all others that I have seen, in which a man of imagination may carve out his own pleasures; there are so many inhabited solitudes.'
DOROTHY WORDSWORTH, in her journal of August 1803

An informed and thought-provoking profile of Scotland's unique landscapes and the impact of humans on what we see now and in the future. James McCarthy leads us through the many aspects of the land and the people who inhabit it: natural Scotland; the rocks beneath; land ownership; the use of resources; people and place; conserving Scotland's heritage and much more.

Written in a highly readable style, this concise volume offers an under-standing of the land as a whole. Emphasising the uniqueness of the Scottish environment, the author explores the links between this and other aspects of our culture as a key element in redis-

covering a modern sense of the Scottish identity and perception of nationhood.

'This book provides an engaging introduction to the mysteries of Scotland's people and landscapes. Difficult concepts are described in simple terms, providing the interested Scot or tourist with an invaluable overview of the country... It fills an important niche which, to my knowledge, is filled by no other publications.'

BETSY KING, Chief Executive, Scottish Environmental Education Council.

The Highland Geology Trail
John L Roberts

ISBN 0946487 36 7 PBK £4.99

Where can you find the oldest rocks in Europe?
Where can you see ancient hills around 800 million years old?
How do you tell whether a valley was carved out by a glacier, not a river?
What are the Fucoid Beds?
Where do you find rocks folded like putty?
How did great masses of rock pile up like snow in front of a snow-plough?
When did volcanoes spew lava and ash to form Skye, Mull and Rum?
Where can you find fossils on Skye?

'...a lucid introduction to the geological record in general, a jargon-free exposition of the regional background, and a series of descriptions of specific localities of geological interest on a 'trail' around the highlands.
Having checked out the local references on the ground, I can vouch for their accuracy and look forward to investigating farther afield, informed by this guide.
Great care has been taken to explain specific terms as they occur and, in so doing, John Roberts has created a resource of great value which is eminently usable by anyone with an interest in the outdoors...the best bargain you are likely to get as a geology book in the foreseeable future.'
Jim Johnston, PRESS AND JOURNAL

Rum: Nature's Island
Magnus Magnusson

ISBN 0 946487 32 4 £7.95 PBK

Rum: Nature's Island is the fascinating story of a Hebridean island from the earliest times through to the Clearances and its period as the sporting playground of a Lancashire industrial magnate, and on to its rebirth as a National Nature Reserve, a model for the active ecological management of Scotland's wild places.

Thoroughly researched and written in a lively accessible style, the book includes comprehensive coverage of the island's geology, animals and plants, and people, with a special chapter on the Edwardian extravaganza of Kinloch Castle. There is practical information for visitors to what was once known as 'the Forbidden Isle'; the book provides details of bothy and other accommodation, walks and nature trails. It closes with a positive vision for the island's future: biologically diverse, economically dynamic and ecologically sustainable.

Rum: Nature's Island is published in co-operation with

Scottish Natural Heritage to mark the 40th anniversary of the acquisition of Rum by its predecessor, The Nature Conservancy.

Red Sky at Night

John Barrington

ISBN 0 946487 60 X   £8.99

'I read John Barrington's book with growing delight. This working shepherd writes beautifully about his animals, about the wildlife, trees and flowers which surround him at all times, and he paints an unforgettable picture of his glorious corner of Western Scotland. It is a lovely story of a rather wonderful life'.
JAMES HERRIOT

John Barrington is a shepherd to over 750 Blackface ewes who graze 2,000 acres of some of Britain's most beautiful hills overlooking the deep dark water of Loch Katrine in Perthshire. The yearly round of lambing, dipping, shearing and the sales is marvellously interwoven into the story of the glen, of Rob Roy in whose house John now lives, of curling when the ice is thick enough, and of sheep dog trials in the summer. Whether up to the hills or along the glen, John knows the haunts of the local wildlife: the wily hill fox, the grunting badger, the herds of red deer, and the shrews, voles and insects which scurry underfoot. He sets his seasonal clock by the passage of birds on the loch, and jealously guards over the golden eagle's eyrie in the hills. Paul Armstrong's sensitive illustrations are the perfect accompaniment to the evocative text.

'Mr Barrington is a great pleasure to read. One learns more things about the countryside from this account of one year than from a decade of The Archers'.
THE DAILY TELEGRAPH

'Powerful and evocative... a book which brings vividly to life the landscape, the wildlife, the farm animals and the people who inhabit John's vista. He makes it easy for the reader to fall in love with both his surrounds and his commune with nature'. THE SCOTTISH FIELD

'An excellent and informative book.... not only an account of a shepherd's year but also the diary of a naturalist. Little escapes Barrington's enquiring eye and, besides the life cycle of a sheep, he also gives those of every bird, beast, insect and plant that crosses his path, mixing their histories with descriptions of the geography, local history and folklore of his surroundings'. TLS

'The family life at Glengyle is wholesome, appealing and not without a touch of the Good Life. Many will envy Mr Barrington his fastness home as they cruise up Loch Katrine on the tourist steamer'. THE FIELD

Listen to the Trees

Don MacCaskill

ISBN 0 946487 65 0   £9.99 PBK

Don MacCaskill is one of Scotland's foremost naturalists, conservationists and wildlife photographers. *Listen to the Trees* is a beautiful and acutely observed account of how his outlook on life began to change as trees, woods, forests and all the wonders that they contain became a

focus in his life. It is rich in its portrayal of the life that moves in the Caledonian forest and on the moorlands – lofty twig-stacked heronries, the elusive peregrine falcon and the red, bushy-tailed fox – of the beauty of the trees, and of those who worked in the forests.

'Trees are surely the supreme example of a life-force stronger than our own,' writes Don MacCaskill. 'Some, like the giant redwoods of North America, live for thousands of years. Some, like our own oaks and pines, may live for centuries. All, given the right conditions, will regenerate their species and survive long into the future.'

In the afterword Dr Philip Ratcliffe, former Head of the Forestry Commission's Environment Branch and a leading environment consultant, discusses the future role of Britain's forests – their influence on the natural environment and on the communities that live and work in and around them.

'Listen to the Trees will inspire all those with an interest in nature. It is a beautiful account, strongly anecdotal and filled with humour.' RENNIE McOWAN

'This man adores trees. 200 years from now, your descendants will know why.'

JIM GILCHRIST, THE SCOTSMAN

ON THE TRAIL OF
On the Trail of Queen Victoria in the Highlands

Ian R. Mitchell

UK ISBN 0 946487 79 0 PBK £7.99

How many Munros did Queen Victoria bag?

What 'essential services' did John Brown perform for Victoria?

(and why was Albert always tired?)

How many horses (to the nearest hundred) were needed to undertake a Royal Tour?

What happens when you send a republican on the tracks of Queen Victoria in the Highlands?

a.. you get a book somewhat more interesting than the usual run of the mill royalist biographies!

Ian R. Mitchell took up the challenge of attempting to write with critical empathy on the peregrinations of Vikki Regina in the Highlands, and about her residence at Balmoral, through which a neo-feudal fairyland was created on Upper Deeside. The expeditions, social rituals and iconography of that world are explored and exploded from within, in what Mitchell terms a Bolshevisation of Balmorality. He follows in Victoria's footsteps throughout the Cairngorms and beyond, to the further reaches of the Highlands. On this journey, a grudging respect and even affection for Vikki ('the best of the bunch') emerges.

The book is designed to enable the armchair/motorised reader, or walker, to follow in the steps of the most widely-travelled royal personage in the Highlands since Bonnie Prince Charlie had wandered there a century earlier.

Index map and 12 detailed maps

21 walks in Victoria's footsteps

Rarely seen Washington Wilson photographs

Colour and black and white reproductions of contemporary paintings

On the Trail of Queen Victoria in the Highlands will

also appeal to those with an interest in the social and cultural history of Scotland and the Highlands - and the author, ever-mindful of his own 'royalties', hopes the declining band of monarchists might also be persuaded to give the book a try.

On the Trail of John Muir

Cherry Good

ISBN 0 946487 62 6   PBK   £7.99

Follow the man who made the US go green. Confidant of presidents, father of American National Parks, trailblazer of world conservation and voted a Man of the Millennium in the US, John Muir's life and work is of continuing relevance. A man ahead of his time who saw the wilderness he loved threatened by industrialisation and determined to protect it, a crusade in which he was largely successful. His love of the wilderness began at an early age and he was filled with wanderlust all his life.

'Only by going in silence, without baggage, can on truly get into the heart of the wilderness. All other travel is mere dust and hotels and baggage and chatter.' JOHN MUIR

Braving mosquitoes and black bears Cherry Good set herself on his trail – Dunbar, Scotland; Fountain Lake and Hickory Hill, Wisconsin; Yosemite Valley and the Sierra Nevada, California; the Grand Canyon, Arizona; Alaska; and Canada – to tell his story. John Muir was himself a prolific writer, and Good draws on his books, articles, letters and diaries to produce an account that is lively, intimate, humorous and anecdotal, and that provides refreshing new insights into the hero of world conservation.

John Muir chronology

General map plus 10 detailed maps covering the US, Canada and Scotland

Original colour photographs

Afterword advises on how to get involved

Conservation websites and addresses

Muir's importance has long been acknowledged in the US with over 200 sites of scenic beauty named after him. He was a Founder of The Sierra Club which now has over ½ million members. Due to the movement he started some 360 million acres of wilderness are now protected. This is a book which shows Muir not simply as a hero but as likeable humorous and self-effacing man of extraordinary vision.

'I do hope that those who read this book will burn with the same enthusiasm for John Muir which the author shows.' WEST HIGHLAND FREE PRESS

On the Trail of William Wallace

David R. Ross

ISBN 0 946487 47 2   PBK   £7.99

How close to reality was Braveheart?

Where was Wallace actually born?

What was the relationship between Wallace and Bruce?

Are there any surviving eye-witness accounts of Wallace?

How does Wallace influence the psyche of today's Scots?

On the Trail of William Wallace offers a refreshing insight into the life and heritage of the great Scots hero whose proud story is at the very heart of what it means to be Scottish. Not concentrating simply on the hard historical facts of Wallace's life, the book also takes into account the real significance of Wallace and his effect on the ordinary Scot through the ages, manifested in the many sites where his memory is marked.

In trying to piece together the jigsaw of the reality of Wallace's life, David Ross weaves a subtle flow of new information with his own observations. His engaging, thoughtful and at times amusing narrative reads with the ease of a historical novel, complete with all the intrigue, treachery and romance required to hold the attention of the casual reader and still entice the more knowledgable historian.

74 places to visit in Scotland and the north of England

One general map and 3 location maps

Stirling and Falkirk battle plans

Wallace's route through London

Chapter on Wallace connections in North America and elsewhere

Reproductions of rarely seen illustrations

On the Trail of William Wallace will be enjoyed by anyone with an interest in Scotland, from the passing tourist to the most fervent nationalist. It is an encyclopaedia-cum-guide book, literally stuffed with fascinating titbits not usually on offer in the conventional history book.

David Ross is organiser of and historical adviser to the Society of William Wallace.

'Historians seem to think all there is to be known about Wallace has already been uncovered. Mr Ross has proved that Wallace studies are in fact in their infancy.' ELSPETH KING, Director the the Stirling Smith Art Museum & Gallery, who annotated and introduced the recent Luath edition of *Blind Harry's Wallace*.

'Better the pen than the sword!'

RANDALL WALLACE, author of *Braveheart*, when asked by David Ross how it felt to be partly responsible for the freedom of a nation following the Devolution Referendum.

MUSIC AND DANCE
Highland Balls and Village Halls

GW Lockhart

ISBN 0 946487 12 X   PBK   £6.95

Acknowledged as a classic in Scottish dancing circles throughout the world. Anecdotes, Scottish history, dress and dance steps are all included in this *'delightful little book, full of interest... both a personal account and an understanding look at the making of traditions.'* NEW ZEALAND SCOTTISH COUNTRY DANCES MAGAZINE

'A delightful survey of Scottish dancing and custom. Informative, concise and opinionated, it guides the reader across the history and geography of country dance and ends by detailing the 12 dances every Scot should know – the most famous being the Eightsome Reel, 'the greatest longest, rowdiest, most diabolically executed of all the Scottish country dances' .' THE HERALD

'A pot-pourri of every facet of Scottish country dancing. It will bring back memories of petronella turns and poussettes and make you eager to take part in a Broun's reel or a dashing white sergeant!' DUNDEE COURIER AND ADVERTISER

'An excellent an very readable insight into the traditions and customs of Scottish country dancing. The author takes us on a tour from his own early days jigging in the village hall to the characters and traditions that have made our own brand of dance popular throughout the world.' SUNDAY POST

POETRY

The Luath Burns Companion
John Cairney
ISBN 1 84282 000 1 PBK £10.00

'Robert Burns was born in a thunderstorm and lived his brief life by flashes of lightning.' So says John Cairney in his introduction. In those flashes his genius revealed itself.

This collection is not another 'complete works' but a personal selection from 'The Man Who Played Robert Burns'. This is very much John's book. His favourites are reproduced here and he talks about them with an obvious love of the man and his work. His depth of knowledge and understanding has been garnered over forty years of study, writing and performance.

The collection includes sixty poems, songs and other works; and an essay that explores Burns's life and influences, his triumphs and tragedies. This informed introduction provides the reader with an insight into Burns's world.

Burns's work has drama, passion, pathos and humour. His careful workmanship is concealed by the spontaneity of his verse. He was always a forward thinking man and remains a writer for the future.

HISTORY

Blind Harry's Wallace
William Hamilton of Gilbertfield
Introduced by Elspeth King
ISBN 0 946487 43 X HBK £15.00
ISBN 0 946487 33 2 PBK £8.99

The original story of the real braveheart, Sir William Wallace. Racy, blood on every page, violently anglophobic, grossly embellished, vulgar and disgusting, clumsy and stilted, a literary failure, a great epic.

Whatever the verdict on BLIND HARRY, this is the book which has done more than any other to frame the notion of Scotland's national identity. Despite its numerous 'historical inaccuracies', it remains the principal source for what we now know about the life of Wallace.

The novel and film *Braveheart* were based on the 1722 Hamilton edition of this epic poem. Burns, Wordsworth, Byron and others were greatly influenced by this version 'wherein the old obsolete words are rendered more intelligible', which is said to be the book, next to the Bible, most commonly found in Scottish households in the eighteenth century. Burns even admits to having 'borrowed... a couplet worthy of Homer' directly from Hamilton's version of BLIND HARRY to include in 'Scots wha hae'.

'A true bard of the people'.

TOM SCOTT, THE PENGUIN BOOK OF SCOTTISH VERSE, on Blind Harry.

'A more inventive writer than Shakespeare'.
RANDALL WALLACE

'The story of Wallace poured a Scottish prejudice in my veins which will boil along until the floodgates of life shut in eternal rest'. ROBERT BURNS

'The return of Blind Harry's Wallace, a man who makes Mel look like a wimp'. THE SCOTSMAN

A Passion for Scotland
David R. Ross
ISBN 1 84282 019 2 PBK £5.99

David R. Ross is passionate about Scotland's past. And its future. In this heartfelt journey through Scotland's story, he shares his passion for what it means to be a Scot.

Eschewing xenophobia, his deep understanding of how Scotland's history touches her people shines through. All over Scotland, into England and Europe, over to Canada, Chicago and Washington – the people and the places that bring Scotland's story to life, and death – including
The Early Scots
Wallace and Bruce
The Union
Montrose
The Jacobites
John MacLean
Tartan Day USA
and, revealed for the first time, the burial places of all Scotland's monarchs.

This is not a history book. But it covers history.

This is not a travel guide. But some places mentioned might be worth a visit.

This is not a political manifesto. But a personal one.

Read this book. It might make you angry. It might give you hope. You might shed a tear. You might not agree with David R. Ross.

But read this book. You might rediscover your roots, your passion for Scotland.

'The biker-historian's unique combination of unabashed romanticism and easy irreverence make him the ideal guide to historical subjects all too easily swallowed up in maudlin sentiment or 'demythologized' by the academic studies.' THE SCOTSMAN

'Ross writes with an immediacy, a dynamism, that makes his subjects come alive on the page.'
DUNDEE COURIER

FICTION

The Bannockburn Years
William Scott
ISBN 0 946487 34 0 PBK £7.95

The Great Melnikov
Hugh MacLachlan
ISBN 0 946487 42 1 PBK £7.95

The Strange Case of R L Stevenson
Richard Woodhead
ISBN 0 946487 86 3 HBK £16.99

But n Ben A-Go-Go
Matthew Fitt
ISBN 1 84282 014 1 PBK £6.99

CURRENT ISSUES

Notes from the North
incorporating a Brief History of the Scots and the English
Emma Wood
ISBN 0 946487 46 4 PBK £8.99

Trident on Trial
the case for people's disarmament
Angie Zelter
ISBN 1 84282 004 4 PBK £9.99

Broomie Law
Cinders McLeod
ISBN 0 946487 99 5 PBK £4.00

TRAVEL & LEISURE

Edinburgh and Leith Pub Guide
Stuart McHardy
ISBN 0 946487 80 4 PBK £4.95

Pilgrims in the Rough: St Andrews beyond the 19th Hole
Michael Tobert
ISBN 0 946487 74 X PBK £7.99

Let's Explore Edinburgh Old Town
Anne Bruce English
ISBN 0 946487 98 7 PBK £4.99

ON THE TRAIL OF

On the Trail of Robert the Bruce
David R. Ross
ISBN 0 946487 52 9 PBK £7.99

On the Trail of Mary Queen of Scots
J. Keith Cheetham
ISBN 0 946487 50 2 PBK £7.99

On the Trail of Bonnie Prince Charlie
David R. Ross
ISBN 0 946487 68 5 PBK £7.99

On the Trail of The Pilgrim Fathers
J. Keith Cheetham
ISBN 0 946487 83 9 PBK £7.99

HISTORY

Reportage Scotland: History in the Making
Louise Yeoman
ISBN 0 946487 61 8 PBK £9.99

The Quest for Arthur
Stuart McHardy
ISBN 1 84282 012 5 HBK £16.99

The Quest for the Celtic Key
Karen Ralls-Macleod
Ian Robertson
ISBN 0 946487 73 1 HBK £18.99

SOCIAL HISTORY

Shale Voices
Alistair Findlay
foreword by Tam Dalyell MP
ISBN 0 946487 63 4 PBK £10.99
ISBN 0 946487 78 2 HBK £17.99

Crofting Years
Francis Thompson
ISBN 0 946487 06 5 PBK £6.95

A Word for Scotland
Jack Campbell
foreword by Magnus Magnusson
ISBN 0 946487 48 0 PBK £12.99

FOLKLORE

The Supernatural Highlands
Francis Thompson
ISBN 0 946487 31 6 PBK £8.99

Tall Tales from an Island
Peter Macnab
ISBN 0 946487 07 3 PBK £8.99

Tales from the North Coast
Alan Temperley
ISBN 0 946487 18 9 PBK £8.99

Highland Myths & Legends
George W Macpherson
ISBN 1 84282 003 6 PBK £5.00

FOOD AND DRINK

The Whisky Muse
Scotch Whisky in Poem and Song
Collected and introduced by Robin Laing
Illustrated by Bob Dewar
ISBN 0 946487 95 2 PBK £12.99

Edinburgh and Leith Pub Guide
Stuart McHardy
ISBN 0 946487 80 4 PBK £4.95

NATURAL SCOTLAND

Wildlife: Otters – On the Swirl of the Tide
Bridget MacCaskill
ISBN 0 946487 67 7 PBK £9.99

Wildlife: Foxes – The Blood is Wild
Bridget MacCaskill
ISBN 0 946487 71 5 PBK £9.99

BIOGRAPHY

Tobermory Teuchter: A first-hand account of life on Mull in the early years of the 20th century
Peter Macnab
ISBN 0 946487 41 3 PBK £7.99

Bare Feet and Tackety Boots
Archie Cameron
ISBN 0 946487 17 0 PBK £7.95

The Last Lighthouse
Sharma Kraustopf
ISBN 0 946487 96 0 PBK £7.99

POETRY

Caledonian Cramboclink: verse, broadsheets and in conversation
William Neill
ISBN 0 946487 53 7 PBK £8.99

Poems to be read aloud
Collected and with an introduction by Tom Atkinson
ISBN 0 946487 00 6 PBK £5.00

Scots Poems to be read aloud
Collected and with an introduction by Stuart McHardy
ISBN 0 946487 81 2 PBK £5.00

Men & Beasts
Poems and Prose by Valerie Gillies
Photographs by Rebecca Marr
ISBN 0 946487 92 8 PBK £15.00

Luath Press Limited
committed to publishing well written books worth reading

LUATH PRESS takes its name from Robert Burns, whose little collie Luath (*Gael.,* swift or nimble) tripped up Jean Armour at a wedding and gave him the chance to speak to the woman who was to be his wife and the abiding love of his life. Burns called one of *The Twa Dogs* Luath after Cuchullin's hunting dog in *Ossian's Fingal.* Luath Press grew up in the heart of Burns country, and now resides a few steps up the road from Burns' first lodgings in Edinburgh's Royal Mile.

Luath offers you distinctive writing with a hint of unexpected pleasures.

Most UK and US bookshops either carry our books in stock or can order them for you. To order direct from us, please send a £sterling cheque, postal order, international money order or your credit card details (number, address of cardholder and expiry date) to us at the address below. Please add post and packing as follows: UK – £1.00 per delivery address; overseas surface mail – £2.50 per delivery address; overseas airmail – £3.50 for the first book to each delivery address, plus £1.00 for each additional book by airmail to the same address. If your order is a gift, we will happily enclose your card or message at no extra charge.

Luath Press Limited
543/2 Castlehill
The Royal Mile
Edinburgh EH1 2ND
Scotland
Telephone: 0131 225 4326 (24 hours)
Fax: 0131 225 4324
email: gavin.macdougall@luath.co.uk
Website: www.luath.co.uk